Nonrational Logic in Contemporary Society

Nonrational Logic in Contemporary Society explores modern examples of beliefs that defy logic but nevertheless are enthusiastically embraced by legions of contemporary people living in technologically advanced societies. The appeal of nonrational logic is based upon C.G. Jung's ideas regarding archetypes, considered to be unconscious thought and behavioral patterns universal to all of humanity and expressed in dreams, art, religion, and reports of supernatural and paranormal experiences such as the belief in UFOs, conspiracy theories associated with child sacrifice and devil worship, lizard people who secretly rule the world, and internet demons whom many insist are real.

C.G. Jung insisted that archetypal reality must be acknowledged for what it is: expressions of universal truths about the human condition. He also warned about the dangers inherent in denying these truths as well as taking these archetypal expressions as literal facts about the workings of physical reality. *Nonrational Logic* includes a multitude of examples from world folklore and reports of traditional customs from around the world collected in the multivolume anthropological classic, *The Golden Bough*, by James Frazer, comparing these traditional reports with contemporary ones to underscore the human psyche's obsessive desire to embrace the fantastic, the extraordinary, and the unbelievable.

Nonrational Logic in Contemporary Society is important reading for analytical psychologists, Jungian psychotherapists, and other professionals as well as the general public seeking to understand how prevalent nonrational thinking is in modern societies and how it reflects traditional expressions.

Jim Kline received his PhD in Psychology with Jungian Studies Specialization, Saybrook University, San Francisco, CA. He is a professor of psychology at the Northern Marianas College, Northern Mariana Islands. His previous publications have appeared in such Jungian-themed Journals as *Psychological Perspectives*, *Jung Journal*, *Spring Journal*, and *The International Journal of Jungian Studies*. He is also the author of *The Otherworld in Myth, Folklore, Cinema, and Brain Science*.

Nonrational Logic in Contemporary Society

A Depth Psychology Perspective on Magical Thinking, Conspiracy Theories, and Folk Devils Among Us

Jim Kline

Routledge
Taylor & Francis Group

LONDON AND NEW YORK

Designed cover image: Karl Freund

First published 2023
by Routledge
4 Park Square, Milton Park, Abingdon, Oxon OX14 4RN

and by Routledge
605 Third Avenue, New York, NY 10158

Routledge is an imprint of the Taylor & Francis Group, an informa business

British Library Cataloguing-in-Publication Data
A catalogue record for this book is available from the British Library

ISBN: 978-1-032-22187-8 (hbk)
ISBN: 978-1-032-22190-8 (pbk)
ISBN: 978-1-003-27148-2 (ebk)

DOI: 10.4324/9781003271482

Typeset in Times New Roman
by MPS Limited, Dehradun

For James Hollis

Mentor, friend, and guide through the depths

Contents

Introduction: What Is Nonrational Logic?

In the 1927 German silent film classic, *Metropolis* (Lang), a super-modern, technologically advanced city hides a dark secret.

Figure I.1 Movie poster for Metropolis (Lang 1927).

Source: *Creative Commons.*

DOI: 10.4324/9781003271482-1

Squeezed within the dazzling avenues dominated by mile-high skyscrapers and multi-laned highways teeming with supersonic vehicles sits a straw-thatched hut from a long-lost forgotten past. This is the home of Rotwang, the genius inventor of the city of Metropolis.

Rotwang's genius for the creation of this ultra-modern city is a blending of science and occult practices. While in the presence of Joh Frederson, the ruler of Metropolis, Rotwang shows him his latest invention: an automaton that he claims he can animate and transform into a life-like human with the resemblance of Rotwang's lost love who ultimately became the wife of Frederson before she died giving birth to their son.

Rotwang is successful in bringing to life his coldly sleek humanoid-automaton, transforming it into a sensually vibrant and soulless temptress. The obsessive desires stirred up by his creation ultimately lead to the destruction of this glittering super city. Lust, greed, envy, wrath—all of the seven deadly sins are unleashed by Rotwang's creation which reveals the vanity, gluttony, and sloth of Metropolis' privileged, self-indulgent elites.

Figure I.2 Rotwang, the mad genius who designed the city of Metropolis, creates a robot with the likeness of his dead lover by infusing his creation with the likeness of the film's heroine, Maria.

Source: *Creative Commons.*

Figure I.3 Rotwang's robot creation, transformed into a sexually vibrant destructive force, sits upon a throne held up by figures representing the seven deadly sins as she incites lust, envy, and wrath in the elites of the city, resulting in mass rioting and destruction.

Source: *Creative Commons.*

In one fantastic scene, these deadly sinful entities all come alive and prance through the modern landscape in the fever dream of Frederson's son, Freder, now a young, privileged societal elite. In another one of his lurid fantasies, Freder imagines the exploited underclass denizens of the city—responsible for keeping the city functioning—being swallowed up by the ancient cannibal god Moloch who appears as an iron-made monster eagerly eating up the oppressed citizens as they wearily stagger up a stairway and tumble into its gaping mouth.

Metropolis illustrates what many of us already know about modern technologically advanced societies: they are fabulously innovative marvels of the human imagination, offering a seemingly endless array of gadgetry and goodies designed to provide ease, luxury, and comfort to those lucky enough to have been born in such societies with the resources to afford such luxuries. For the rest of the citizens, a sense of being not good enough, of living in a world rigged for the elite, pervades their thoughts and fuels envy, lust, and rage, which erupts far too often in violent and self-destructive acts.

Figure I.4 The ancient cannibal god Moloch appearing as a modern iron monster eating the exploited underclass citizens of Metropolis.

Source: *Creative Commons.*

As our surroundings continue to take on the look of the futuristic city featured in *Metropolis*—a look inspired by director Fritz Lang's first sight of New York's Manhattan skyline—our sense of being out of sorts, of something missing from this man-made marvel of invention and imagination, leads to imaginative speculation of what exactly is missing. Like Rotwang's medieval hut squeezed between the dazzling skyscrapers of Metropolis, hidden within all of us is a primeval point of view, one based not on sophisticated reasoning but on what can only be referred to as the source of fever dreams that lead to suspicions about something monstrous lurking within the gleaming gewgaws surrounding us.

According to researchers who have probed the psychic landscape of the human brain, there are two basic types of thinking: fantasy thinking and analytical thinking (Jung, 1952/1967, p. 18; Freud, 1900/1998, pp. 269, 639; Heshmat, 2017, n.p.). The latter is considered more evolutionary advanced, the former more primitive. Modern technologically advanced societies tend to emphasize analytical thinking, which relates to solving problems that result in achieving goals considered important to advancing in these societies. The life course recommended by modern societies seems to be: study hard in school by using analytical thinking so you can get a good college education and land that high-paying tech job with Apple or Google that promises a life in which you can freely indulge yourself with the latest gadgetry while living comfortably for the rest of your life in a high-rise overlooking Central Park or San Francisco Bay.

However, every now and then, that more primitive part of the brain speaks up: something is missing. Something crucial has been left out of this high-tech life course, something untamed, wild, irrational, and soulfully unsettling. Sometimes these irrational thoughts trigger fever dreams featuring monstrous figures endlessly chasing the dreamer through a dark landscape. In these types of dreams, no matter how fast you run, no matter where you hide, no matter what sophisticated weaponry you use to stop this thing, the monster endures and chases you down to kill you.

The fever dream just described is considered the most common of all dream motifs. What is it telling us? Why is it so common? And why does it feel so threatening and real when we are asleep and dreaming?

The most vivid dreams we have occur in REM or rapid eye movement sleep, a reference to the movement of a sleeping person's eyes while the eyelids are closed, indicating that the sleeper is following the action of a dream. The REM stage of sleep is sometimes referred to as paradoxical sleep; this is due to the fact that, when sleep researchers record the brain waves of research volunteers on an electroencephalograph to determine the various sleeping cycles that a volunteer goes through during the night, the brain waves of the REM stage look nearly identical to the waking stage. It's as if the person is consciously awake during REM, and yet the person is obviously asleep. In addition, areas of the brain that promote analytical thinking—most notably the prefrontal cortex—are almost entirely inactive, while the emotional center of the brain—the amygdala—is sometimes more active in REM than in the waking stage. This is why a person can become agitated, even terrified, by a REM-stage dream: the dreamer believes whatever is occurring in the dream is real. It doesn't matter if the dream monster chasing you looks like Godzilla and talks like your mother. You believe it. That is, until you wake up. And then, thankfully, you can shrug it off as just a stupid dream, an attitude toward dreams usually promoted in modern societies that champion the superiority of logical, analytical thinking over fantasy thinking.

And yet, in many cases, because of the disturbing, emotional intensity of such dreams, it's sometimes hard to dismiss them as nonsense. There seems to be an underlying *nonrational logic* to them.

I had an acquaintance who told me about a recurring dream he had from his childhood that expressed the most common dream motif of being pursued by an unstoppable monster. The dream began to occur after he watched a science fiction horror show on TV about giant alien reptiles taking on the look of humans in order to enslave the world. In his dream, one of the giant reptiles chased him through a decimated landscape until he woke up in terror. The recurring dream faded over time, but then began to haunt him again decades later after he was a young adult. After suffering from this recurring dream for months, he finally had a revelation: the reptilian monster chasing him down was an aspect of his own personality that he had repressed for decades and was now demanding to be recognized as an integral part of who he was. In this example, a frightening TV show that he'd watched as a child triggered a dream that incorporated the most common dream motif to convey a deeply important message to him: recognize and accept the repressed shadow aspect of your personality or be haunted by it indefinitely. What had once been a nightmare from his childhood had now become a message from his unconscious as a way to help him become more tolerant of his more troubling personality characteristics.

Dreams vividly illustrate the logic inherent in what appears to be random, illogical fantasy scenarios with no relationship to a person's waking concerns. If one takes the time to understand the nonrational language of dreams, it becomes apparent that even the most bizarre scenarios express an underlying significance. One's reaction to a dream is key to its importance; usually, the stronger the emotional reaction, the more significant the dream is to the dreamer.

C.G. Jung (1952/1967) linked instincts to dreams, even going so far to state that dreams are pictorial expressions of instincts, not only underscoring their importance to survival but also linking them to what he called the archetypal substratum of the psyche (pp. 28–29). Like instincts, archetypes are thought and behavioral patterns universal to all of humanity and can express themselves in dream motifs and symbols. Also like instincts, they are spontaneous reactions to phenomena beyond the control of ego consciousness; their intent is to maintain a healthy relationship between the unconscious and consciousness.

The unconscious, therefore, is the source of nonrational logic, linked to universal archetypal patterns infused with symbolic meaning and relevance. However, if one consistently ignores dreams and makes no attempt to determine their significance to the dreamer's life and well-being, a psychological imbalance could result. Something feels "off" in one's life, making a person feel unbalanced, incomplete. In other words, too much focused, analytical thinking can trigger a response from the unconscious to inject more fantasy thinking in one's worldview.

Jung referred to fantasy thinking as the inspiration for all of what humanity has created:

> When you observe the world ... all of the houses, everything [made by humanity] was fantasy to begin with, and fantasy has a proper reality. This should not be forgotten. Fantasy is not nothing. It is, of course, not a tangible object, but it is a fact nevertheless. It is like a form of energy,

despite the fact that we can't measure it .... So psychic events are facts, are realities, and when you observe the stream of images within [while dreaming], you observe an aspect of the world, the world within. Because the psyche ... is a quality of matter, just as our body consists of matter. It is simply the world seen from within. It was just as though you were seeing into another aspect of matter. (Evans, 1976, p. 302)

Jung's emphasis upon psychic material having a relationship with the material objects we see and create while conscious underscores the connection between waking reality and the reality of dreams experienced while in the REM stage: no matter how bizarre and irrational a dream might appear to be, it is "not nothing." Out of these bizarre scenarios come innovations, different ways to interpret and shape our waking reality so it reflects psychic reality, the "world within."

The creative imagination is based upon fantasy thinking. And since fantasy thinking is related to archetypal reality, which in turn is linked to instincts, one begins to realize how crucial this type of thinking is. It's also important to remember that we naturally react to phenomena from an intuitive, instinctual perspective before processing the phenomena from a more rational perspective (Heshmat, 2017, n.p.). Fantasy thinking and daydreaming, therefore, are the brain's default mode. The problem arises when too much fantasy thinking—or too much analytical thinking—occurs in an individual. There is also the problem of interpreting fantasy scenarios from the unconscious, which requires analytical thinking along with a knowledge of archetypal thought patterns, motifs, and symbols to guard against taking fantasies as literal rather than figurative views of how the waking world works.

Just as there are those prone to too much analytical thinking, there are those prone to too much fantasy thinking. A subgroup of fantasy-prone thinkers illustrates how too much fantasy thinking and not enough analytical interpretation of phenomena can result in a distorted view of reality. This subgroup has gained much support and attention over the last several decades, thanks to a large degree to the technological advancements in communication, specifically the influence of the Internet and social media to connect like-minded thinkers across the globe. This subgroup of fantasy thinkers is known as conspiracy theorists.

Conspiracy thinking has a long history, dating back to ancient times when, for example, the ancient Roman Republic accused a religious cult—called Christianity—of practicing human sacrifice and cannibalism during so-called orgies referred to by the early Christians as Agape feasts. Early Christians were also accused by the ancient Romans of attempting to take over the government (Cohn, 1977, pp. 1–7).

Some modern conspiracy theorists have the same view of reality: evil-doers with the intent of corrupting belief systems with inhuman practices such as cannibalism and worship of demons are hiding within the current U.S. governmental system. One of these theories echoes the plot to the science fiction TV horror show referred to previously: shape-shifting reptilian aliens from another planet with the ability to take on human form have infiltrated every aspect of our society with the intent to enslave humanity (Roberts, 2013, n.p.). As irrational as this belief appears to be, there is a nonrational logic underlying it: we are influenced by our reptilian nature—our instinctual, intuitive nature—and yet we deny this powerful influence, preferring to cover it up with analytical and rational explanations of phenomena.

Conspiracy thinkers habitually reject factually based explanations of controversial and innovative occurrences—assassinations, terrorist attacks, unusual aerial phenomena, significant advancements in science and technology such as moon landings, and breakthroughs in the control of the spread of viruses. They remain suspicious of mainstream explanations because these more factually based explanations insist upon the superiority of analytical thinking rather than fantasy thinking. And yet, we must remember: all of us first react to phenomena through fantasy or intuitive, gut-reaction thinking processes. The conspiracy theorists prefer to process new phenomena in this manner, which leads to more imaginative speculations based on nonrational logic—or, the unconscious, the realm of archetypes.

Archetypal reality is also linked to what Jung called the mythopoetic imagination, responsible for the creation of myths, folklore, legends, and—yes—conspiracy theories. This is why many conspiracy theories have an archetypal dimension to them. For example, the conspiracy known as Pizzagate is based upon the belief that sexually perverse individuals associated with the Democratic Party are kidnapping children and forcing them into sexual slavery, and these debauched Democrats are warehousing the children in the basement of a pizza parlor outside of Washington D.C. These corrupt government officials are also Satan worshippers and their ultimate goal is to force all of humanity to bow down and worship their supreme satanic leader (Kline, 2017, 186–195). One can note how this theory echoes the claims made by the ancient Romans against the early Christians. Both are based upon religious beliefs associated with sacrifice to, and sacred communion with, a supernatural figure of supreme power.

When fantasy thinking is denied importance, determined to be inferior to analytical thinking, it can manifest itself in the most unusual areas of waking reality. For example, members of the two major U.S. political parties essentially look upon members of the opposing party as made up of downright evil people out to destroy U.S. society. In other words, religious expression, which in many cases embraces nonrational beliefs in supreme or supernatural beings, has been projected upon the evil "other" and channeled into a righteous war against the forces of evil.

Unusual and shocking events also trigger nonrational thoughts about the intent and causes of such events, leading to faulty cause-effect assumptions. The September 11, 2001, terrorist attack on the U.S., for example, inspired wild speculations about the collapse of New York's Twin Towers which conspiracists claimed to be the result of timed explosions within the buildings rather than the result of the towers being hit by hijacked commercial airliners; such a theory led to another one: the attack was orchestrated by government officials as a way to justify declaring war on Iraq to take over Middle Eastern oil production (McGreal, 2011, n.p.).

C.G. Jung recognized the importance of identifying the nonrational element in archetypal expressions from the unconscious, and how individuals living in modern industrial societies tend to lack an understanding of this element. Since the nonrational element continues to be devalued in contemporary cultures, it is important to point out how it still exists and influences our everyday lives. It is also important to recognize how it has been expressed by other cultures throughout human history. By looking at these earlier nonrational examples as they have been expressed in myths, folklore, and ritual customs—the mythopoetic imagination—and comparing them to contemporary examples, I hope to demonstrate the enduring appeal and relevancy of nonrational logic in contemporary society.

A key source filled with traditional examples of customs, rituals, and practices illustrating how nonrational thinking expresses underlying truths about the human condition is James Frazer's classic compendium of myth, ritual, and magical thinking, *The Golden Bough*, which I will be referring to throughout this presentation to demonstrate the power of nonrational logic to effect human beliefs and influence human behavior. Another key guide through this examination of both early and contemporary expressions of the nonrational will be what I refer to as the figure of the *folk devil*.

Traditionally, a folk devil is an outcast figure in his or her society, considered to be untrustworthy, rebellious, conniving, deranged, and sometimes in possession of supernatural powers. A folk devil disrupts, distorts, and exploits the values of society, and therefore is also associated with what sociologist Stanley Cohen refers to as the creation of moral panic within a society. In *Folk Devils and Moral Panics* (1972/2002), Cohen extensively explored the panic that erupted in Great Britain in the 1960s and 1970s, triggered by groups of rival British teen gangs called mods and rockers (the inspiration for the British rock group The Who's concept album, *Quadrophenia*, released in 1973 and later made into a film released in 1979).

As the name implies, a folk devil is a common figure in folklore. In fact, an encounter with a devil figure is one of the most popular folk tale subtypes (Thomson, 1973). In addition, researchers have traced what is considered the oldest folk tale which features a blacksmith making a pact with the devil. The researchers traced variations of this tale as far back as 6000 B.C. (Yong, 2016, n.p.).

I'm sure that a good number of us have encountered folk devils in our modern times. Ever fallen for a sales pitch by a telemarketer who turned out to be a con artist? Ever had your computer or your company's computer system hacked or infected with malware? Ever fallen for a news report that you later learned was created by a spreader of fake news? Ever been tempted to try hydroxychloroquine or bleach after hearing them recommended by a president of the United States as proven methods to prevent catching the COVID-19 virus?

The film *Metropolis* vividly illustrates the power of a folk devil figure—the genius-inventor Rotwang—to disrupt and ultimately destroy the established mores of a modern society. Rotwang uses nonrational, occult methods, combined with sophisticated technological advancements, to create marvels for his city; yet he remains an outcast in his society and is ultimately driven mad by the lustful desires he still harbors for his long-lost love. His madness, however, reveals what is missing from his ultra-modern world, and perhaps what is missing from other modern societies. I will explore the "missing part" in subsequent chapters with additional references to this film.

A more contemporary example of a folk devil who causes panic and destruction in a modern society is the former president of the United States. In his final days of office, Donald Trump began spreading the "big lie" conspiracy theory that the 2020 presidential election had been rigged against him by the opposing Democratic political party. Although no significant evidence of any widespread election fraud was found, such findings were rejected by Trump and his legions of loyal supporters who instead proposed some very creative alternative theories about how the election was rigged, one of which involved ballot-counting computer systems, allegedly manufactured in Venezuela, programmed to flip a vote for Trump to his Democratic rival, Joe Biden (Jones, 2020, n.p.). Another fanciful theory involved fake pro-Biden ballots somehow flown in from Southeast Asia that could be detected as phony by looking for traces of bamboo fibers on the ballots (Levine, 2021, n.p.).

On January 6, 2021, while Congress was in the process of certifying the presidential election results for each state, Trump held a rally attended by his most fervid supporters outside the U.S. Capitol building. All of those attending the rally emphatically embraced Trump's conspiracy theory, with many of them also supporters of the QAnon conspiracy which considers Trump a messiah figure leading a secret campaign to eliminate key members of the Democratic Party who are child-sacrificing Satan-worshippers (a variation of the Pizzagate theory referred to previously). Like the soulless automaton from *Metropolis*, Trump stirred up his crowd into a frenzy, resulting in nearly one thousand of them storming and invading the U.S. Capitol building in an attempt to overturn the election results in Trump's favor. Five people died and hundreds were injured in the melee, one of the most vivid modern examples of how nonrational logic untempered with analytical thinking can result in a distortion of reality, leading to violence and assault on the mores of a society. It also illustrates how political beliefs can become sacred beliefs tinged with religious fervor, expressing a righteous cause.

A poll taken in March 2021, months after the Capitol riot, found that two-thirds of Republican voters still believed the election was rigged against Trump (PRRI, 2021, n.p.), proving that charismatic folk devils expressing a nonrational view of reality are alive and doing quite well in modern, technologically advanced society. Understanding the power of nonrational thinking, therefore, is critical not only for an individual's psychological well-being but also for the well-being of modern society.

References

Cohen, S. (1972/2002). *Folk devils and moral panics: The creation of the mods and the rockers*. New York: Routledge.

Cohn, N. (1977). *Europe's inner demons: An enquiry inspired by the great witch-hunt*. New York: New American Library.

Evans, R.I. (1976). The Huston films [1957]. From *Jung on elementary psychology*. In W. McGuire, & R.F.C. Hull, eds. (1977), *C.G. Jung speaking: Interviews and encounters*, pp. 276–352. Princeton, NJ: Princeton University Press.

Freud, S. (1900/1998). *The interpretation of dreams*. New York: Avon.

Heshmat, S. (2017, September 15). Explaining delusional thinking: A reasoning deficit. *Psychology Today*. Retrieved from https://www.psychologytoday.com/us/blog/science-choice/201709/explaining-delusional-thinking.

Jones, D.W. (2020, December 24). Five myths about voting machines. *Washington Post*. Retrieved from https://www.washingtonpost.com/outlook/five-myths/five-myths-about-voting-machines/2020/12/24/ac2e02a2-453f-11eb-b0e4-0f182923a025_story.html

Jung, C.G. (1952/1967). *Symbols of transformation. Collected Works, volume 5* (2nd ed.). H. Read, M. Fordham, G. Adler (eds.), W. McGuire (senior Ed.).Princeton, NJ: Princeton University Press.

Kline, J. (2017). C.G. Jung and Norman Cohn explain pizzagate: The archetypal dimension of a conspiracy theory. *Psychological Perspectives*, 60(2), 186–195. 10.1080/00332925.2017.1314699

Lang, F. (Director). (1927). *Metropolis* [Film]. UFA Studios.

Levine, S. (2021, May 6). Arizona Republicans hunt for bamboo-laced China ballots in 2020 "audit" effort. *The Guardian.com*. Retrieved from https://www.theguardian.com/us-news/2021/may/06/arizona-republicans-bamboo-ballots-audit-2020

McGreal, C. (2011, September 11). 9/11 conspiracy theories debunked. *The Guardian.com*. Retrieved from https://www.theguardian.com/world/2011/sep/05/9-11-conspiracy-theories-debunked.

PRRI Staff (2021, May 12). The "big lie": Most Republicans believe the 2020 election was stolen. *PRRI.org*. Retrieved from https://www.prri.org/spotlight/the-big-lie-most-republicans-believe-the-2020-election-was-stolen/

Roberts, J. (2013, October 17). The biggest secret: Do reptilian-human hybrids run our world? *Collective Evolution.com*. Retrieved from https://www.prri.org/spotlight/the-big-lie-most-republicans-believe-the-2020-election-was-stolen/

Thomson, S. (1973). *The types of the folktale: A classification and bibliography, 3rd ed.* Helsinki, Finland: Suomalainen Tiedeakatemia Academia Scientarium Fennica. Retrieved from https://archive.org/details/typesoffolktalec0000aarn

Yong, E. (2016, January 20). The fairy tales that predate Christianity. *The Atlantic.com.* Retrieved from https://www.theatlantic.com/science/archive/2016/01/on-the-origin-of-stories/424629/

Chapter 1

Folk Devils Among Us

Folk Devils in the Classroom

In the general psychology classes I teach at a community college in the Northern Mariana Islands, one of the requirements is for students to give a formal presentation to the class. I give them a lot of freedom to choose whatever subject that interests them, just as long as it has something to do with psychology.

One presentation that was quite informative for more reasons than expected was given by a young woman about the characteristics, causes, and treatment of sleep deprivation. When she announced her topic to the class, I was grateful to her for choosing such a relevant topic since most students wrestle with sleep deprivation as they attempt to manage their myriad school assignments along with personal must-do tasks which in many cases include working a part-time or even full-time job while also having to take care of responsibilities at home and somehow also maintaining personal relationships with friends and family members.

As with most presentations given in class, this one was in PowerPoint slide format. The student covered the subject quite expertly, giving a clear definition and characteristics of sleep deprivation, reasons for it occurring, and, most interestingly, examining the progressive stages and the symptoms relating to each stage which included lack of energy, inability to concentrate, increased irritability, and, in the later stages after a person hasn't slept for several days, experiencing hallucinations. She also included the physiological effects of prolonged lack of sleep which, if not corrected, could result in significant damage to one's health. She ended with treatment methods and encouraged all of us to seek help for prolonged bouts with this disorder.

After she concluded her slide presentation, she said, "I have a short video I'd like to share with you about an experiment done several decades ago in Russia about the effects of severe sleep deprivation." She said she'd found the video on YouTube and thought it did an amazing job of illustrating how hazardous it is to go without sleep for significant periods of time.

DOI: 10.4324/9781003271482-2

The video, entitled "The Russian Sleep Experiment," was a documentary narrated by an Englishman with a polished, even eloquent speaking voice. According to the narrator, the experiment was conducted in the late 1940s and involved five men, all of them political prisoners. The sleep experiment was to last 30 days, during which time the participants were confined to a bare, barracks-like structure with thick, one-way see-through glass portholes for monitoring their behavior, as well as microphones hooked up throughout the barracks area to pick up their conversations. They were given cots to relax on and enough food and other supplies to last their confinement. They were also given gas masks to wear and periodically forced to breathe a type of gas that would ensure that they remained awake throughout the duration of the experiment.

According to the narrator, the first five days of the experiment proceeded relatively normally with no overt problems among the participants except for whisperings among them relating to the crimes they had been accused of committing that had resulted in their being considered enemies of the state. They were also highly critical of their being monitored which added to their already paranoid states of mind.

On the ninth day, there was a dramatic turn of events: one of the participants began screaming uncontrollably, prompting two others to join in. The other two tore up books they had been given to read and covered up the glass portholes with pages smeared with their own feces. After hours of nonstop screaming, suddenly everything became quiet, so quiet that those monitoring the participants believed their microphones had either been destroyed or were malfunctioning in some manner.

After three days of complete silence, the overseers made the decision to enter the barracks to test the microphones. They attempted to make an announcement to the participants in order to inform them of the plan to enter the chamber. In response to this announcement, the overseers picked up a barely audible whisper from one of the participants: "We no longer want to be freed."

Before the experimenters entered the barracks to double-check their monitoring equipment and to remove the paper that covered up the portholes, they made sure to flush the area of the gas that was keeping the participants awake. This action caused all of the participants to start screaming again and begging to have the gas turned back on. When the experimenters finally entered the chamber, they found four of the five participants alive, but in a state that challenged the definition of "alive." The survivors had torn their bodies apart with their bare hands so their entrails were clearly visible. The food they had been given remained untouched; instead, they had been feeding on themselves as well as the body of the one participant who had died.

It was at this point in the documentary that the student stopped the video, saying, "It gets really graphic after this, but I just wanted you to see how dangerous it is to go sleepless for too long."

I was glad the student stopped the video at that point because my brain was turning inside out, trying to reconcile her scientifically sound and expertly presented slide presentation with this documentary featuring sleep deprived, self-mutilating cannibals. All I could muster at that point was to thank her for her presentation.

After class, I tried to figure out why my brain was flip-flopping from a rational view of sleep deprivation to one that insisted on including symptoms of uncontrollable screaming and a hunger for human flesh. I decided to do some Googling to check on the source of the video, and it took only a few clicks to discover that it had been produced by a contributor to the Creepypasta internet site. This popular site is devoted to fans with a strong passion for creating and sharing horror stories and neo urban legends. Many contributors to the site post a scare story or video and invite others to elaborate on their original posting.

The Russian Sleep Experiment had first appeared on Creepypasta in 2010, and since then has been viewed by tens of millions of people, some of whom, like my student—and now, thanks to her, my entire general psychology class—believed it was a real experiment. To be honest, I too was primed to accept the video as factual, right up to the point where she turned it off and, thankfully, gave me time to check the state of my mind which, as I mentioned, was having a hard time accepting cannibalism as a symptom of sleep deprivation.

As I continued to ponder this incident, I realized it was a perfect example of how nonrational logic is such a prominent aspect of not only contemporary society but also an aspect of the human psyche in general. The incident is also a strong example of how the figure of the folk devil is actually a dimension of our psychological make up.

The word devil is normally used in the context of what should be feared, denied, and avoided at all costs. The traditional devil figure is an entity that is out to corrupt your morals by tempting you with something you know you must resist accepting or possessing but still have a strong desire to believe in whatever is being proposed, or to be tempted to indulge in acts that can ultimately damage your self-esteem and threaten your life.

Normally, we might associate devil figures with con artists and individuals with psychopathic tendencies who know that what they are doing is to take advantage of someone with a strong moral grounding and firm understanding of what is proper and improper behavior but nevertheless can be tempted to succumb to behavior that transcends their moral values. However, in the case of the creator of the Russian Sleep Experiment mock documentary, there was no initial intention to corrupt or take advantage of viewers. At the end of the video, the narrator clearly states his intention: it's an entertainment.

In the case of my student's intention, I believe she sincerely accepted the documentary as factual and then with her sincere demeanor enticed others to believe in its legitimacy as well. In doing so, she became an unwitting spreader of a false view of reality. And yet, she could have only done this if her audience were not primed to believe in this false reality in the first place. Ultimately, she underscored what is inherent in all of us: we have a tendency to want to believe in the fantastic, the bizarre, the grotesque. With her example, she illustrated the enduring appeal of nonrational logic by her briefly taking on the persona of a modern folk devil figure.

The Fear and Appeal of the Dark Side

As I mentioned in the Introduction, information and experiences are first processed by the brain from more an instinctual, survival-mode way of interpreting phenomena, after which information is, hopefully, processed from a more logical point of view. This is exactly what happened to me when I was confronted with something that was, frankly, frighteningly disturbing, challenging my usual way of viewing human beings as friendly and good natured. My brain switched into survival mode, putting me on alert to something threatening, even demonic, about what humans are sometimes capable of.

We are certainly aware of the dark side of human behavior. We know that atrocities have occurred in the past, some perpetrated by so-called rationally thinking professionals: scientists, including psychologists, and certainly members of our government whom we expect to be concerned for the well-being of its citizens. Viewing the Russian Sleep Experiment triggered unseemly thoughts about what certain governmental officials and scientists have perpetrated in the past. We know that the Nazis during World War II conducted atrocious experiments on some of the prisoners confined in concentration death camps. And we also know that the US government sanctioned experiments involving physical and psychological torture on participants who, in some cases, weren't even informed that they were part of the experiment being conducted. For example, another student presented an excellent investigation of the infamous MK-Ultra mind control and truth serum development experiments conducted in the 1950s and 1960s by the CIA on both consenting and nonconsenting participants; some of the participants were given high doses of LSD, others forced to submit to sensory isolation and, that's right, sleep deprivation experiments. These types of US-sanctioned experiments were a paranoid reaction to alleged mind control experiments being developed and conducted by those pesky commies in the Soviet Union, North Korea, and China (Gross, 2019, n.p.).

The Creepypasta fake sleep deprivation documentary was, no doubt, inspired by these real and alleged mind control experiments. The blending of fake and factual is vividly on display in this scary entertainment that has inspired several other talented creative artists to produce their own versions of this never-conducted experiment, thus furthering the blurry boundaries separating the real and verifiable with the unreal and uncanny. This vague mental boundary between real and unreal is actually encouraged by the brain since imaginary thinking is the brain's default mode: when it's not focusing attention on a particular task, the brain is deeply engaged in daydreaming.

The Appeal of Nonrational Thinking

In addition to the presentations I assign on topics relating to general psychology, I also have students give presentations as well as write research papers relating to conspiracy theories in order to encourage them to determine the unsound arguments and unverifiable supportive evidence associated with these theories. My ultimate goal is to help them develop better critical thinking practices, a crucial component in all academic as well as scientific and psychological studies. The problem with these types of assignments is that many students end up believing in the conspiracies.

One student, for example, wrote about the conspiracy surrounding one of modern humanity's greatest scientific achievements: the 1969 Apollo 11 moon landing, an achievement credited to approximately 400,000 individuals working for years under the guidance of the US National Aeronautics and Space Administration (NASA) (Hollingham, 2019, n.p.). After researching the conspiracy, which included citing several reliable and credible sources, the student concluded that the moon landing had been faked. NASA scientists working on the project realized it was impossible to succeed with such an innovative and technologically sophisticated endeavor. In order to justify the massive amount of time and funds spent on the project, along with the use of nearly half a million participants, and also to cover up the failure from those pesky commie competitors, the leaders of the project turned to the one person they believed could solve their problem: film director Stanley Kubrick.

It was Kubrick who, in 1968—one year before the Apollo 11 moon landing—directed the spectacularly innovative science fiction classic *2001: A Space Odyssey* (1968). The film created a sensation with its sophisticated and awe-inspiring special effects featuring a crew of humans traveling through space in an ultra-modern space ship in search of extraterrestrial life. One of the key scenes from the film took place on the moon. Obviously, if some major organization such as NASA needed to save face for botching a manned moon landing project, Kubrick rather than some rocket scientist was the man for the job.

According to my student, the faked moon landing was filmed on some of the same stage sets Kubrick used for filming *2001*. This elaborate cinematic cover-up would never have come to light if Kubrick—supremely proud of his accomplishment but obviously sworn to secrecy like the rest of the

400,000 workers involved in NASA's moon landing debacle—hadn't left clues to his participation in the cover-up in another film he directed: *The Shining* (1980), released 11 years later in 1980. Based upon the horror novel by Stephen King, Kubrick dropped clues throughout the film that had references to his involvement with faking the Apollo 11 moon landing mission.

Perhaps *The Shining's* most convincing clue involved a series of scenes featuring the film's young protagonist, Danny, whose father has been hired as the caretaker of a spooky old resort hotel, the Overlook, located in the Colorado Rocky Mountains. At one point, Danny is featured playing in one of the halls of the hotel, whose octagonal carpet pattern has an uncanny resemblance to a rocket launch pad. Even more conclusive evidence is the sweater Danny is wearing which features an image of the Apollo 11 rocket. At one point, Danny rises up from the carpet and stands as straight as the rocket depicted on his sweater, as if he is enacting the launching of the rocket.

The final convincing evidence occurs moments after this scene when Danny enters one of the hotel rooms; the room number is 237, an abbreviated reference to 237,000 miles, the near-exact distance between the Earth and the moon (Cohen, 2019, n.p.).

After reading the student's evidence for the moon landing cover-up, I encouraged her to do a second draft and dig deeper into the evidence about this elaborate conspiracy, looking at both sides of the controversy. I then made the mistake of giving her a large hint: Stanley Kubrick nor anyone else had anything to do with faking the moon landing. I mention that it was a mistake to tell her she was wrong for reaching such a conclusion because I was basically insulting her point of view, not a very tactful approach to encourage a person to be more open-minded before embracing the legitimacy of a conspiracy theory. She probably did interpret my unsubtle hint as an insult because she decided that she was not interested in researching the subject any further.

This example again illustrates how we are captivated by nonrational explanations for phenomena because our brains are triggered to first comprehend such phenomena from an unconscious, archetypal perspective. In this case, the film *The Shining*, considered to be one of the most unsettlingly bizarre films made about the uncanny, acts as a stimulant upon the psyche, giving rise to a flight-or-fight survival reaction to supernatural goings-on, resulting in the release of unconscious, archetypal energies linked to the mythopoetic imagination. The key scene featuring Danny wearing a sweater emblazoned with an Apollo 11 image thus becomes a clue to something overlooked by the masses who have accepted a more rational explanation of the moon landing mission, linking other conspiracy theories about this project being faked by NASA to a film director who, just one year prior to the Apollo 11 moon landing project, released a film that included such a landing.

For conspiracy thinkers, there are no random events. As I will explore in more detail in Chapter 2, conspiracy theorists see cause and effect relations between phenomena that defy rational explanations. Everything is connected to everything else. Major world events are all linked to forces working behind the scenes to manipulate our view of what is real, similar to what Kubrick dramatized so vividly in *2001* which included scenes of humans confronting aliens who have manipulated human evolution for millions of years. While some consider these manipulative forces as essentially benign—an all-powerful God entity—conspiracy theorists interpret these forces as evil linked with the devil.

Evil and the Origin of the Folk Devil

Jung essentially defined the origins of the folk devil inclinations that exist within all of us while explaining how humans become individuals based upon a person's inherent dominant personality characteristics. Jung stated that the key to developing and understanding one's singular personality is to be tempted by evil. He referred to this evil force as originating in the unconscious. During times of conflict or turmoil, the homeostatic balance between consciousness and the unconscious becomes unstable. Jung indicated that the unconscious in these instances acts as an "inner voice" as it whispers what appears to be disruptive thoughts and stirs up irrational impulses that disturb ego consciousness but which ultimately have an underlying intent to restore homeostasis and even encourage the expansion of consciousness.

Jung (1934/1981) described three possible outcomes when the inner voice of the unconscious whispers what at first appears to be evil to the ego:

> What the inner voice whispers to us is generally [perceived as] something negative, if not actually evil .... The inner voice brings the evil before us in a very tempting and convincing way in order to make us succumb. If we do not partially succumb, nothing of this apparent evil enters into us, and no regeneration or healing can take place .... If we succumb completely, then the contents expressed by the inner voice act as so many devils, and a catastrophe occurs. But, if we can succumb only in part, and if by self-assertion the ego can save itself from being completely swallowed, then it can assimilate the voice, and we realize that the evil was, after all, only a semblance of evil, but in reality a bringer of healing and illumination. In fact, the inner voice is "Lucifer" [i.e. 'light bringer'] in the strictest and most unequivocal sense of the word, and it faces people with ultimate moral decisions without which they can never achieve full consciousness and become personalities. (pp. 184–185)

In Jung's explanation of how individuality is attained, one can recognize the archetypal figure of the devil as tempter who whispers evil intentions that cause moral panics within us. Jung's third outcome is obviously the preferred one. He refers to the ego ultimately interpreting the whisperings from the unconscious as a force with the intent of encouraging the individual to question his or her current moral code or world view, not to corrupt it but to challenge its soundness and relevancy. As a person consciously struggles to interpret these whisperings from the unconscious, there is the potential to expand one's consciousness, leading to a better understanding of one's individuality. Jung referred to this wrestling with the devilish intent of the unconscious as a confrontation with Lucifer, one of the names given to the devil but whose original meaning referred to light bringer: the force that triggers inner insight and wisdom.

The second outcome Jung mentions is what occurs when the ego is swamped by nonrational inclinations, allowing archetypal energies to dominate one's world view. This happens too often with those who embrace conspiracy theories. But, as the student examples illustrate, it can also occur when conscious, critical thinking skills are not applied to interpreting questionable sources, especially when these sources refer to uncanny and bizarre explanations for rather mundane topics such as sleep deprivation or historical events such as moon landings; these off-the-mainstream sources transcend the rational and incorporate supernatural—i.e. archetypal—elements. It's obviously more interesting to think that sleep deprivation can lead to cannibalism rather than merely exhaustion. It's also mind-blowing to discover that a massive cover-up occurred to hide the truth about the moon landing project and how the cover-up was finally revealed years later in a horror movie.

Slenderman as Internet Folk Devil

A vivid example of how a refusal to challenge unconscious whisperings can lead to what Jung called a psychological catastrophe is illustrated by an incident influenced by another contributor to the Creepypasta web site. This contributor, Eric Knudson, first developed his Creepypasta contribution on another internet site, SomethingAwful.com, in 2009, as part of a contest that involved manipulating or photo-shopping images and then creating a story based on these manipulated images (Emery, 2017, n.p.). Knudsen used a cheery, decades-old photo from Australia featuring children playing in a playground. Knudsen inserted the figure of a dark, slim, multi-tentacled man standing in the shadows amid the frolicking children. He referred to this sinister, supernatural creature as Slenderman.

Figure 1.1 Photoshopped image featuring Slenderman.
Source: *Creative Commons.*

His effort was so successful that, like the Russian Sleep Experiment, it ended up inspiring legions of others to create variations of the Slenderman figure lurking in the shadows of benign settings as well as urban environments bordering dense forest areas. Gradually, stories of the supernatural origins of Slenderman, along with tales of his sinister intentions and hypnotic abilities to influence others to do evil, created a series of neo urban legends about this fictional folk devil figure. One of the many variations featured a manipulated wood cut by medieval artist Hans Holbein, circa 1497, featuring the figure of death, depicted as a skeleton dressed in knight's armor, running a lance through another knight. The modern Slenderman artist expertly manipulated the medieval image to give the skeleton figure the appearance of having four spindly, bony legs (Emery, 2017, n.p.).

Like many urban legends, the Slenderman phenomenon became so elaborate and convincing in some of its details that certain people began to believe he was real. Some projected god-like powers upon this bogeyman, and then devoted themselves to obeying and acting out his thought-manipulating commands. Two 12-year-old girls from Waukesha, Wisconsin, became so sure about Slenderman's existence, they convinced themselves that he lived in a long-abandoned mansion in the woods outside of Waukesha, and that they could prove their devotion to him by killing one of their fellow students.

On May 31, 2014, the two lured one of their friends into the woods, telling their companion that they wanted her to join them in a birdwatching expedition. Once they had penetrated deep into the wooded area, the two turned on their friend and one of them stabbed her repeatedly while the other encouraged her on; the two then left their companion for dead. Fortunately, the girl survived and the two perpetrators were arrested and tried as adults for attempted murder. After they were convicted, they entered mental institutions since the girl who had done the stabbing had been diagnosed with schizophrenia. On July 1, 2021, the girl who had not participated in the stabbing assault was released from confinement, while the other diagnosed with schizophrenia remained in a mental institution (Richmond, 2021, n.p.).

Although this incident is an extreme example of allowing archetypal inclinations stirred up by modern depictions of supernatural beings to influence evil acts, it does illustrate the necessity to challenge these whisperings from the unconscious. It's likely that the one girl who committed the stabbings and diagnosed as schizophrenic could have been influenced by auditory hallucinations; many who suffer from this disorder have also struggled with similar hallucinations.

Confronting the Unconscious

At one point in his life, Jung also grappled with such auditory as well as visual hallucinations that he felt were initial signs of a schizophrenic break with reality. He was familiar with such delusions from a clinical point of view, having worked with schizophrenic patients for a decade at the Burgholzli Psychiatric Hospital in Zurich, Switzerland, during the early years of his psychiatric career. In October 1913, not long after dissolving his friendship with Sigmund Freud, he began to experience a series of hallucinations depicting oceans of blood inundating the Swiss landscape and drowning millions of citizens. Fearing he was near a psychotic break, he isolated himself so he could better deal with these horrible apocalyptic visions by actively encouraging them through meditation techniques that allowed his unconscious to dominate his conscious state of mind. During these sessions, he experienced the sensation of descending into the underworld and encountering bizarre figures, talking serpents, as well as prophets who spoke with him about what he was experiencing and the importance of incorporating these types of encounters with the unconscious into his consciousness for further examination. His experiences ultimately led to his singular psychological philosophy including his ideas about the importance of listening to the whisperings of the unconscious to further psychological growth (see Jung, 2009).

The technique Jung developed during this period became known as active imagination, now used by certain psychologists dealing with schizophrenic patients who hear voices (Luhrmann, 2013, n.p.). The modern technique encourages patients to dialog with these voices, the same advice Jung expressed in his comments about how to deal with unconscious whisperings first interpreted as evil.

The Slenderman phenomenon illustrates how the archetypal imagination can overpower ego consciousness and lead to catastrophic outcomes; it also demonstrates how so many of us are interested in the phenomenon of mind control and the fear of being overpowered by so-called evil thought patterns. Conspiracy thinkers usually deny that evil thoughts are coming from them. On the contrary, they're all coming from somewhere out there, dictated by evil powers eager to manipulate us and control our minds and actions. History has proven that such forces do exist, with the CIA's MK-Ultra experiments as just one example. But conspiracy thinkers believe they are much more prevalent: they dominate the world.

One of the best series of films that vividly illustrate a folk devil figure out to create chaos throughout the civilized world with the use of evil mind control techniques is the series from Germany directed by Fritz Lang featuring the genius criminal mastermind, Dr. Mabuse. My personal favorite of the series is *The Testament of Dr. Mabuse*, released in 1933, during the early years of Hitler's influence on the German nation and beyond. Like many people during that time, Lang was deeply disturbed by the rise of Nazism and incorporated his hatred for Hitler's diabolical influence upon the German nation by including scenes featuring a psychiatrist under the hypnotic power of Dr. Mabuse who, in this film, has been incarcerated in a mental institution as a madman after having perpetrated many violent assaults, assassinations, robberies, and other criminal acts on the German establishment. While confined to the mental institution, Dr. Mabuse lies in a coma, yet still able to manipulate the mind of the chief psychiatrist, Professor Blum, who watches over him; in some scenes, Mabuse projects his evil thoughts, heard as whisperings, to Professor Blum, compelling Blum to, in turn, influence others to carry out evil acts of terrorism and destruction on the Germans. At one point, Professor Blum gives a powerful diatribe praising the genius of Dr. Mabuse, appearing unhinged as he mimics some of the frenzied speech inflections and expressively wild hand gestures of Hitler. According to Lang, he had to leave the country after the film premiered in order to avoid Nazi persecution.

One of the most potent scenes from the film occurs after Mabuse has died while confined in the mental institution. After Mabuse's death, Professor Blum sits in his office poring over the final writings of Mabuse, then begins to hear Mabuse's voice. Suddenly, Blum sees a ghostly Mabuse, dressed in his mental patient dressing gown sitting across from Blum. Mabuse's eyes appear like glowing saucers, and the top of his brain is visible and appears to pulsate. As the psychiatrist stares as if in a trance at the ghostly specter, Mabuse whispers to him about how Blum must continue to carry out Mabuse's criminal activities, all of which are designed to create terror and chaos in the population in order to underscore how the entire world is "doomed to annihilation" (Lang, 1933). As the psychiatrist continues to sit wide eyed and hypnotized by this specter whispering pure evil, the ghost of Dr. Mabuse finally rises up and enters Blum's body.

Here is a vivid illustration of the power of the unconscious to whisper evil intentions leading to a complete psychological catastrophe in a man who was once a brilliant psychiatrist, a fate that Jung himself might have succumbed to as he struggled to comprehend the overwhelming visions of apocalypse and annihilation that began inundating him beginning in October 1913. Unlike the fictional Professor Blum, Jung resisted becoming "completely swallowed" by the persuasive power of the unconscious through the assertion of his ego, refusing to interpret these visions as coming from a source with purely evil intentions.

The Legend and Fantasy of Spring-heeled Jack

Dr. Mabuse is a fictional character, a madman with supremely evil intentions inspired in part by a real madman who ultimately brought Germany and much of Western civilization to the brink of annihilation. However, as Slenderman and the Russian Sleep Experiment illustrate, purely fictional creations can take on a life of their own, especially if these specters from the archetypal imagination have a supernatural, even diabolical, allure that infuses the ordinary and mundane life in which we normally live with the uncanny. As Jung mentioned, "The inner voice brings the evil before us in a very tempting and convincing way in order to make us succumb."

There seems to be almost a necessity to view life as having a potential nonrational dimension to it, even if this dimension appears to threaten our well-being. As I mentioned in the Introduction, the most common of all dream scenarios is to be pursued by a demonic force out to kill the dreamer. One can interpret this dream scenario in many ways and in doing so one must always take into consideration the dreamer's life situation at the time the dream occurred. However, in some cases, a perceived threat that is interpreted as diabolical can manifest itself in our waking lives and then later become embellished and elaborated upon by others as both the Slenderman and Russian Sleep Experiment entertainments were, by fans who both interpreted these entertainments as real and fictional.

One alleged demon, clearly inspired by the traditional conception of the devil, haunted the city of London and surrounding areas as a living being for nearly 70 years, beginning in the early 19th century. This figure continues to inspire speculations surrounding its flesh and blood reality: the folk devil figure known as Spring-heeled Jack.

Figure 1.2 Spring-heeled Jack featured on the cover of *Police Gazette News, London*, circa 1840, depicted as the devil incarnate.

Source: *Creative Commons.*

Before he became a full-fledged folk devil, Jack went through many imaginative metamorphoses. The first report of him occurred in September 1837 in a village south-west of London, where he appeared as "'a ghost, imp or devil' in the shape of 'a large white bull,'" allegedly attacking several people, mostly women (Dash, 1996, n.p.). He was later described as a bear, a ghost covered in a white sheet and blue fire, and a devil-like figure with iron claws dancing on the walls of Holland Park at midnight (Dash, 1996, n.p.).

The reports became more serious in the early months of February 1838 when the 18 year-old daughter of a family living in a town east of London answered the door one evening and was attacked by a man wearing a helmet and a cape draped around a tight-fitting outfit with a lantern tied around his chest. The ominous figure belched blue fire into the girl's face, then began tearing at her clothes with fingers fitted with metal claws. Other family members came to her rescue and later called the police. After the police investigated the incident, they concluded that the girl had been attacked by an eccentric drunk and her description of her attacker was somewhat exaggerated.

Other attacks, primarily on women, began to be reported with descriptions of the assailant closely matching the young woman's. No one was arrested since many conflicting details made it hard to determine exactly what the assailant looked like. What seemed to be certain was that the man was quite agile with the seeming ability to jump over hedges, fences, and walls to escape from any persons chasing after him. Some believed he must be wearing springs on his shoes; thus, the name Spring-heeled Jack became associated with this mysterious assailant.

Numerous other reports, all unsubstantiated, were filed over the next several months. Then claims of Jack's activities went dormant for over 30 years until a woman from Peckham filed a report in October 1872, claiming to have been attacked by a tall man who appeared in a ghost-white cloak. After this report, others began pouring in, with one man claiming he had been chased by a seven-foot man dressed in white with his "face in a blaze" (Dash, 1996, n.p.), while another was chased by a similarly-described man whom he saw leap over a six-foot fence. Still another man who was accosted insisted that the man must have been wearing "spring-heeled or India-rubber soled boots, for no man living could leap so lightly, and, I might say, fly across the ground in the manner he did last night" (Dash, 1996, n.p.).

Reports like these died down once again until March 1877 when a British Army camp at Aldershot reported numerous incidents of a dark, demonic figure taunting and terrifying some of the recruits on sentry duty. Some of the soldiers actually fired at him but the figure scampered away apparently unharmed.

Jack's final appearance was in Liverpool over 20 years later in September 1904, where many saw him prancing up and down Everton Street, and finally leaping "clean over the terraced houses from Stitt Street to Haigh Street, and then [hopping] back across the slate roofs to Salisbury Street, after which he was never seen again" (Dash, 1996, n.p.).

Author Mike Dash did extensive research on Jack, inspired in part by Dash's familiarity with publications devoted to reports of UFOs and alien visitations; some of the authors of these types of reports began to look at the legends surrounding Spring-heeled Jack within the context of their fascination with alien visitors, ultimately considering Jack as a possible alien from another planet who ended up stranded in the early 19th-century London area after his space ship crashed.

Dash, however, considers Spring-heeled Jack more closely associated with devil figures from folklore:

> To the inhabitants of London, in the first months of Victoria's reign, Jack was actually several different monsters – "a ghost, a bear and a devil." The earliest rumors say Jack first appeared to be a bull and a bear, and also as "an unearthly warrior, clad in armor of polished brass." Variations on these themes were also reported; for example on one occasion Spring-heeled Jack was described as "a figure clad in a bear's skin, which being drawn aside, exhibited a human body in a suit of mail, and with a long horn, the emblem of the king of hell himself ...." The Devil was commonly believed to disguise himself as a ghost and that "evil spirits may appear as a lion, bear, black dog, toad, serpent or cat." This reading of the initial reports would suggest that, in the popular imagination at least, Jack-the-demon was always the "real" Spring-heeled Jack, and Jack-the-bear, Jack-the-bull and Jack-the-ghost simply disguises. It would therefore seem unsurprising that it was the leaping, fire-breathing devil-figure that emerged from the welter of early rumor as the definitive Jack. (1996, n.p.)

Dash's implication is that, although no one was ever arrested as the perpetrator of Jack-like attacks, the early attacks on the public were perpetrated perhaps by eccentric or drunken assailants but then combined with rumors of supernatural beings lurking around the London area. Gradually, over a period of 70 years, more fantastic characteristics were ascribed to this figure until he became some sort of super, alien-like demon who, like Superman, could leap tall buildings in a single bound and bounce bullets off his chest; he also seemed to be immortal since he never aged, and had the ability to spit blue flames, a common attribute of the traditional devil from folklore.

What essentially began as violent attacks on the citizens of the London area became the inspiration for what Dash called a variation of the "phantom attacker ... with reference to 'urban terrors' and other social panics" (1996, n.p.). Social panics are what folk devils are expert at inciting, a type of mass hysteria. The Spring-heeled Jack phenomenon, therefore, was the result of eccentric criminal activity with no hard evidence to accuse anyone of the crimes, combined with the archetypal imagination associated with the figure of the folk devil.

Folk Devils Within the Psyche

What the legend of Spring-heeled Jack ultimately illustrates, along with the rest of the examples in this chapter, is that, despite how unsettling and frightening the nonrational can be, we are drawn to it as it whispers unsettling thoughts stirred up by panic, uncertainty, and unusual phenomena that seem to defy logical explanations. In these situations, the unconscious becomes more activated, its whisperings more pronounced, and its demands on our egos to resist succumbing to these whisperings more crucial than ever.

Jung's own example of allowing unconscious forces to overtake his ego in order to better understand the intent of unconscious activities that threaten to overwhelm our conscious perceptions of reality gives us a real-life example of the challenges and benefits these forces offer to the human psyche. His example also gives us a way to deal with these forces when their whisperings become too obvious to ignore.

References

Cohen, R. (2019, July 18). How Stanley Kubrick faked the moon landing. *Paris Review.org*. Retrieved from https://www.theparisreview.org/blog/2019/07/18/how-stanley-kubrick-staged-the-moon-landing-and-other-stories/

Dash, M. (1996). Spring-heeled Jack: To Victorian bugaboo from suburban ghost. *Fortean Studies*, vol. 3, pp. 7–125. London, UK: John Brown Publishing. Retrieved from https://www.mikedash.com/research

Emery, D. (2017, January 20). The truth about Slenderman. *Snopes.com*. Retrieved from https://www.snopes.com/fact-check/slenderman/

Gross, T. (2019 September 9). Author interviews: The CIA's secret quest for mind control: LSD and a 'Poisoner in chief.' *NPR.org*. Retrieved from https://www.npr.org/2019/09/09/758989641/the-cias-secret-quest-for-mind-control-torture-lsd-and-a-poisoner-in-chief

Hollingham, R. (2019, June 19). Apollo in numbers: The workers. *BBC.com*. Retrieved from https://www.bbc.com/future/article/20190617-apollo-in-50-numbers-the-workers

Jung, C.G. (1934/1981). The development of personality. In H. Read, M. Fordham, G. Adler (Eds.), W. McGuire (Senior ed.), *The development of personality. Collected Works, volume 17*, pp. 165–186. Princeton, NJ: Princeton University Press.

Jung, C.G. (2009) *The red book: Liber novus* (S. Shamdasani, ed.). New York: W.W. Norton.

Kubrick, S. (Director). (1968). *2001: A space odyssey* [Film]. MGM

Kubrick, S. (Director). (1980). *The shining* [Film]. Warner Brothers.

Lang, F. (Director). (1933). *The testament of Dr. Mabuse* [Film]. Germany: Nero-Film.

Luhrmann, T.M. (2013, September 19). The violence inside our heads. *New York Times*. Retrieved from https://www.nytimes.com/2013/09/20/opinion/luhrmann-the-violence-in-our-heads.html

Richmond, T. (2021, July 1). Judge orders woman released in Slender Man case. *APnews.com* Retrieved from https://apnews.com/article/wisconsin-0fbe59b1f2f3505092b1a523055ec120

Magical Thinking = Primary Process Thinking = Delusional Thinking = Hysterical Thinking

Intentionality and Confirmation Biases

On June 23, 2021, John McAfee committed suicide in a Barcelona jail cell. At the time of his death, McAfee, the British-born computer software wizard and creator of one of the most successful antivirus software programs, was awaiting extradition to the United States for tax evasion charges. His suicide, therefore, seemed to be related to his imminent extradition to the U.S. to face more jail time for his attempt to escape tax evasion prosecution. However, approximately 24 hours after his death, McAfee's suicide morphed into something far more sinister.

On June 24, one day after McAfee's suicide in a Barcelona jail, a 12-floor condominium complex in the Miami, Florida suburb of Surfside partially collapsed, killing 98 people. The U.S. government-affiliated National Institute of Standards and Technology (NIST) immediately began investigating the causes of the collapse but since its investigation was estimated to take quite some time before an official cause could be determined, speculation about the causes began to circulate. One of the more reasonable explanations focused on another structural collapse that had occurred at the condominium complex three years earlier involving the swimming pool deck which had plummeted into the underground parking garage; investigative reporters from the *Washington Post* indicated that this earlier collapse had weakened the complex's surrounding key structural columns, causing the more devastating collapse to occur (Swaine, J, Brown, E, et.al, 2021, n.p.). However, this explanation was hardly satisfying to those with conspiratorial thinking tendencies, especially since it failed to take into consideration the connection between this tragedy and the so-called suicide of John McAfee.

According to some conspiracy theorists, McAfee had left messages on his Twitter account years prior to his death, claiming to have secret files that allegedly contained compromising information about nefarious activities perpetrated by the CIA and other government officials. McAfee had stored these files in one of the condos at the collapsed complex; this condo was owned by his son Pat. In one of his Twitter messages, he implied that if he

DOI: 10.4324/9781003271482-3

ever ended up dead by suicide, he had most likely been assassinated by government officials (Evon, 2021, n.p.).

Other conspiracy theorists claimed that McAfee had created a "dead man's switch," a device that could automatically set off a detonation at the time of a person's death (Palmer, 2021a, n.p.). The implication was that the switch became activated after someone killed him in his Barcelona cell, which then led to the collapse of the Miami-based condominium complex, destroying his secret files. Obviously, there were some head-scratching questions about the dead man's switch theory beyond the question of how such a device could actually work: why would McAfee want to blow up a condo complex that not only destroyed files linked to those who allegedly killed him, but also killed his son who lived there?

One conspiracy theorist made a noble attempt to summarize the connection between McAfee's alleged suicide in Barcelona and the collapsed condo building in Miami: DeAnna Lorraine, a former candidate for the U.S. House of Representatives and embracer of the QAnon conspiracy that claims certain members of Congress are deep-state Satanists who practice child sacrifice and cannibalism among other atrocities. While being interviewed on a right-wing-leaning talk show, Lorraine rejected the dead man's switch theory while emphasizing the deep-state Satanist connection and also linking the Miami condo collapse with the collapse of New York's Twin Towers that occurred 20 years prior on September 11, 2001. According to Lorraine, because both incidents involved buildings collapsing in "one fell swoop," they must have been the result of timed explosions set by the deep state. In the case of the Miami condo collapse and its link with John McAfee, the deep-state Satanists blew up the complex to destroy the information he had stored there in his son's condo. Lorraine concluded that the facts as she's presented them are "pretty damn obvious" as they were with the alleged 9/11 terrorist attacks: "We know how the deep state operates ... . [They're] dirty, they're satanic, and they're disgusting ... " (Palmer, 2021b, n.p.).

Lorraine and the other like-minded thinkers who embraced the causal relationship between McAfee's death and the collapse of the Miami condo complex failed to take into consideration the lack of evidence pertaining to those seemingly prophetic tweets that McAfee allegedly tweeted years before his death. There is no evidence of their existence. Nor is there evidence that his son Pat owned one of the condos in the collapsed complex. In fact, there is no evidence that McAfee even had a son named Pat (Evon, 2021, n.p.). However, there is evidence that those who embrace these types of nebulous causal relationships between phenomena are more likely to be attracted to conspiracy theories such as this one.

One of the key characteristics of conspiracy theorists is that they are highly influenced by the *intentionality bias,* the common belief that everything happens for a purpose: a force—someone or something—has caused an event to happen. Psychologist Rob Brotherton (2016 n.p.) describes this bias as a universal cognitive process that keeps us alert to possible threats that could harm us, but one that is much more of a cognitive influence in those who embrace conspiracy theories.

To determine how influential the intentionality bias is, not only for conspiracy thinkers but for humanity in general, a series of experiments were conducted by researchers at the Yale Mind and Development lab who asked participants to reflect back on significant events from their lives: falling in love, getting married, serious illnesses, and other impactful, life-changing events. After gathering their evidence, the researchers reported that:

> ... a majority of religious believers said they thought that these events happened for a reason and that they had been purposefully designed (presumably by God). But many atheists did so as well, and a majority of atheists in a related study also said that they believed in fate — defined as the view that life events happen for a reason and that there is an underlying order to life that determines how events turn out. (Banerjee & Bloom, 2014, p. SR12)

A similar study conducted by researchers at Queen's University in Belfast reached similar conclusions: "British atheists were just as likely as American atheists to believe that their life events had underlying purposes, even though Britain is far less religious than America" (p. SR12).

Another common bias affecting how we interpret events that impact our views and beliefs is the *confirmation bias*. The tendency to believe that events have underlying purposes encourages us to look for information that confirms that view while disregarding information that doesn't support it. In DeAnna Lorraine's case, for example, her tendency to see random big events as connected and having an underlying sinister purpose compels her to disregard evidence that contradicts her already established view that deep-state Satanists are the actual cause of these events.

Just like the intentionality bias, the confirmation bias is hardly reserved for conspiracy theorists. The internet and social media thrive on confirmation bias, thanks to algorithmic programs that link a user's preferred content with complementary content and merchandise. The reasoning is that if you liked this product or supported that left-leaning or right-leaning candidate, then you'll also like this similar product or this other similarly-leaning candidate too, resulting in confirming your already established biases. That's why if, for example, you accidentally click on an ad for a baby monitor, you will see pop-up ads for sites selling baby monitors for the rest of your life.

Many scientists have had their research tainted by confirmation bias; if certain data doesn't confirm their already established hypothesis, then sometimes a scientist will disregard conflicting data as irrelevant. A fellow scientist attempting to replicate the findings of an experiment or study tainted with confirmation bias will find it impossible to do so, thus calling into question the original researcher's evidence and research design, as well as the researcher's reputation.

An insidious example of confirmation bias in research was the Eugenics movement that was extremely influential in the early decades of the 20th century. Eugenicists were racists primarily from the U.S. and Britain, some of them well-regarded university professors, legal experts, and scientists who, inspired by Darwin's theory of evolution, set out to confirm the evolutionary superiority of Caucasians with a Western European heritage. To pseudo-scientifically prove their bias, they created quack devices and instruments to measure the physiological characteristics of individuals from non-white races and ethnic groups to compare them with Western Europeans, then interpreted their findings to confirm their racial biases.

Because of the prevalence of racism in the U.S. at that time, the Eugenics movement confirmed the already well-established racist biases of whites with Western European backgrounds, receiving support for their pseudo-scientific findings from government officials. The result was laws passed to limit immigration from countries with predominantly Asian, African, and Eastern European populations. Eugenicists were also able to get laws passed banning interracial marriages and allowing for the sterilization of so-called unfit and inferior members of the population in order to prevent these inferior members from contaminating the gene pool of the white race: individuals with learning disabilities, individuals with autism, people born into poverty, family members with a history of antisocial tendencies, family members with substance abuse issues, and people suffering from certain psychological disorders such as schizophrenia (Kirsch, 2014, p. D, 6). One of the individuals who fell into the latter category was my maternal grandfather. Incarcerated in an Iowa State mental institution for most of his adult life, he was sterilized in 1949 by order of the Eugenics Board for that state. Fortunately, my mother had already been born; otherwise, I wouldn't be here and no one would be reading these words.

The Eugenics movement not only dramatically illustrates how confirmation bias can affect those who are considered rational thinkers such as scientists and legal experts, but it also illustrates the nonrational logic that underlies paranoia over contagion, contamination, and so-called inferior members of a society who end up scapegoats for society's ills, all of which will be further explored in Chapter 3.

Sympathetic Magic

In *The Golden Bough*, first published in 1895, pioneering anthropologist James Frazer expressed similar attitudes in regards to the confirmation and intentionality biases toward people living in traditional cultures. Frazer pejoratively referred to members of indigenous and traditional cultures as savages and primitives which could be interpreted as a racist attitude reflecting those who embraced the Eugenicist movement. However, Frazer was not so much referring to the beliefs and traditions of these indigenous cultures as inferior to modern, Western European cultures; he was well aware that these so-called primitive attitudes were still very much alive and embraced by the people of his time. Frazer was essentially interested in the concept of *animism* which is a dominant belief system among members of traditional cultures that accept the belief in a life power or force that permeates and animates all life, including inanimate objects. As he stated: "As the savage commonly explains the processes of inanimate nature by supposing that they are produced by living beings working in or behind the phenomena, so he explains the phenomena of life itself" (1895/1981, p. 121, P1).

One can see how Frazer's comments on animism pertain to the intentionality bias; processes within nature are intentionally "produced by living beings." Conspiracy theorists who believe in deep-state forces "working in or behind the phenomena" would interpret these "living beings" as evil, out to corrupt, destroy, and dominate those unaware of these forces. In many cases, people living in traditional cultures held similar attitudes toward these living beings; however, for the most part, they exhibited a much more benign attitude toward these invisible powers.

Frazer refrains from passing judgment on the intent of these living beings; instead, he provides endless examples of how people interpret the intent of these influential, invisible forces. He also provides a multitude of examples that illustrate how people are obsessed with performing rituals and behaving in certain ways to control and manipulate the invisible forces.

Frazer refers to these types of ritualistic acts as examples of *sympathetic magic*. There are two basic types of sympathetic magic: contagious and imitative. The first has to do with manipulating an object that has come in contact with a person; if the person in possession of the object manipulates it in some way, it can have an effect on the other person who has been in contact with the object. Voodoo dolls, for example, which are made in part from some item belonging to an individual, can be manipulated by someone else to affect that individual in some way.

Imitative magic has to do with imitating a natural process in a way that has an effect on that natural process. Frazer gives many examples of members of traditional cultures who, for example, perform rituals that simulate thunder, lightning, and rainfall—banging pots together, creating sparks with pieces of rocks, and sprinkling water on the ground—to imitate a rainstorm with the intent to have nature respond with a downpour.

A more elaborate example occurred shortly after World War II on certain islands in Melanesia. U.S. soldiers fighting the Japanese in that area had set up military camps in many of the islands, bringing with them equipment and supplies that natives of the island had never seen before. Cargo planes began dropping off what seemed to be endless supplies from some distant land where these incredible objects and supplies originated. After the war when American soldiers packed up and disappeared and the cargo planes stopped landing with their array of goods, the inhabitants began building replicas of the planes out of bamboo, cleared jungle areas to create landing strips, and fashioned wooden control towers that included boxes made from straw to replicate radio transmitters in order for the natives to contact the cargo planes and entice them to return with their bounteous goods.

This elaborate example of imitative magic became known as the cargo cult tradition (Raffaele, 2006, n.p.), which vividly illustrates how a belief in living beings working behind the scenes to control the world we live in can somehow be manipulated by imitating the behavior exhibited by these living beings. Sometimes this power can infuse the imitators so they possess it themselves. Modern examples include dressing and imitating the movements and mannerisms of a rock star to capture the star's charisma and talents. There is probably no rock guitarist wanna-be who hasn't tried imitating the flamboyant, guitar-playing mannerisms of Eddie Van Halen, Jimi Hendrix, or Jimmy Page. And there probably isn't a fashion-diva wannabe who hasn't dressed in a slinky, sparkly designer dress and strutted around in public hoping to embody the spirit of a supermodel.

Contagious magic also permeates modern, materialistic cultures. It's common to collect objects allegedly endowed with a special contagious power by its maker. It's why a piece of gum or cigarette discarded by a celebrity is swooped up by a fan and hawked on eBay for thousands of dollars. It's also why an art collector will sometimes pay millions of dollars for an original Picasso or van Gogh.

A favorite example involves biologist and proud atheist Richard Dawkins who admitted that one of his most prized possessions was a first-edition copy of Charles Darwin's *On the Origin of Species*. Many rare book collectors would agree with Dawkins that such a rare first edition, published during the time in which Darwin lived, holds much more value than any other edition, even though other editions contain the same text. The assumption here is that the first edition must be endowed with more of Darwin's revered, contagious spirit since it had been published during his lifetime. Andrea Kitta, an expert on contagion examples from folklore, echoes Frazer's ideas about contagious magic when describing how an ordinary object becomes contaminated with special power by its close proximity to something or someone considered sacred or holy; although she refers to Christian saints touching, for example, a piece of clothing and therefore endowing the clothing with the saint's holiness (2019, p. 17), one can see how this same idea could apply to the first edition of Darwin's book: his "close proximity" to this edition published during his lifetime made it more "holy" and thus much more of a coveted sacred object than all other editions. Commenting on his prized possession, Dawkins stated: "This book has made it possible no longer to feel the necessity to believe in anything supernatural" (Hutson, 2013, pp. 16–17).

Primitive Energetics

Frazer summarized the belief and practice of sympathetic magic from both the contagious and imitative perspectives: "Both branches of magic ... may be conveniently comprehended under the general name of sympathetic magic, since both assume that things act on each other at a distance through a secret sympathy, the impulse being transmitted from one to the other by means of what we may conceive as a kind of invisible ether, that which is postulated by modern science for precisely similar purpose, namely to explain how things can physically affect each other through a space which appears to be empty" (1900 & 1906–15/2018, pp. 27–28). What Frazer was emphasizing is that humans are obsessed with making cause-and-effect relationships between phenomena to explain the workings of the world. Science uses rational methods to determine causal relationships, while many others use nonrational methods for the same reason. The intended conclusions reached by rational logic and nonrational logic are identical: to explain how the world works in order to predict and replicate these workings, and to explain behavior that we all share as human beings as well as behavior that, according to those with superior rational insight, only superstitious people exhibit, and according to those with superior nonrational insight, only evil people indulge in.

Frazer's reference to an invisible ether that connects phenomena through empty space is the animistic spirit. It could be compared to what scientists call the Higgs-boson particle, a subatomic bonding particle responsible for providing mass to form the universe. Higgs-boson was kiddingly referred to as the God particle, a fitting name since it could be considered having similar characteristics associated with the god entity from ancient Greece credited with enticing all objects to bond with each other in various combinations to create the universe and keep it recreating and renewing itself: the god known as Eros.

Jung (1943/1972) referred to the concept of ether as an archetypal motif, not only conceived as an invisible force permeating empty space to connect all that exists within the universe, but also as an inner force that keeps a person alive and connected to the source of life itself: " ... *aether* [is] the primordial breath or soul-substance ... a concept found all over the world ... " (p. 95). In addition, Jung used the term *primitive energetics* (p. 68), in reference to traditional beliefs about controlling and manipulating the invisible forces to which Frazer referred, also by use of "magic power" (p. 95):

> This concept [i.e. primitive energetics] is the equivalent to the idea of soul, spirit, God, health, bodily strength, fertility, magic, influence, power, prestige, medicine, as well as certain states of feeling which are characterized by the release of affects .... This power-concept is also the earliest form of a concept of God ... and is an image that has undergone countless variations in the course of history. (p. 68)

Jung linked the primitive energetics concept with the dominant archetypal motif of the collective unconscious: the Self, or inherent god image or concept. Because the Self is the concept or image of god that acts as an all-powerful organizing force inherent in the human psyche, Jung considered religious expression as a universal impulse.

Grand Delusions

Like Frazer, Jung (1943/1972) used unflattering terms when referring to those who allow archetypal reality and the religious impulse to overpower their view of reality, calling them "primitives" or "simple-minded," yet also insisted that anyone who completely ignores the religious impulse can suffer from psychic instability; on a collective scale, it could lead to mass destruction:

> Simple-minded folk have never, of course, separated these things [i.e. archetypal influences] from their individual consciousness, because the gods and demons were not regarded as psychic projections and hence the contents of the unconscious, but as self-evident realities. Only in the age of enlightenment did people discover that the gods did not really exist but were simply projections. Thus the gods were disposed of. But the corresponding psychological function was by no means disposed of; it lapsed into the unconscious, and men were thereupon poisoned by the surplus of libido [i.e. archetypal energies] that had once been laid up in the cult of divine images. The devaluation and repression of so powerful a function as the religious function [in preference for the reasoning function] naturally have serious consequences for the psychology of the individual. The unconscious is prodigiously strengthened by this reflux of libido, and, through its collective contents, begins to exercise a powerful influence on the conscious mind. The period of the Enlightenment closed, as we know, with the horrors of the French Revolution. And at the present time, too, we are once more experiencing this uprising of the unconscious

destructive forces of the collective psyche. The result has been mass murder on an unparalleled scale. (p. 94)

Jung's references to the Enlightenment and the French Revolution, which promoted such Enlightenment ideals as reason, logic, and scientific principles, were intended to emphasize how the denigration of the religious impulse can lead to mass slaughter as it did during the French Revolution's reign of terror during which over 16,000 people were executed, many of whom were religious leaders and their supporters. Jung first wrote the above passages in 1916, during World War I, which is why he mentioned that "we are once more experiencing this uprising of the unconscious destructive forces of the collective psyche," leading to "mass murder on an unparalleled scale." Jung later added a footnote to this passage in 1943 during the height of World War II: "… superfluous to remark that it is still true today" (p. 94).

And yes, it is still true today, since many insist that the religious impulse is based on nonrational logic that should be denied expression in favor of pure logic, reason, and the scientific method. Richard Dawkins, for example, refers to those who insist upon expressing the religious impulse as delusional; his book, *The God Delusion* (2006), is just one of many he has written that condemn people who embrace this nonrational, "primitive energetics" belief: "There is no reason for believing that any sort of gods exist and quite good reason for believing that they do not exist and never have. It has all been a gigantic waste of time and a waste of life. It would be a joke of cosmic proportions if it weren't so tragic" (2014, n.p.). Dawkins recites a long list of atrocities committed in the name of God, but neglects to include the French Revolution's reign of terror and the two World Wars on his list; as Jung stated, these conflicts that triggered "mass murder on an unparalleled scale" were, in part, the result of the demonization of the nonrational dimension of the human psyche.

Obviously, nonrational logic is hardly an adequate method for interpreting all aspects of the workings of the human psyche and natural world. But neither is pure logic. In this context, Jung (1943/1972) referred to the concept of *enantiodromia*: whatever psychic power is denied expression, it will eventually become its opposite power in equal strength. Like the earlier quote, Jung first wrote the following in 1916 during World War I:

Thus the rational attitude of culture necessarily runs into its opposite, namely the irrational devastation of culture. We should never identify ourselves [solely] with reason, for man is not and never will be a creature of reason alone, a fact to be noted by all culture-mongers. The irrational cannot and must not die … . The enantiodromia that always threatens when a movement attains to undisputed power offers no solution of the problem, for it is just as blind in its disorganization as it was in its

organization. The only person who escapes the grim law of enantiodromia is the man who knows how to separate himself from the
unconscious ... by putting it clearly before him as *that which he is not.*
(pp. 72–73)

Jung insisted that we must recognize the nonrational, archetypal dimension
of the human psyche as separate from ego consciousness. If we cannot separate our singular selves from unconscious forces, we risk embracing these
nonrational concepts as legitimate interpretations of how the physical world
works rather than how the archetypal world works. The nonrational is
based upon sympathetic magic, faulty cause-effect relationships between
phenomena that nevertheless express an underlying meaning and intent for
the individual. The archetypal dimension expresses profoundly significant
metaphorical concepts that cannot be proven by rational methods such as
the concept of God and the animistic spirit.

If ego fails to make the distinction between itself and the realm of archetypes, it risks identifying itself with the Self: all-knowing, all-powerful,
and unforgiving when challenged by mere mortal opinions. Richard
Dawkins and others who continue to demonize those who express religious
views, and conspiracy theorists who demonize those who don't, both ex-
emplify the "God delusion:" in both instances, ego has identified with the
god image within.

In the case of conspiracy theorists who champion religious beliefs, seeing
God in all aspects of the secular world can lead to interpreting purely secular
causes as imbued with the divine. For example, members of the QAnon
conspiracy, previously referred to in connection with DeAnna Lorraine's
theory about John McAfee's death, consider Donald Trump a messiah
figure who will someday bring about the arrest and punishment of deep-state
Democrats who worship Satan and sacrifice children in order to drink their
adrenalin-infused blood as a way to achieve immortality. This view of
politics as a holy war between the forces of good and evil incorporates New
Testament references to Holy Communion—symbolic cannibalism associated with eating Christ's flesh in the form of bread and drinking his blood
in the form of wine to become one with his teachings and ultimately achieve
immortality. However, the QAnon supporters have demonized this holy rite,
while at the same time making Trump the new savior of the free world.

A new layer of religious references were added to the QAnon belief system
in early November 2021, when faithful adherents began descending upon
Dealy Plaza in Dallas, Texas. They had come to witness the appearance of
John F. Kennedy and his son, John Jr. Many of us might remember that the
former president was assassinated at Dealy Plaza in November 1963, and
that his son died in a plane crash in 1999. However, these QAnon adherents
insisted that John and John Jr. had both faked their deaths. Apparently, yet

another Kennedy, Jacqueline, faked her death as well because she also was scheduled to make an appearance alongside her husband and son.

After the holy Kennedy trinity made their appearance at the site of the assassination, John Jr. was to give a speech in which he officially reinstated his father as the current president and also declared Donald Trump as the King of Kings, essentially the second coming of Christ. The three Kennedys then were scheduled to embark on a tour of the world for seven days, after which the newly reinstated President Kennedy would *really* die, leaving his son to reign in his place as the next president. John Jr. would then immediately resign and reinstate Trump as the current president with John Jr. then becoming vice president. Now, with Trump as both current president and the King of Kings, it was only a matter of time before the deep-state Satan-worshippers were banished to the deepest pit of hell (McKay, 2021, n.p.).

If this convoluted, secularized second-coming scenario sounds familiar, it's because it incorporates key motifs from the New Testament's Book of Revelation in which Christ returns to defeat Satan and bring in a new world order of peace and justice for true believers. Jung's (1943/1971) comments about what happens when the inner god image becomes a reality that dominates the secular world-view summarizes this example of political figures envisioned as divine entities:

> The idea of God is an absolutely necessary psychological function of an irrational nature, which has nothing whatever to do with the question of God's existence … . [For] the idea of an all-powerful divine Being is present everywhere, unconsciously if not consciously, because it is an archetype … . I therefore consider it wiser to acknowledge the idea of God consciously, for if we do not, something else is made God, usually something quite inappropriate and stupid such as only an "enlightened" intellect could hatch forth. (p. 71)

Jung's assessment of the sometimes "inappropriate and stupid" expressions of the religious impulse may seem harsh, but his emphasis is upon those who are gripped by the god archetype and exhibit a superior attitude toward those who fail to see God in the manner they do, which is sometimes to trivialize this inherent and universal expression of the nonrational.

Magical Thinking

In my capacity as a psychology professor at a community college located on the island of Saipan in the Northern Mariana Islands, I feel fortunate to live in a location where the religious impulse is expressed from both a traditional and organized religion perspective. I sometimes give my students an assignment featuring a nonrational example and ask them to explain the nonrational logic inherent in the scenario. The majority of students can usually spot the nonrational logic because of its relationship to their traditional religious views which emphasize ancestral worship of the first inhabitants of the islands, the Chamorros. The following is one of the examples I have used for this assignment, reported by a student:

> Every Sunday, I go to the cemetery to visit my elders and light a candle for each of them. I have five different graves to visit. Last weekend, I forgot to bring a lighter with me and I honestly don't know what I was thinking about, but I saw a lighter on the grave right next to my great-grandma's grave and I said to myself that I was going to borrow it. Before I took the lighter I forgot to ask [for permission] and I just said: "dispensa yu" which means "sorry" in Chamorro. After taking the lighter, I lit the candle for my great-grandma and took the lighter so I could burn the other candles. When nighttime came, I went to take a shower and I could feel someone's presence watching me. I suddenly remembered about the lighter I took and felt scared. I rushed out of the shower. As I got in my room, I felt dizzy and my back hurt really badly. I couldn't sleep well. I kept moving around to be comfortable but it didn't help. I prayed before I closed my eyes to force myself to sleep. The next day, I rushed to the store and bought a candle. I went to the cemetery to return the lighter and also burn a candle for the grave that I took the lighter from. I apologized to the grave and felt relieved when I got back into my car. (A. Flores, 2020, personal correspondence with author)

What follows are student responses to this example:

> By reading the case study I can conclude that the woman featured in this example feels uneasy and disoriented after she returns home with a lighter she took from a grave site ... because of a nonrational view of how the world works, known as "magical thinking ... ." Elderly spirits on the island are known as Taotao Mo'na and local people hold a strong belief that before you enter a Taotao Mo'na's territory, you have to ask for permission and not do anything to make them feel offended. With the woman taking the lighter home, the spirits might've felt disrespected thus making her feel uneasy and watched. (A.N. Borlongan, 2021, personal correspondence with author)

> The spirits of the dead have been known, in superstition, to attach themselves in the things that "belong" to them, especially in a cemetery where they are buried. In this case, the lighter does not belong to the woman but to a grave next to her great-grandma's. So, when she took it home, she also took the spirit of the grave with her. Which is why she

was so bothered when she was at home, to the extent that someone was watching her. Her worries were even heightened when she realized that she took the lighter home and pieced it together that it must be the spirits that's making her feel uneasy. She could've been scared too because she may have angered the grave on which she took the lighter from. When she returned it the next day, she felt relieved because she believed that she had returned it to the owner and that the spirits no longer followed her nor it would bother her. It is this belief that she assumed on the reason why those things happened to her the previous night, and it is the same reason why she felt at eased because she had set it right. (C. M. Matta, 2921, personal correspondence with author)

The student responses emphasize respect for ancestral spirits, especially when entering areas where these spirits are likely to dwell, such as a cemetery. Ancestral spirits, known as taotaomona, also dwell within the island's jungle areas, specifically where there are banyan trees which residents sometimes refer to as taotaomona trees. James Frazer had much to say about sacred trees, most notably the "golden bough," which I will discuss in more detail in Chapter 4 on Totemism.

What the student responses also illustrate is Frazer's ideas about sympathetic magic, specifically contagious magic. The last student comment refers to a spirit becoming angry out of being disrespected by the woman's act of taking the lighter from the spirit's grave without asking for permission and how the spirit attached itself to the lighter to follow her home. In many other student examples about ancestral spirits, sometimes students report having experienced or witnessed a possession by one of these disrespected spirits which can lead to the possessed person acting contrary to his or her normal way of behaving, even sometimes becoming violent and attacking other family members. Possession will be explored more in depth in Chapter 5 in connection with the concept of the soul.

Another student makes a reference to *magical thinking*, which is related to Frazer's two categories of magic, but it specifically refers to the thought processes involved in accepting these concepts relating to sympathetic magic. Magical thinking has also been linked with *primary process thinking* (Vandenberg, 2014, n.p.), a term used by Freud who considered it associated with instinctual responses governed by the id, which Freud considered the ruler of the unconscious as opposed to Jung's concept of the archetype of the Self as regulator of the unconscious and its relationship with ego consciousness. Because it is linked with instincts, the id demands immediate fulfillment of a need or desire and can override what the ego considers of primary importance until the desire is fulfilled.

Magical thinking compels the individual to believe he or she is endowed with psychic powers: if a desire is truly important, and if the person can think hard enough about it—visualize it coming true—the universe will respond and fulfill that wish. The intentionality bias is also related to magical thinking since it assumes that one's thought processes are linked to the outside world and that the outer world can pick up on one's thoughts to grant desires and arrange outcomes, underscoring the idea that everything is interconnected and everything happens for a purpose. A common example is to be thinking about an old friend you haven't seen for years and suddenly the phone rings and it's your old friend calling you. The implication is that you have sent out a thought beam aimed at your friend and the friend has received the psychic message and responded by calling you. What is overlooked is the hundreds of other times you've thought about that friend over the years and the friend hasn't called, except for this time, an attitude that reflects the confirmation bias since you've dismissed all those other incidents as irrelevant because they don't confirm the nonrational belief you secretly hold regarding your psychic powers.

As the above example illustrates, magical thinking is extremely common. A personal example occurred one morning just before dawn when I was asleep in my apartment in Saipan while my wife and our beloved cats were far away in Washington State where our house is located. As I was sleeping, I heard my favorite cat Little Red meow loudly as if he were perched on my pillow next to my left ear. Because I fervently believe that I have a special instinct-grounded bond with him, I recognized his distinct meow and woke up startled, actually expecting him to somehow be perched right there on my pillow. When I realized the truth of the situation, I panicked, believing he had sent me a psychic call for help. I immediately phoned my wife to see if Little Red was sick or in danger. My wife assured me that he was fine, sleeping in the home office next to her desk. I was so sure that my favorite cat had sent out an emergency signal to me that it took me a while to accept the fact that what I had experienced was this very common magical-thinking thought process.

Folk devil figures have taken advantage of the universal desire to embrace magical thinking, becoming millionaires by promising legions of people that, yes, you can think yourself rich, or think yourself thin, or think yourself into the perfect job, or attract the perfect mate by envisioning a supremely suitable someone. Just buy my book or subscribe to my web page or take my seminar on the secret to fulfilling your most cherished desires by harnessing the power of your mind.

The Secret (2006/2018), by Rhonda Byrne, is one of the most successful and widely read books promoting magical thinking. Since its publication in 2006, it has sold well over 30 million copies worldwide. Byrne promotes the idea that our thought processes can somehow link up with a source of power permeating and guiding the universe and entice this power to bring about a desired wish. Byrne's ideas essentially echo Frazer's definition of sympathetic magic: "things act on each other at a distance through a secret sympathy, the impulse being transmitted from one to the other by means of what we may conceive as a kind of invisible ether."

Another highly successful book using this same type of nonrational logic is *Think and Grow Rich* (1937/2005), by Napoleon Hill, written during the time of the Great Depression when millions of people struggling to make a living were willing to try anything to survive, even attempting to think themselves out of poverty.

Another folk devil figure who attempted to put into practice the magical thinking ideals promoted by Byrne and Hill was mass murderer Elliot Rodger. At age 22, before he went on his killing spree in the town of Isla Vista near the campus of the University of Santa Barbara, California, in May 2014, Rodger attempted what legions of others do who are keen on becoming rich overnight: he tried desperately to visualize himself winning the lottery so he could become an instant millionaire and achieve his ultimate desire of becoming irresistible to beautiful blondes. In his auto-biography, *My Twisted World* (2014), which he sent to the *Santa Barbara News-Press* the day before he rode through Isla Vista looking for beautiful blondes to shoot since they had failed to respond to his wish to become the object of their desires, Rodger detailed the appeal of *The Secret* and another successful book promoting magical thinking, *The Power of Your Subconscious Mind* (1963/2010), by Joseph Murphy. According to Rodger (2014):

> My father gave me a book called *The Secret* … . He said it will help me develop a positive attitude. The book explained the fundamental concept known as the Law of Attraction … . The theory stated that one's thoughts were connected to a universal force that can shape the future of reality … . The prospect that I could change my future just by visualizing in my mind the life I wanted filled me with a surge of hope that my life could turn out happy. The idea was ridiculous of course, but the world is such a ridiculous place already that I figured that I might as well give it a try … . I proclaimed how I wanted to be a millionaire, so I could live a luxurious life and finally be able to attract the beautiful girls I covet so much. I wished to make up for the years of youth that I wasted in bleak loneliness, and by doing so, I would get revenge on everyone who thought they were better than me, just by becoming better than them through the accumulation of wealth … . After a lot of deep thinking … I [fixated on] the current jackpot for the Mega-millions Lottery … . As it so happened, I had over $6,000 saved up at the time … . [After spending thousands of dollars on lottery tickets] I was certain I would be the winner. It was destiny … fate. But no, the world continued to give me no justice or salvation whatsoever. I sank into the worst depression of my life … .

[Weeks later] I happened to come across a book called *The Power of Your Subconscious Mind,* by Joseph Murphy. This book would fill me with hope for the next few months. It was very similar to *The Secret* ... and it had the same effect on me. It gave an even more in-depth view on the law of attraction ... . I [once again] began to visualize myself winning the lottery ... . After reading this book, I wanted to believe that there was some sort of supernatural power that I could harness to change reality as I saw fit ... . I took frequent walks ... dreaming and visualizing about winning the lottery ... .

I didn't win ... . That night, I threw a tantrum, screaming and crying for hours on end ... .

[After destroying my laptop in the rampage] I decided to go to the shooting range in Oxnard ... . I walked into the range, rented a handgun from the ugly old redneck cashier, and started to practice shooting at paper targets. As I fired my first few rounds, I felt so sick to the stomach. I questioned my whole life and I looked at the gun in front of me and asked myself, *"What am I doing here? How could things have led to this ... ?"* There I was, practicing shooting with real guns because I had a plan to carry out a massacre ... . I questioned the very fabric of reality. *Why did this all exist?* I wondered. *How did life come to be? What was the nature of reality? What was my place in all of it ... ?*

The life I could have ceased to exist. I will never have sex, never have love, never have children. I will never be a creator, but I could be a destroyer ... . The human species had rejected me all my life, despite the fact that I am the ideal, magnificent gentleman. Life itself is twisted and disgusting, I mused. Humans are brutal animals. If I can't live among them, then I will destroy them all ... . (n.p.)

I include this lengthy quote from Rodger because it not only illustrates the temptation many of us have to believe that our inner thought processes can somehow be understood by the invisible beings working behind the scenes so they can bring about a desired outcome for us, but also because it illustrates someone who feels that this is the only way to achieve anything in life: magical thinking is really how life works. As Rodger stated, he felt he could "change reality as I saw fit" by linking his thought patterns with the powers responsible for fashioning reality and manipulating these powers to change reality in a way that fulfilled his desires. His feelings of having been betrayed by these invisible forces shattered his view of reality triggering an existential crisis. The powers had betrayed him by refusing to act in his best interests. Therefore, the invisible forces who dictate the rules of life itself must be *conspiring* to do him harm. He had already suspected this malicious intent because, for years, the invisible forces had refused to allow beautiful girls to become attracted to him, "the beautiful girls I covet so much."

Rodger made a crucial comment that relates to someone who exhibits a cluster of personality characteristics associated with conspiracy thinkers: he believed he was an "ideal, magnificent gentleman," someone superior to the humans who cannot see his magnificence because they are mere mortals and he is actually closer to being an omnipotent god. In other words, Rodger failed to distinguish his ego identity from the Self and fell under the spell of the God delusion. As he stated in perhaps the most chilling passage from his autobiography:

> I am not part of the human race. Humanity has rejected me. The females of the human species have never wanted to mate with me, so how could I possibly consider myself part of humanity? Humanity has never accepted me among them, and now I know why. I am more than human. I am superior to them all. I am Elliot Rodger ... Magnificent, glorious, supreme, eminent ... Divine! I am the closest thing there is to a living god. Humanity is a disgusting, depraved, and evil species. It is my purpose to punish them all. I will purify the world of everything that is wrong with it. On the Day of Retribution, I will truly be a powerful god, punishing everyone I deem to be impure and depraved. (n.p.)

Such a megalomaniacal attitude was an expression of Rodger's view of the invisible forces that he imagined ruling the world: they are vengeful, un-merciful, and diabolical. His attitude is similar to how DeAnna Lorraine described the dirty, disgusting, deep-state cannibals working behind the scenes to destroy America. So, in an act of imitative magic, Rodger ab-sorbed their diabolical power in order to destroy those whom he deemed impure and depraved.

The Schizotypal Personality

Rodger's embracement of magical thinking, his God delusion, and his paranoid belief that the forces of life were conspiring against him, all express a type of personality related to a study designed to determine the personality characteristics of conspiracy thinkers. The study appeared in the June 2020 issue of the *Journal of Personality,* and involved researchers giving various types of personality tests to approximately 2,000 participants. According to the findings, a significant feature of individuals exhibiting conspiratorial thinking was their relationship to characteristics associated with the *schi-zotypal personality.* People with this type of personality are highly attracted to magical thinking along with a stubborn, egotistical attitude about the validity of personal beliefs that defy logic; they also exhibit paranoid thoughts, suffer from depression and social anxiety, and therefore isolate themselves from others while holding onto a superior-than-thou view of themselves (Carey, 2020, D3).

It's relatively easy to note how the characteristics associated with con-spiracy thinkers relate to Elliot Rodger: he exhibited an entitled, self-centered attitude, was supremely cold-hearted, and suffered from elevated levels of depressive moods. He was also gripped by magical thinking as a way to "change reality" that would align with his worldview so he could achieve his desired goals in life which, again, were supremely egotistical and self-centered. Ultimately, his thought processes led to a full-blown psy-chosis, a delusional state in which he imagined himself a vengeful god out to punish those whom he believed were unworthy of any mercy and in doing so would purify the world of the depraved and unfit.

Obviously, Rodger's example is far from the typical conspiracy theorist point of view. However, it does conform to the schizotypal personality which, in its extremes, is considered a psychological disorder. Another key characteristic of the schizotypal personality reflects the intentionality and confirmation biases but with an emphasis upon how all events dictated by the invisible forces are for the individual's benefit, giving the person clues about what direction in life to take, making references to the person in subtle ways through secret signs, and providing clues about what is really going on in the world that only someone with an "enlightened intellect" can pick up on (Casabianca, 2021, n.p.). In other words, everything happens for "my" purpose. The trick is to interpret the signs and signals sent by the invisible forces for "my" benefit and disregard all others as irrelevant.

Members of the QAnon conspiracy excel at this personality characteristic, interpreting cryptic messages left by the mysterious "Q" who allegedly works within the U.S. government and passes on his or her findings about deep-state Satanists via "Q drops" on fringe internet sites which the fol-lowers then attempt to interpret with their enlightened intellectual powers (Evon, 2021, n.p.). So far, the Q followers have exhibited a less than sterling record for interpreting their leader's vague prophecies; the return of the dead Kennedys to proclaim Trump as the King of Kings is just one such example of getting the signals wrong. A more serious misinterpretation of Q's mes-sages occurred on January 6, 2021, when many QAnon followers took part in the riot at the U.S. Capitol which left five people dead and hundreds wounded. They believed that a Biblical-type Armageddon, which Q had referred to as "The Storm," had finally come. As one Q supporter posted via Twitter prior to the event: "Nothing will stop us. They can try and try and try but The Storm is here and it is descending upon D.C. in less than 24 hours … . Dark to light!" (Barry, Bogel-Burroughs, & Philipps, 2021, n.p.). This message was the last one posted by Ashli Babbitt, one of the casualties of the riot.

A Master of Magical Thinking

I cannot emphasize enough how this type of thinking is hardly anything new since it's an integral part of how all human beings think. Certainly in its extremes it can lead to extreme conclusions about the workings of the universe and how, if we are attuned to the invisible forces responsible for universal causation, we can decipher their subtle messages and manipulate them for our benefit, or at least better understand the riddles of human existence. However, if one can temper this type of thinking with analytical thought processes, a more coherent and insightful view of life can be the result.

One of the greatest examples of someone who was able to balance and blend nonrational logic with pure reasoning was one of humanity's greatest recognized geniuses: Isaac Newton. The Enlightenment's mathematical wizard who explained to the world the laws of universal causation, and who founded the concept of scientific positivism (processes are valid only if they can be confirmed mathematically), was also someone who not only indulged in magical thinking but practiced a type of magic known as alchemy, one of Jung's favorite esoteric philosophies. Newton firmly believed in animism, a living spirit permeating and animating the universe. As he explained in one of his personal writings: "A certain infinite spirit pervades all space into infinity, and contains and vivifies the entire world" (Fiorio, 2020, n.p.). This belief impacted his theories about universal causation. According to historian Soraya Field Fiorio, Newton "believed an immaterial force guided the whole of creation, its presence manifesting through such phenomena as motion and gravity" (n.p.).

A collector of Newton's more esoteric writings summed up Newton's preoccupations with the workings of the universe:

> He was the last of the magicians ... . He looked on the whole universe and all that is in it as a riddle, as a secret that could be read by applying pure thought to certain evidence, certain mystic clues that God had laid about the world to allow a sort of philosopher's treasure hunt to the esoteric brotherhood ... He regarded the universe as a cryptogram set by the Almighty. (n.p.)

As I mentioned, Newton dabbled in alchemy as a way to decipher the crypto-grammatical clues left by God for humanity as a way to solve the mysteries inherent in the natural world. As he described it in his private writings: "There is a vital agent diffused through everything in the earth, a mercurial spirit, extremely subtle and supremely volatile" (n.p.). Newton's description of the "vital agent" as a "mercurial spirit" is a direct reference to alchemy which considers the entity known as Mercurius, associated with the Roman messenger god Mercury and his Greek counterpart Hermes, as the god-spirit that guides the alchemist in his pursuit of the knowledge of the material elements that make up the universe. Alchemical philosophy is infused with esoteric symbols and references to chemical formulas that, with the right combination, can unlock the secret source of life and produce a type of substance called the philosopher's stone. This substance can be deciphered in ways that not only explain the forces inherent in nature, but can be manipulated to control nature.

Newton's thought processes underscore how nonrational logic complements rather than offends and wars against pure mathematical reasoning and the scientific method. We need both methods of thinking to better understand the mysteries of human existence.

Conspiracy thinkers such as the QAnon followers err in their insisting that their approach to deciphering the cryptic messages of their leader is grounded in pure logic when in fact it is pure nonrational logic. They also insist that what they have uncovered about the true nature of reality is linked to the source of all evil. In this regard, they are correct since the source of evil is the human psyche overwhelmed by nonrational logic and devoid of analytical thinking. Or vice versa.

What the QAnon believers report about deep-state Satanists, for example, are indeed linked to traditional ideas about the source of evil. Their belief about Satanists embedded in government echo reports made by the ancient Romans about a fringe religious cult of cannibalistic pedophiles known as Christians. Just like the QAnon followers, early Romans demonized the practice of Holy Communion, accusing Christians of killing babies to eat their flesh and drink their blood as a way to honor their Satanic leader Jesus Christ who sometimes appeared to them in the form of a donkey (Cohn, 1977, p.1). An early anti-Christian writer from 2nd century A.D. described the Christian initiation ceremony as:

> ... disgusting as they are well known. A child covered in dough to deceive the unwary, is set before the would-be novice. The novice stabs the child to death ... . Then—it's horrible!—they hungrily drink the child's blood, and compete with one another as they divide [and devour] his limbs ... . It is well known too what happens at their feasts ... . On the feast day they foregather with all their children, sisters, mothers, people of either sex and all ages. When the company is all aglow from feasting, and impure lust has been set afire by drunkenness ... [the] light, which would have been a betraying witness, is overturned and goes out. Now, in the dark, so favorable to shameless behavior, they twine the bonds of unnamable passion, as chance decides. And so all alike are incestuous, if not always in deed at least by complicity ... . Precisely the secrecy of this evil religion proves that all these things, or practically all, are true. (p. 1)

A nonrational conclusion to reach about any secret organization, especially if one is not part of that organization, is that secrecy of any sort is proof of evil practices. Secrecy ignites fantasy thinking, and when one is paranoid, fantasy thinking can lead to the conclusion that Satanic practices are perpetrated by these secretive evildoers working behind the scenes to corrupt the world with their evil. Note how Jung's earlier statements from Chapter 1, about how archetypal thinking can lead to embracing evil intentions if one does not temper such thinking with reason, apply to this type of thinking.

Hysterical Thinking

The early references to Christians practicing Satanic rites in honor of their shape-shifting donkey leader also refer to the Christian cult as intending to overtake the dominant governmental system (Cohn, 1977, p. 7), a common accusation associated with all so-called secret cults. The deep-state Satanists embedded in the U.S. governmental system are just the latest secret cult to allegedly perpetrate what is obviously a deep-seated archetypal pattern.

It's interesting to note that conspiracy theories about sinister forces embedded within the U.S. governmental system can be traced nearly as far back as the founding of the American government itself. In 1798, a type of mass hysteria erupted over rumors about members of the Illuminati infiltrating the governmental system, attempting to spread its evil intentions that echoed some of the Enlightenment principles that demonized religious practices in favor of reason and the scientific method. George Washington, then retired from government, made statements in which he fervently believed that members of the Illuminati were infiltrating various U.S. institutions (Hodges, 2011, n.p.). Washington feared the Illuminati might be attempting to infiltrate his own beloved secret organization, the Freemasons, whose symbol, the all-seeing eye of God atop an unfinished pyramid—which appears on the back of the U.S. dollar bill—had allegedly been adopted by the Illuminati (Lloyd, 2018, n.p.).

The real Illuminati was founded in Bavaria in 1776, by philosopher Adam Weishaupt. His intent was to create an organization of intellectuals, philosophers, and freethinkers to promote enlightened thinking modeled after the Enlightenment movement. Many famous individuals from that period became members, including Bavarian royalty, along with doctors, lawyers, and literary figures, one of whom was arguably Jung's favorite author, Johann Wolfgang von Goethe. However, infighting among these elite members resulted in rumors of nefarious goings-on.

One disgruntled former member sent a letter to the Bavarian government accusing the organization of being in favor of such illegal practices as abortions and assisted suicide, and that members were encouraged to hunt down enemies and secretly poison them. Members also regarded religious practices as absurdities based on superstition. Worst of all, the disgruntled former member accused the Illuminati of conspiring to overthrow the Bavarian government. The letter resulted in Bavarian governmental leaders ordering the organization to disband. A raid on the headquarters of the organization turned up documents that seemed to verify the accusations made by the disgruntled member, including a defense of suicide, atheism, and medical instructions dealing with performing abortions. In 1787, the government officials released an edict stating that anyone associated with the Illuminati would be arrested and put to death (Hernandez, 2016, n.p.).

Although the original Illuminati organization probably never had a membership of over 2,000, their influence upon paranoid thinking about secret organizations attempting to infiltrate and corrupt governmental institutions in order to put into practice their alleged anti-religious, and anti-life practices (i.e. suicide, abortions, and poisonings of enemies) created a panic among European nations.

A rumor that members of the Illuminati were allegedly responsible for the French Revolution and its reign-of-terror mass murders spread through Europe and ultimately reached America, thanks to a large degree by two influential books published in Great Britain in 1798 and 1799. Both detailed the evil intent of the now-disbanded organization. Influential clergymen in the U.S. then began preaching about the spread of the Illuminati in America. One minister interpreted this spread of anti-Christian principles as a sign of the end of times as predicted in the New Testament's Book of Revelation based upon "numerological calculations" (Hershey, 2016, p. 74), echoing the practices of current QAnon members and their obsessions over deciphering Q drops and interpreting them as prophecies of Armageddon. Yet another minister went on to proclaim that, "… it is now generally believed, that the present day is unfolding a design the most extensive, flagitious, and diabolical that human art and malice have ever invented. Its object is the total destruction of all religion and civil order. If accomplished, the earth can be nothing better than a sink of impurities, a theatre of violence and murder, and a hell of miseries" (p. 76).

Fortunately, this mass hysteria that gripped America in 1789 lasted only a few years, probably due to the lack of reliable and more sophisticated communication and media networks to spread such unsubstantiated, paranoid-infused rumors, unlike what we have today. It wasn't until the rise of communism beginning in the 1920s that such paranoid-fueled thinking about a godless, one-rule dictatorial governmental system with intent to enslave all of humanity erupted once again in the U.S.

Red Hysteria: The Russians Are Coming

The fear of communist domination of the world was, in many regards, a justifiable fear. Communist sympathizers in the U.S. were not that uncommon prior to World War II. The Communist Party USA was established in 1919 and prided itself in advocating for fair labor practices and welfare for workers especially during the Great Depression. Communist party members became active leaders in various cultural and even student group organizations (Devinatz, 2013, n.p.). However, attitudes toward communist sympathizers changed drastically after World War II when the U.S. became a dominant world power and the only country with nuclear weaponry, a secret that the U.S. wanted to keep exclusively for itself, and one that was nearly stolen by communist sympathizers. Julia and Ethel Rosenberg were Communist Party members who passed on secret nuclear bomb information to Soviet contacts and, in 1953, became the only two American civilians executed for conspiracy to commit espionage (Jenkins, 1998, n.p.).

Despite its legitimacy in the U.S. prior to World War II, communism was always considered a potential threat to U.S. political, moral, and ethical principles since, like the 18th-century Bavarian Illuminati, it had little tolerance for religious views. In addition, Soviet communism was dictatorial, and leaders such as Josef Stalin were intolerant and unmerciful to those who dared to criticize rulership, with legions of dissenters ending up either assassinated or in Siberian concentration camps.

The perceived threat of Russian infiltration in all avenues of American society led to the great Red Scare paranoia of the post-World War II era, inflamed and exploited by such folk devil figures as Senator Joseph McCarthy of Wisconsin who claimed to have a long list of communist sympathizers working behind the scenes in American government, military, education, media, and entertainment institutions. Like the campaigns that were created to support U.S. troops fighting Nazis and Japanese soldiers during World War II and to encourage citizens to look out for any suspicious activities that could be the work of Nazi and pro-war Japanese sympathizers, Red Scare campaigns warned citizens to remain alert to any activity that could be the work of communist sympathizers.

As Red Scare hysteria grew, so did the fear that Soviet communism's ultimate goal was to create what the Illuminati had been accused of attempting: establishing a New World Order dictatorial governmental system that would enslave the world, banning all religious activities, encouraging so-called anti-life causes such as abortions and euthanasia, and eliminating unfit members of the population—seniors, the mentally impaired, and critics who objected to leadership dictates.

Like the suspected influence of communism in all facets of American society, Red Scare propaganda was created for every fabric of American culture, some of it obviously contradictory in its messages. For example, the film and television industries were accused of massive pro-communist infiltration, with many of those affiliated with Hollywood ending up blacklisted and unable to find work for decades, yet Hollywood also produced numerous anti-communist films such as *I Married a Communist, The Red Menace*, and *I Was a Communist for the FBI*.

Figure 2.1 An anti-communist poster from the Red Scare hysteria era, circa 1950. Note the reference to Dr. Fred Schwarz who was an anti-communist proponent and founded the Christian Anti-Communism Crusade.

Source: *Creative Commons.*

In addition, anti-communist comic books were produced to reach young people featuring scare stories about what American life would be under communist rule. A favorite from that era, published in 1947, was titled, *Is This Tomorrow: America Under Communism* (1947), a truly nightmarish story that detailed how the infiltration of communists in all aspects of

Figure 2.2 Scene from the anti-communism comic book *Is This Tomorrow* (1947) depicting the torture of dissenters and their enslavement in concentration and labor camps.

Source: *Internet Archive.*

American society led to the complete overthrow of the government and enslavement of dissenters who were tortured, rounded up in cargo ships and cattle cars, and transported to concentration camps in Alaska and forced labor camps in the Dakotas (pp. 40–41).

Red Scare hysteria continued into the 1960s, the era in which I became aware of its influence, thanks to my father's enthusiastic embrace of what tomorrow could bring if God-fearing, red-blooded Americans didn't demand a more aggressive anti-communist stance from the government. My father's favorite book from that era was *None Dare Call It Treason* (1964), by John Stormer, a pastor and superintendent of a Christian school in Florissant, Missouri who also held a B.A. in journalism and founded a publishing company, Liberty Bell Press, to put forth his view that communists were subtly infiltrating and corrupting every American institution.

None Dare Call It Treason was essentially the adult version of *Is This Tomorrow,* filled with sensationalist details about what would occur once the commies took over America: "Once the takeover comes, you, like millions of others, who believe in God and man's responsibility for his own life and actions can be slaughtered like diseased animals or worked to death in slave labor camps or brothels for the Red Army" (p. 20). Because my father was an independent businessman, he believed he would be one of the first to be arrested and "slaughtered like a diseased animal."

Because the book was released in February 1964, nine months before the presidential election of that year, the book had a major influence on those who were critical of Democratic incumbent Lyndon Johnson whom many conservative thinkers believed was far too soft on communism. Anti-communist champions like my father preferred the Republican candidate Barry Goldwater whom Democrats felt leaned so far to the right, he could end up causing World War III in his attempts to wipe out communism across the globe. As election day neared, my father became more agitated, at one point telling me that if Barry Goldwater wasn't elected, it could be the last free election America ever had.

My father's attitude toward communist influence was a product of the Red Scare era which championed gut-reaction primary process thinking over analytical thinking. In fact, analytical or intellectual thinking was thought to be aligned with commie thinking. As Stormer pointed out, communism is " ... a disease of the intellect. It promises universal brotherhood, peace and prosperity to lure humanitarians and idealists into participating in a conspiracy which gains power through deceit and deception and stays in power with brute force ... . It is a conspiracy in which hate-driven men participate" (p. 16).

According to Stormer, universal brotherhood and humanitarianism in the form of such international organizations as the United Nations and its many branches were communist fronts: "Much American aid to communists is hidden in U.S. grants to the United Nations and its specialized agencies" (p. 8). Stormer referred to these international groups as "one-world propaganda organizations" (p. 208) and linked them to supporting communism's ultimate goal of world domination. Once again, the same accusations leveled against the Illuminati 200 years prior to Stormer's claims were now made against these types of international institutions.

One of the most aggressive anti-communist organizations of the 1960s was the John Birch Society. My father attended meetings of this organization but refused to become a member out of fear that commies had infiltrated it and he could once again end up "slaughtered like a diseased animal." The John Birch Society was famous for accusing former presidents—Franklin Roosevelt, Harry Truman, Dwight Eisenhower, John

WANTED

FOR

TREASON

THIS MAN is wanted for treasonous activities against the United States:

1. Betraying the Constitution (which he swore to uphold):
   He is turning the sovereignty of the U.S. over to the communist controlled United Nations.
   He is betraying our friends (Cuba, Katanga, Portugal) and befriending our enemies (Russia, Yugoslavia, Poland).
2. He has been WRONG on innumerable issues affecting the security of the U.S. (United Nations-Berlin wall-Missle removal-Cuba-Wheat deals-Test Ban Treaty,etc.)

3. He has been lax in enforcing Communist Registration laws.
4. He has given support and encouragement to the Communist inspired racial riots.
5. He has illegally invaded a sovereign State with federal troops.
6. He has consistantly appointed Anti-Christians to Federal office: Upholds the Supreme Court in its Anti-Christian rulings. Aliens and known Communists abound in Federal offices.
7. He has been caught in fantastic LIES to the American people (including personal ones like his previous marraige and divorce).

Figure 2.3 A "Wanted for Treason" poster created and distributed by a member of the John Birch Society only weeks prior to Kennedy's assassination in November 1963.

Source: *Creative Commons.*

Kennedy—and the incumbent president at that time, Lyndon Johnson, as communist sympathizers. Only weeks prior to Kennedy's assassination in Dallas, Texas in November 1963, a member of the John Birch Society in the Dallas area distributed flyers in the form of a "wanted" poster with mug-shot style photos of Kennedy accusing him of being a traitor and thus "Wanted for Treason."

The list of accusations included in the flyer read like a modern-day meme that one would find posted on social media aimed at demonizing a political figure with lies, innuendos, and contradictory information. For example, the flyer accuses Kennedy of betraying certain friendly nations, one of which is Cuba; in 1962, Cuba nearly became the site of a Soviet-sponsored nuclear missile base until Kennedy and his administration put a stop to it, which many people at that time felt was the closest the world had ever come to nuclear war. Other accusations reflect those associated with the Illuminati: Kennedy is anti-Christian; he supports the "communist-controlled United Nations;" and is favorable to people who believe in equality and humanitarian causes but who are really communist sympathizers interested in civil unrest.

Red Scare Hysteria: The Deep State Version

Fortunately, the Red Scare hysteria that gripped America for decades ended with the fall of Soviet communism in the 1990s. Unfortunately, a new brand of Red Scare hysteria grew out of it and is still with us. Now, instead of commies trying to destroy America from within, we have those Satanic, deep-state Democrats, Hollywood elites, the left-leaning press, and ultra-liberal educators who indoctrinate our youth with socialist propaganda instead of teaching them about the my-country-right-or-wrong greatness of America. As former President Trump summed up the state of the union in a speech held at Mount Rushmore on July 3, 2020, during a time in which the largest protest against racial injustice was erupting all over America and other parts of the world:

> Our nation is witnessing a merciless campaign to wipe out our history, defame our heroes, erase our values, and indoctrinate our children ... . In our schools, our newsrooms, even our corporate boardrooms, there is a new far-left fascism that demands absolute allegiance. If you do not speak its language, perform its rituals, recite its mantras, and follow its commandments, then you will be censored, banished, blacklisted, persecuted, and punished ... . Make no mistake: this left-wing cultural revolution is designed to overthrow the American Revolution ... . The radical ideology attacking our country advances under the banner of social justice. But in truth, it would demolish both justice and society. It would transform justice into an instrument of division and vengeance, and it would turn our free and inclusive society into a place of repression, domination, and exclusion. (Trump, 2020)

According to Trump's summation of the anti-American forces working to destroy the nation, the commies are still here. Or, make that the Illuminati. Or Satanists. Legions of Americans fervently believe in evil forces permeating American society with the intent to "overthrow the American Revolution." Just connect the dots, decipher that latest Q drops, wish for guidance from the invisible forces, and you too will come to the "pretty damn obvious" conclusion of the existence of an evil cabal within America with its own secret rituals such as killing and drinking the blood of kidnapped children. They might preach social justice and equality for all but their real intent is enslavement if you don't follow the New World Order commandments.

At one time, Americans fervently protesting against communist infiltration proclaimed: "I'd rather be dead than Red." Now, those who deem influential Democrats as deep-state Satanists proclaim: 'I'd rather be a Russian than a Democrat" (Evon, 2018, n.p.).

It appears that the conflict gripping America is not so much between warring political, social, and moral belief systems, but the human psyche itself with its twin dimensions of rational and nonrational thinking.

As Jung stated during the height of the Red Scare era:

> The world hangs on a thin thread, and that thread is the psyche of man. Suppose certain fellows in Moscow lose their nerve or their common sense for a bit, then the whole world is in fire and flames. Nowadays we are not threatened by elementary catastrophes. There is no such thing as an H-bomb; that is all man's doing. We are the great danger. The psyche [of man] is the great danger. What if something goes wrong with the psyche? (Evans, 1976, pp. 303–304)

References

Banerjee, K., & Bloom, P. (2014, Oct. 17). Does everything happen for a reason? *New York Times*, SR12.

Barry, E., Nicholas Bogel-Burroughs, N., & Dave Philipps, D. (2021, January 20). Woman killed in capitol embraced Trump and QAnon. *New York Times*. Retrieved from https://www.nytimes.com/2021/01/07/us/who-was-ashli-babbitt.html

Brotherton, R. (2016, May 22). The appeal of conspiracy theories about EgyptAir MS804. *Psychologytoday.com*. Retrieved from https://www.psychologytoday.com/intl/blog/suspicious-minds/201605/the-appeal-conspiracy-theories-about-egyptair-ms804

Byrne, R. (2006/2018). *The secret*. New York: Atria/Simon & Schuster.

Carey, B. (2020, September 29). A theory about conspiracy theories. *New York Times*, D3.

Cohn, N. (1977). *Europe's inner demons: An enquiry inspired by the great witch-hunt*. New York: New American Library.

Dawkins, R. (2006). *The God delusion*. New York: Bantam Books.

Dawkins, R. (2014, June 17). The improbability of God. *Free Inquiry Magazine*, 8(3), n.p. Retrieved from https://richarddawkins.net/2014/06/the-improbability-of-god/

Devinatz, V. (2013, November 13). Communist party of the United States of America. *Britannica.com*. Retrieved from https://www.britannica.com/topic/Communist-Party-of-the-United-States-of-America

Evans, R.I. (1976). The Huston films [1957]. From *Jung on elementary psychology*. In W. McGuire, & R.F.C. Hull, eds. (1977). *C.G. Jung speaking: Interviews and encounters*, pp. 276–352. Princeton, NJ: Princeton University Press.

Evon, D. (2018, August 6). Are these "I'd rather be Russian than a Democrat" shirts real? *Snopes.com*. Retrieved from https://www.snopes.com/fact-check/russian-than-democrat-shirts/.

Evon, D. (2021, June 25). Did John McAfee hide files at collapsed Miami building? *Snopes.com*. Retrieved from https://www.snopes.com/fact-check/john-mcafee-files-miami-building/

Fiorio, S.F. (2020, November 1). Isaac Newton: Magician. *Parabola*. Retrieved from https://parabola.org/2020/11/01/isaac-newton-magician/

Frazer, J. (1895/1981). *The golden bough: The roots of religion and folklore*. New York: Avenel Books.

Frazer, J. (1900 & 1906-15/2018). *The golden bough: A study in magic and religion, an abridgment from the 2nd and 3rd editions* (R. Fraser, Ed.). London, UK: Folio Society.

Hernandez, I. (2016, November 1). Meet the man who started the Illuminati. *Nationalgeographic.com*. Retrieved from https://www.nationalgeographic.com/history/history-magazine/article/profile-adam-weishaupt-illuminati-secret-society

Hershey, R.W. (2016). Sources and secrecy: The Illuminati scare in New England, 1798–1800. In *The conspiracy papers: Essays on conspiracy theory*, pp. 62–104. Burlington, Amsterdam: Wishcraft Books.

Hill, N. (1937/2005). *Think and grow rich*. New York: Tarcher/Penguin.

Hodges, J. (2011, September 5). George Washington on the Illuminati. *Leadershipbygeorge.com*. Retrieved from https://leadershipbygeorge.blogspot.com/2011/09/george-washington-on-illuminati.html.

Hutson, M. (2013). *The 7 laws of magical thinking: How irrational beliefs keep us happy, healthy, and sane*. New York: Plume.

Is this tomorrow: America under communism (1947). St. Paul, MN: Catechetical Guild Educational Society. Retrieved from https://archive.org/details/IsThisTomorrowAmericaUnderCommunismCatecheticalGuild/page/n41/mode/2up.

Jenkins, J.P. (1998, December 14). Julius and Ethel Rosenberg: American spies. *Britannica.com*. Retrieved from https://www.britannica.com/biography/Julius-Rosenberg-and-Ethel-Rosenberg.

Jung, C.G. (1943/1972). *Two essays on analytical psychology. Collected Works, volume 7*. H. Read, M. Fordham, G. Adler (Eds.), W. McGuire (Senior ed.). Princeton, NJ: Princeton University Press.

Kitta, A. (2019). *The kiss of death: Contagion, contamination, and folklore*. Logan, UT: Utah State University Press.

Krisch, J. (2014, October 14). When racism was a science. *New York Times*, Sec. D, 6.

Lloyd, E. (2018, February 13). Eye of providence - powerful secret symbol with deep meaning. *AncientPages.com*. Retrieved from https://www.ancientpages.com/2018/02/13/eye-providence-powerful-secret-symbol-deep-meaning/

McKay, T. (2021, November 2). Fingers crossed! QAnon faithful await the return of JFK Jr. on the grassy knoll in Dallas. Retrieved from https://gizmodo.com/fingers-crossed-qanon-faithful-await-the-return-of-jfk-1847982576

Murphy, J. (1963/2010). *The power of your subconscious mind.* New York: Tarcher/ Penguin.

Palmer, E. (2021a, June 24). John McAfee "Q" Instagram post sparks dead man's switch conspiracy. *Newsweek.com.* Retrieved from https://www.newsweek.com/ john-mcafee-suicide-q-instagram-dead-mans-switch-1603638

Palmer, E. (2021b, June 30). DeAnna Lorraine thinks Miami condo collapse was "deep state operation." *Newsweek.com.* Retrieved from https://www.newsweek. com/deanna-lorraine-qanon-florida-condo-collapse-john-mcafee-conspiracy-1605519

Raffaele, P. (2006, February). In John they trust. *Smithsonianmag.com.* Retrieved from https://www.smithsonianmag.com/history/in-john-they-trust-109294882/

Rodger, E. (2014). *My twisted world.* Retrieved from https://www.documentcloud. org/documents/1173808-elliot-rodger-manifesto.

Stormer, J. (1964) *None dare call it treason.* Florissant, MO: Liberty Bell Press.

Swaine, J., Brown, E., Lee, J.S., Mizra, A., & Kelly, M. (2021, August 12). How a collapsed pool deck could have caused a Florida condo building to fall. *Washington Post.* Retrieved from https://www.washingtonpost.com/investigations/interactive/2021/pool-deck-condo-collapse/

Trump, D.J. (2020, July 4). Remarks by President Trump at South Dakota's 2020 Mount Rushmore fireworks celebration, Keystone, South Dakota. *TrumpWhiteHouse.archives. gov.* Retrieved from https://trumpwhitehouse.archives.gov/briefings-statements/ remarks-president-trump-south-dakotas-2020-mount-rushmore-fireworks-celebration-keystone-south-dakota/.

Vandenberg, B. (2014, August 1). Magical thinking. *Britannica.com.* Retrieved from https://www.britannica.com/science/magical-thinking/additional-info#history

Chapter 3

Don't Touch, Think, or Do That—Contagion, Contamination, and Taboo

Pandemic Pandemonium

The COVID-19 pandemic that plagued the world beginning in late 2019 dramatically illustrated James Frazer's contention that magical thinking pervades human cultures and that one of the expressions of magical thinking is contagious magic: the belief that the life essence of a person or other living entity can contaminate another object or living being with which it has come into contact. Frazer used the phrase "invisible ether" to refer to the person's essence that can permeate the environment indefinitely, indicating that contagion is an archetypal pattern.

Former president Trump, who was in office when the COVID-19 pandemic was first reported in the Wuhan district of China, underscored the "invisible ether" concept when, in March 2020, he used Twitter to refer to the virus as an "invisible enemy" over which the world is at war (Trump, 2020, n.p.). Although micro-organisms weren't discovered until the 17th century, ideas about the prevalence of powers and substances invisible to the human eye were theorized to exist as early as 5th century BC (Bryan, 2020, n.p.). Perhaps this is why conspiracy theorists strongly embrace a paranoid world view: they are more sensitive to the presence of undetectable "invisible forces" out there with the intent to contaminate us. And perhaps this is also why so many people embraced paranoid-fueled conspiracy theories about the pandemic: questions about its true origins, doubts about the severity of its impact on the world population, and alternative ways to guard against becoming infected by it rather than getting the dreaded "zombie jab," as some people called the COVID-19 vaccination after its availability became widespread in early 2021, implying that the vaccine had the power to destroy a person's cognitive abilities rather than boost the person's immune system (Fauzia, 2021, n.p.).

Because of the furor raised by legions of antivaccination advocates, numerous alternative remedies began to be promoted, beyond those advocated by Trump which included hydroxychloroquine—primarily used to treat malaria—and cleaning bleach—primarily used to clean your clothes. One of

DOI: 10.4324/9781003271482-4

the more interesting alternative remedies was ivermectin, a substance normally used to kill parasites in cows and horses. Its rise in popularity in the summer of 2021 overwhelmed the usual supply carried by bovine feed stores and pharmaceutical companies. Along with the surprising upsurge in demand for the drug, there was also a massive misinformation war over the drug's effects on the COVID-19 virus. In other words, while a global pandemic raged, infecting hundreds of millions and either killing or contributing to the deaths over 13 million—as of May 2022 (Cheng, 2022, n.p.)—another deadly epidemic spread with even more ferocity: the epidemic of misinformation, enabled by the Internet.

Misinformation about the pandemic's causes and cures became so infectious that the Centers for Disease Control (CDC), the World Health Organization (WHO), and the Food and Drug Administration (FDA) all made futile attempts to counter the potentially harmful rumors and conspiracy theories about the pandemic permeating Internet websites and social media platforms. At one point, misinformation about how ivermectin was an effective cure for COVID inspired the FDA to post warnings to those who preferred it to the vaccine, stating, "You are not a horse. You are not a cow. Seriously, y'all. Stop it" (FDA, 2020, n.p.).

Other conspiracy theories about the origins of the virus included accusations against the US government, that it had contributed funds to China's Wuhan Institute of Virology to study COVID-related viruses and that the virus either accidentally escaped from the lab into the general population or was released on purpose by the Chinese government as a bioweapon that would result in China gaining an advantage over nations hostile to its world influence. Despite the evidence indicating that the virus originated in bats that ended up infecting an open livestock market in the Wuhan district, followers of former president Trump promoted both the lab and bioweapon conspiracy theories (Kasprak, 2020, n.p.).

Trump's most fervent supporters then began an Internet-enabled demonization campaign against the government's head infectious disease expert, Dr. Anthony Fauci, who had served as director of the National Institute for Allergic and Infectious Diseases since 1984. Fauci himself expressed bewilderment over the surge of misinformation about the virus, indicating that at first many of the rumors were so outrageous that he was tempted to dismiss them as nonsense, but ultimately they became deadly since they were threatening the lives of individuals hesitant to protect themselves from infection (Fu, 2021, n.p.).

To be honest, another virus origins conspiracy theory *was* funny at first, the one proclaiming that 5G cellular towers were responsible for creating virus-like symptoms, indicating that there really was no virus, only manipulative evildoers attempting to control the minds of the general population with cellular technology by sending out signals to scramble a person's brain. This conspiracy theory became less funny, however, when people actually began to destroy 5G cellular towers by lighting them on fire (Chan, Dupuy, & Lajka, 2020, n.p.).

Another disturbing conspiracy theory involving ways to prevent the spread of the virus had to do with masking requirements. As the virus continued to spread throughout the world, country leaders began to demand certain restrictions on public outdoor and indoor gatherings which included wearing protective masks. Conspiracy theorists objected to the mask requirements, believing it was a government-related conspiracy to control the population by restricting personal freedoms. The masks were even thought to be a type of Satanic "mark of the beast," forced upon the population by those in government who worshipped Satan (Dwoskin, 2021, n.p.). The antimask movement grew out of this conspiracy theory, once again encouraged by former president Trump who resisted wearing a mask until he became infected with the virus. After he recovered, Trump finally attempted to promote the use of masks and vaccines during some of his political rallies but was booed for doing so, once again by his most loyal supporters who, by that time, had fully embraced the antimask, antivaccine movements originally promoted by their leader (Smith, 2021, n.p.).

The result of the avalanche of conspiracy theories about the pandemic was to provide support for another theory, this one introduced by biologist Richard Dawkins. In his book *The Selfish Gene* (1976/2016), Dawkins coined the term *meme* (rhymes with gene), calling it a "unit of cultural transmission" (p. 249) to theorize how certain cultural trends are embraced by the public and then spread to other cultures in ways similar to how a virus spreads, through human transmission. The following meme (see Figure 3.1) provides more information about the term:

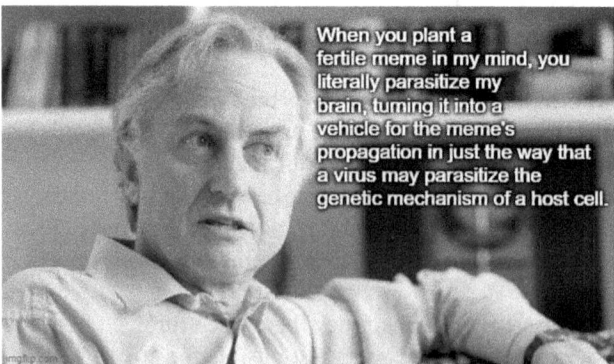

When you plant a fertile meme in my mind, you literally parasitize my brain, turning it into a vehicle for the meme's propagation in just the way that a virus may parasitize the genetic mechanism of a host cell.

Figure 3.1 A meme featuring Richard Dawkins and his definition of meme from *The Selfish Gene* (1976/2016, p. 249).

Source: *Creative Commons.*

Using biological terminology, Dawkins emphasized how infectious certain cultural trends are, comparing them to parasites that infect a physical body and impact the "genetic mechanism of a host cell," implying that cultural trends and ideas can impact a person's thought processes to the point where they can significantly alter a person's neurological network. This idea was actually embraced by antivaccers who insisted that the vaccine—not the virus itself—alters a person's DNA code, resulting in dulled-brain, zombie-like symptoms that evildoers take advantage of by making those who have been vaccinated easier to manipulate and indoctrinate. In fact, the opposite turned out to be true when research into the long-term effects of the virus indicated that, in some cases, it could lead to lingering cognitive and behavioral issues (Budson, 2021, n.p.).

Psychic Epidemics

As I indicated in Chapter 2 when examining the personality characteristics of those who excel at accepting conspiracy theories as legitimate explanations for controversial events, one of the key characteristics of this personality type is to accept the validity of unproven rumors about big news events from an intuitive, gut-level thinking process rather than from a more rational-thinking perspective. Thanks to the Internet, gut-level reactions to complex world issues and big news events can be sent expeditiously via social media platforms and within a few minutes accumulate a couple hundred thousand "likes" to its distorted perspective. With this type of lightning-bolt exposure and immediate acceptance by legions of like-minded thinkers, distorted information can take on more of a sense of legitimacy.

Jung had a term for the spread and acceptance of this type of skewed information, one that complements Dawkins' own use of biological terms to describe cultural trends that spread like a virus. Jung used the term *psychic epidemics*. He originally used the term in 1932 when lecturing in Vienna, Austria:

> The gigantic catastrophes that threaten us today are not elemental happenings of a physical or biological order, but psychic events. To a quite terrifying degree we are threatened by wars and revolutions which are nothing other than psychic epidemics. At any moment several millions of human beings may be smitten with a new madness, and then we shall have another world war or devastating revolution. Instead of being at the mercy of wild beasts, earthquakes, landslides, and inundations, modern man is battered by the elemental forces of his own psyche. This is the World Power that vastly exceeds all other powers on earth. (1934/1981, p. 177)

Since he was delivering the lecture in Adolf Hitler's home country just prior to Hitler becoming chancellor of Germany, Jung no doubt had the rise of Nazism on his mind when he spoke of millions of people suddenly embracing the beliefs of someone like Hitler who took as fact one of the oldest and most virulent of all conspiracy theories: the Jewish plot to take over the world. As we all know (except for Holocaust deniers), Hitler used this conspiracy theory to justify exterminating six million Jews in Nazi concentration camps.

Jung's lecture comments echo those he made during the height of the Cold War, quoted in Chapter 2: "We are the great danger. The psyche is the great danger. What if something goes wrong with the psyche?" With the inundation and rapid spread of misinformation surrounding the pandemic, it's not hard to conclude that something was definitely going wrong with the psyche at this time. Or, to be more accurate, something was going on in the psyche that needed to be recognized as a psychic epidemic. This one was spread not by a Nazi madman but by those taking advantage of technological advancements in communication that, in theory, were supposed to bring the world together in "perfect harmony," just like the famous hippie-inspired Coca-Cola commercial of the early 1970s, premiering around the time when the Internet was being made ready for use by the general population.

The point is: there has always been something wrong with—or misunderstood about—the psyche. However, big-brain humans are in denial about it, refusing to accept the influence of unconscious patterns of thought that express archetypal reality, a reality that has been misunderstood ever since Freud rediscovered the unconscious for modern sensibilities at the beginning of the 20th century. Or as James Hillman put it in the title of one of his books, this one co-authored with Michael Ventura: *We've Had a Hundred Years of Psychotherapy and the World's Getting Worse* (1992).

Bodily Fluids and Body Contamination Paranoia

Fears over what might happen if a person receives a vaccination have existed since the invention of the first vaccine in 1796. It was around that time that English doctor Edward Jenner began noticing that a disproportionate number of milkmaids remained free of smallpox which had ravaged the world population for thousands of years. In addition, the complexions of milkmaids remained free of pock marks and other severe rashes associated with both smallpox and cowpox, the latter a milder version of the smallpox virus. Jenner theorized that because milkmaids were in daily contact with cows, and cows suffer from cowpox which has similar symptoms as smallpox, the milkmaids must have developed an immunity to the cowpox disease due to constant exposure to it and, therefore, could also have developed an immunity to smallpox.

Jenner then took cowpox samples and applied it to scrapes he made on a person's arm, thus infecting the person with a small dose of the disease.

The infected person developed mild symptoms of the disease before fully recovering, thus lending credence to Jenner's theory. After obtaining samples of the smallpox virus, Jenner applied it to persons he had infected with cowpox. The individuals again developed mild symptoms of the disease before fully recovering, thus encouraging him to pursue the development of what he called a *vaccine,* a word derived from *vacca,* which is Latin for "cow" (Clarke, 2021, n.p.).

Jenner went on to develop the first vaccine for smallpox and campaigned for its application to the general population. Resistance was immediate. Many people were terrified over the thought of being inoculated with a substance derived from a diseased cow. Religious groups thought that introducing such foreign substances into a person's body was unholy, "a violation of the sacred body made in God's image" (n.p.).

Rumors about the effects of the vaccine began spreading, one of which was that it could corrupt a person's physiological make up so that bovine-like characteristics would begin developing on a person's body. A famous satirical cartoon by James Gillray appeared in 1802 entitled "The Cow Pock, or the Wonderful Effects of the New Inoculation" (see Figure 3.2).

The Cow Pock __ or __ the Wonderful Effects of the New Inoculation !__ vide the Publications of ye Anti Vaccine Society

Figure 3.2 Satirical cartoon from 1802, featuring Dr. Edward Jenner, the inventor of the smallpox vaccine, giving vaccinations to people, after which miniature cows begin bursting out of their bodies.

Source: *Creative Commons.*

The cartoon featured Dr. Jenner inoculating people with his vaccine, resulting in miniature cows bursting out of the bodies of those who had received the vaccine.

It's easy to find comparisons with some of the fears voiced by those who first resisted getting the smallpox vaccination to those who are part of the modern antivaccination movement. A major similarity is that both the early and modern vaccine resisters consider injecting small amounts of viral substances into healthy bodies as a perverse and unholy affront against Our Creator who made us in His likeness and therefore to put anything that is considered a threat to the purity of the body must be resisted. Both groups also share the fear of developing gene-altering symptoms that are more in the fantastic realm of mythology and folklore than reality: one could turn into a hybrid human with bovine features like the Minotaur from Greek myth; or worse yet, turn into a zombie.

The history of vaccines, therefore, must include a history of vaccine resistance. As other vaccines were developed and introduced to the general population, antivaccination protests continued to encourage the public to keep their bodies free from these unholy contaminants.

The current antivaccination movement owes a great deal of its inspiration to a similar movement that began in the United States during the mid-1950s, around the time that the polio vaccine was being developed. Keep in mind the "psychic epidemic" going on in the United States during that period, examined in Chapter 2: the Red Scare hysteria that insisted commies had infiltrated every aspect of American society. And now, with the development of the polio vaccine in the early 1950s, along with the introduction of fluoride in drinking water around the same time, it became far too obvious for Red Scare conspiracy theorists that the commies were trying to poison us with gene-altering vaccines, as well as a substance introduced into our drinking water rumored to cause brain damage. A very telling document from the mid-1950s from an anticommunist organization (see Figure 3.3) warned of America coming under the influence of the "Unholy Three: Fluoridated Water, Polio Monkey Serums, and Mental Hygiene."

The influence of Red Scare hysteria is obvious in the information provided in the poster. The overall message conveys a conspiracy theory still prevalent today: anti-American evildoers are attempting to manipulate the minds of the general public by forcing them to take substances that melt their brains. What is most striking about the poster is that it advocates against mental health treatment, apparently because psychiatrists and other mental health professionals are experts in brain manipulation techniques and, therefore, in a perfect position to corrupt minds and "transform a free and intelligent people into a cringing horde of zombies."

Fluoridation fears complemented vaccine fears despite the benefits it provided for protection against cavities, especially in children. According to antifluoridation propagandists, drinking fluoridated water could lead to a

At the Sign of THE UNHOLY THREE

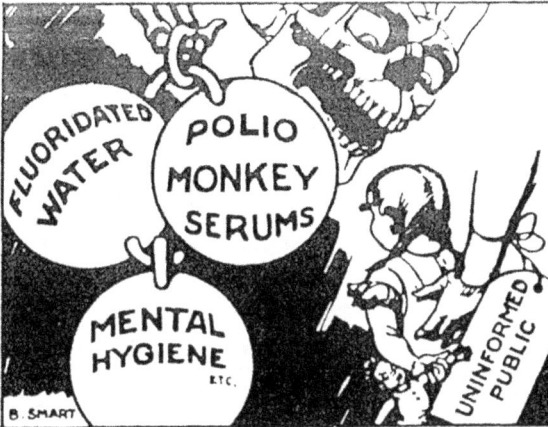

Are you willing to PUT IN PAWN to the UNHOLY THREE all of the material, mental and spiritual resources of this GREAT REPUBLIC?

FLUORIDATED WATER

1—Water containing Fluorine (rat poison—no antidote) is already the only water in many of our army camps, making it very easy for saboteurs to wipe out an entire camp personel. If this happens, every citizen will be at the mercy of the enemy—already within our gates.

POLIO SERUM

2—Polio Serum, it is reported, has already killed and maimed children; its future effect on minds and bodies cannot be guaged. This vaccine drive is the entering wedge for nation-wide socialized medi-cine, by the U. S. Public Health Service, (heavily infiltrated by Rus-sian-born doctors, according to Congressman Clare Hoffman.)   In enemy hands it can destroy a whole generation.

MENTAL HYGIENE

3—Mental Hygiene is a subtle and diabolical plan of the enemy to transform a free and intelligent people into a cringing horde of zombies.

Rabbi Spitz in the American Hebrew, March 1, 1946: "American Jews must come to grips with our contemporary anti Semites; we must fill our insane asylums with anti-Semitic lunatics."

FIGHT COMMUNISTIC WORLD GOVERNMENT by destroying THE UNHOLY THREE ! ! !   It is later than you think!

KEEP AMERICA COMMITTEE
Box 3094, Los Angeles 54, Calif.   H. W. Courtois, Secy.   May 16, 1955

Figure 3.3 Poster from the mid-1950s warning Americans of the danger of such alleged communist-sanctioned programs as vaccines, fluoridated water, and mental hygiene.

Source: *Creative Commons.*

long list of health problems including various cancers, diseases of the kidneys and liver, destruction of thyroid and pineal glands, and, of course, brain damage to zombietize the population (Armfield, 2007, n.p,).

Ultraconservative anticommunist groups such as the John Birch Society promoted the link between the "Unholy Three" and communist infiltration as a plot to make America dumber for easier takeover. Note the reference in the above poster to the New World Order, the ultimate goal of the commies. Or the Illuminati. Or the Deep State Satanists.

Interestingly, a popular film from the early 1960s illustrated the fluoridation controversy, tying it in with the communist plot to destroy America from within, in this case, within the physical bodies of Americans. The film was *Dr. Strangelove, Or: How I Learned to Stop Worrying and Love the Bomb* (Kubrick, 1964), highly successful upon release and perhaps too satirically lighthearted for the subject it was dealing with. In the film, it's not the Russians who "lose their nerve or common sense" and end up pushing the button to start World War III; it's a US Air Force general, Jack D. Ripper, who seriously believes that it's better to be dead than Red. After he gives the command to US Strategic Defense planes carrying nuclear bombs to head for the Soviet Union in preparation for dropping their loads on Soviet targets, he barricades himself in his office along with another officer and begins ranting about how commies are attempting to make all US citizens "impure" by contaminating their bodily fluids through fluoridation (Kubrick, 1964).

General Ripper's rant about protecting one's bodily fluids so they remain free from contamination included a warning to men who have to be extra cautious about losing a key fluid which, if depleted, could compromise a man's life force essence: semen. The good general's advice to men was to never ejaculate. According to this type of thinking, it's better to wipe out all forms of life than risk corruption of one's precious bodily fluids.

General Ripper's concerns about his bodily fluids being corrupted by fluoride and drained by lovemaking are archetypal concepts associated with "primitive energetics," explored in Chapter 2. These archetypal concepts have been called by other names and expressed with symbolic images, one of which is the archetypal image known as the uroboros, or tail-biting serpent. This universal symbol has been interpreted as a representation of an inexhaustible, self-perpetuating energy system likened to the energy found in the universe that keeps it in perpetual motion.

Another term for a person's life essence is *aion,* a favorite concept of Jung's. Aion refers to both the life cycle of the universe, and to an individual's life cycle. The latter is imagined as life fluids circulating throughout the body, with one of these fluids identified as semen. To lose semen in this context is to interrupt the cyclical flow of life fluids. So, in a sense, General Ripper is correct: men must refrain from ejaculating. Masturbation, therefore, is simply out of the question.

The archetypal idea of the aionic flow of fluids within the body and its disruption within a man especially through autoerotic methods contributed to the demonization of this sexual practice, with masturbation called, among other things, an act of self-pollution. These ideas are all unconsciously influential attitudes about how we keep our body free from contamination and from self-pollution (see Hillman, 1975, pp. 105–125).

As I mentioned, *Dr. Strangelove* is a comedy, a very dark one. At one point, director Stanley Kubrick planned to end the film with an elaborate, slapstick-style pie fight within the US strategic command building or war room; military officers waged a custard pie war with the US president and his advisers while bombs dropped on Russia and Russia retaliated with their own bombs. As I have insisted, however, conspiracy theorists take their beliefs deadly seriously and most probably object to the film's trivialization of this commie/Satanist/deep state plot.

Conspiracy thinkers are not wrong to remain suspicious of scientific advancements in combating diseases with substances developed in laboratories and then injected into the bodies of healthy humans. Many conspiracy theorists rightly point to vaccinations and other drugs that have done serious harm to individuals. The polio vaccination, for example, developed in the 1950s, suffered several setbacks when around a dozen test patients died and hundreds of cases of paralysis were reported before the vaccine was halted and refined (Adereyko, 2021, n.p.).

More recently, one of the worst drug scandals in US history centered around hundreds of physicians prescribing pain medication with opioids as the active ingredient, encouraged to do so by the manufacturers of these types of drugs. The result was millions of individuals becoming addicted to these pain drugs, leading to death rates by overdoses that, for several years, became the number one cause of deaths in middle-aged white Americans. These types of deaths were described as "deaths of despair," referring to a rise in reported cases of anxiety, depression, and a sense of hopelessness. The rise in such deaths was so dramatic, beginning in the late 1990s, that it compromised the overall life expectancy of this segment of the population (Rehder, Lusk, & Chen, 2021, n.p.).

Deaths from the opioid epidemic hit new record highs in 2020 and 2021 (Weiland & Sanger-Katz, 2022, n.p.), exacerbated by the COVID-19 pandemic when people were forced to adhere to lockdown restrictions and struggled with isolation issues. Self-medication was the answer for far too many. Unfortunately, due to a lack of hope for the future—which Jung would claim is due to a lack of spiritual grounding, calling it the "spiritual problem of modern man" (see Jung, 1933/1955, pp. 196–220)—too many Americans proved to be too fond of self-medication practices, willfully ingesting substances in doses that endangered their precious bodily fluids. This form of self-pollution, far more life-threatening than a vaccination or autoeroticism, reflects the habits of the human population's fondness for not only polluting themselves to escape from a sense of hopelessness rather than from a virus, but also polluting the Earth.

Contamination: "What you do to the Earth, you do to yourself" [1]

In 2012, a horror film was released that, unlike *Dr. Strangelove*, took the theme of corruption of one's precious bodily fluids very seriously and linked their corruption with the Earth's own, mirroring one of the major themes of Frazer's *The Golden Bough*: we are all dependent upon the Earth for our livelihood, so if we harm or despoil the Earth, we harm ourselves, and if we despoil ourselves, the Earth suffers as well. The film was *The Bay* (Levinson, 2012), inspired by a real event: the contamination of New England's Chesapeake Bay by companies dumping pollutants into the bay. One of the companies was a large chicken farm that dumped tons of chicken excrement into the bay on a daily basis for years; these chickens had been fed steroids to increase growth and rapid maturation, so this hormonal substance also ended up in the bay as a component of the excrement.

The film's director, Barry Levinson, was first approached by a film company to make a documentary about the polluting of Chesapeake Bay. Instead, Levinson created a "found footage" film, one that presented the story as if it were compiled and edited from news reports, police car dashboard cameras, security camera footage, and smartphone videos to give the film narrative a documentary-style realism that turned out to be nearly unwatchable. The graphically realistic depiction of a small New England town dealing with a horribly contaminated water supply was too close to the real-life situation. This time, it wasn't fluoride or a vaccine causing people to experience extreme effects of body contamination. It was mutated parasites.

The film takes place during a July 4 weekend, and as townsfolk celebrate the July 4 holiday with various carnival attractions, water sports events, and special food offerings and eating contests, parasites enter their bodies through contaminated drinking water and from the bay as the citizens' frolic in the brackish water. The parasites then feed on the entrails of their host humans before bursting out of their stomachs, necks, and other body parts like the creatures from the *Alien* series of films and also like the miniature cows from the smallpox vaccine scare. The result is pure panic among the citizens as half-eaten dead bodies litter the streets and many who can still stand roam the town in agony, begging for someone to kill them and put them out of their suffering. The local hospital swarms with people convulsing in pain while the parasites continue to eat their innards and explode out of their stomachs and other body parts.

After the town's head physician calls the CDC for advice on how to treat the hundreds of patients dying in the waiting room and hospital corridors, CDC officials remain baffled by the symptoms and doubt the doctor's report of mutated parasites as the cause. As bodies continue to pile up in the hospital, a CDC official ultimately advises the doctor and his staff to run for their lives to avoid contamination. Unfortunately, by that time, the majority of the staff is dead and the doctor infected.

News of the contamination reaches the outside world via local news reporters covering the July 4 festivities. The result is confiscation of all news footage by the federal government which then seals off the town and floods the bay with chlorine to kill the parasites and thousands of other living organisms, leaving much of Chesapeake Bay a dead zone.

What makes the film so terrifying is its fact-based believability. As I mentioned, director Barry Levinson was first approached by filmmakers to create a documentary about the polluting of Chesapeake Bay; however, after watching another excellent documentary on the subject and realizing the public reaction to it was indifference, he decided to take a fictional approach that dramatized the devastation of the bay from the perspective of various characters experiencing the contamination as it occurred. Determined to adhere to the research findings of scientists who had studied the bay's pollution problem, Levinson chose the "found footage" pseudo-documentary approach to give the film a narrative drive, characters to care for, and a monster based on 90% of the fact-based information known about the parasite featured in the film. Levinson used the steroids-in-the-chicken-excrement angle to present the parasite as having mutated into something much larger than its actual size, sometimes appearing as big as a good-sized cockroach, other times as big as a good-sized Chihuahua.

The oversized mutated parasites are monstrous representations of "man's doing." Reckless disregard for the environment results in a dead zone populated by dead humans and a grossly contaminated large body of water devoid of life, caused by a monstrous power threatening to destroy all other inhabitants living next to the body of water. According to Jung, the monstrous power is the psyche of man.

The public reaction to *The Bay* was similar to the documentary about the pollution of Chesapeake Bay: indifference. Climate scientists have been warning the world for decades about the detrimental effects of human contamination upon the environment. In April 2022, for example, the United Nations released a report by the International Panel on Climate Change that listed a series of failures by nations to curb carbon emissions in order to avoid raising the global temperature and thus disrupting climate cycles leading to extreme weather conditions. UN Secretary-General Antonio Guterres referred to the latest report as a "file of shame, cataloguing the empty pledges that put us firmly on track toward an unlivable world" (Rice & Pulver, 2022, n.p.). Also commenting on the report was Inger Anderson, United Nations Environment Program executive director, who stated that, "The last two decades saw the highest increase in carbon emissions in human history, even though we know the trouble we are in" (n.p.)

The main problem is that humans love their gadgets and their freedoms. A typical reaction to the report, most notably by those who believe that climate change is either grossly exaggerated or nonexistent, might be: "Reduce carbon emissions by giving up my car and taking public transportation instead? Sounds like the government wants to reduce my personal freedoms in order to control my life. Also, just look at who is trying to scare us with these bogus climate change reports: the United Nations. Everyone knows they are a New World Order-controlled international organization, so whatever they report is lies conjured up by commie-loving Satanists."

Impacting this mind set is what developmental psychologist Lawrence Kohlberg called the moral stages of development. According to Kohlberg, there are three main stages of moral development: pre-conventional, conventional, and post-conventional. The pre-conventional stage can be described as, "Why do I have to do this if there's no immediate benefit for me?" It's essentially a child's point of view about why the child is being told to do something by an authority figure that is unpleasant and restrictive. Although it's a moral stage that reflects a self-centered attitude toward doing what is considered the right thing to do, it's an attitude that hardly dies with childhood.

The conventional moral stage can be summarized as, "If that's what the law says I have to do, then I'll do it." Obedience to authority figures and societal laws dominate this stage, but it's also a stage that most everyone must embrace in order for a society to remain functioning.

Post-conventional morality can be summarized as, "Why am I allowed this privilege when others are denied it?" This stage emphasizes equal rights for all citizens of a society, and concern for issues that affect all humans on the planet.

Perhaps one of the most dramatic examples of the post-conventional stage was the reaction to the killing of an unarmed African American, George Floyd, by a white police officer. The event occurred on May 25, 2020, in Minneapolis, Minnesota, and was caught on smartphone and posted on social media. Although there had been numerous fatal encounters between police and unarmed African American men in the past, with riots and protests erupting in the aftermath of some of these killings, the death of George Floyd was unique. At first, there was a heated local reaction to the killing, but as footage of the murder continued to circulate on social media, first the United States, and then the entire world reacted with moral outrage, sparking mass protests across the globe and demands for justice for Floyd and for others subjected to racial and ethnic discrimination. Nothing like this had ever occurred before, an example of social media triggering moral outrage over a local killing that ultimately spread around the world in a matter of days. Here was a life-affirming example of a psychic epidemic.

A less than sterling example of a psychic epidemic occurred during the early months of 2020 when the pandemic first began to seriously threaten the population. Those with a preconventional moral outlook began hoarding basic supply items, depleting stores of toilet paper and other must-have-to-survive products that left many without any of the basic supplies. Many postconventional moralizers objected to the hoarding tactics of the precon's, leading to volatile confrontations and lots of toilet paper-related memes.

Contamination from the Other

It's sometimes hard to remain civil when you believe your life is being threatened by an invisible enemy. As many people of all moral stages learned during the pandemic, survival mode kicks in and dominates all other thinking functions. Freud would call this the reaction of the instinctual dimension of the psyche, which he referred to as the id, and which demands immediate gratification: "I need this—a lot of this!—and I need it now." Such a demand from the unconscious is hard to resist, especially when a person enters a store looking for basic household items and finds a riot going on in the paper products aisle. Seeing people in a panic in this situation can trigger a group-think mentality; in other words, survival panic is highly contagious. In addition, emotional contamination, when a person takes on the dominant emotional state of someone else or a group, is especially difficult to resist in these types of situations.

Social scientists have called the behavior resulting from worries over threats to survival *terror management*. One of the symptoms of this type of psychic epidemic is for a person to surround himself with material objects that gives the person a sense of comfort and security. Like pallets of toilet paper. Other characteristics of terror management behavior include "preference for 'charismatic' [political] candidates who articulate a grand vision that makes people feel like they are part of an important movement of lasting significance" (Weiten, 2011, p. 402).

Such a political movement featuring a charismatic political figure who emphasized traditional American values with the campaign slogan, "Make America Great Again," occurred during the 2016 presidential election, with Donald Trump ultimately winning the election as he campaigned for a return to a time in American history when white privilege ruled with little restraint. It could be argued that Trump had the Eugenics movement in mind as the last time when America was truly great. As I mentioned in Chapter 2, in the early decades of the 20th century, the Eugenics movement worked to maintain white superiority by encouraging the US government to pass laws restricting the influx of non-white racial and ethnic groups into the United States, along with sterilizing those deemed unfit to procreate in order to avoid contaminating the gene pool of those with a Western European heritage. Trump attempted to revive these policies to keep America free from contamination from so-called undesirables emigrating from what he referred to as "shithole countries" that make up Latin America, the Middle East, Africa, and the Caribbean (Kendi, 2019, n.p.).

Trump's overall message was: We must maintain our purity of essence. To do so requires making certain members of the human population scapegoats for whatever issues are troubling a nation or the world. For example, during the pandemic when Trump was president, he consistently blamed China for causing it, referring to the COVID-19 virus as the China virus. Trump then blamed the World Health Organization (WHO) for a too-favorable attitude toward helping China deal with the outbreak, even implying that it worked with the Chinese government to cover up the severity of the pandemic. Trump then suspended US funding for WHO while the pandemic continued to spread; Trump also attempted to influence the US Congress to place restrictive economic sanctions against China for spreading the virus (Neuman, 2020, n.p.). Although a large number of Americans objected to Trump's actions, his loyal fan base, eager for Trump to make America great again for them, strongly supported him. One of the results was an increase in violent incidents involving attacks on Asian Americans, similar to the re-ported increase in attacks on Americans of Middle Eastern descent after the terrorist attacks on the United States that occurred on September 11, 2001, perpetrated by Middle Eastern radicals.

Such behavior is the result of fears over being threatened by an invisible enemy. Even though a person might give such an enemy a face and a na-tionality, the enemy remains invisible, a result of the unconscious projection of racist and prejudicial attitudes upon those who are "not like us," and therefore perceived as a threat.

Trump's most fervid followers never seemed to process his political beliefs and attitudes from a rational perspective, never questioning his reasoning, leading to what Jung called a mob or herd mentality. Jung was intolerant of the herd mentality. As he warned during his speech given in Austria in 1932, psychic epidemics are a product of such a mentality, and have the power to start wars and thus endanger the planet. Jung went into more detail about the herd mentality when he was interviewed in 1938, not long before the beginning of World War II:

> Don't you know that if you choose one hundred of the most intelligent people in the world and get them all together, they are a stupid mob? ... . Not everybody has virtues, but everybody has the low animal instincts, the basic primitive caveman suggestibility, the suspicions and vicious traits of the savage [mind]. The result is that when you get a nation of many millions of people, it is not even human. It is a lizard or a crocodile or a wolf ... . That's what a nation is: a monster. Everybody ought to fear a nation. It's a horrible thing. How can such a thing have honor or a word? That's why I am for *small* nations. Small nations mean small catastrophes. Big nations mean big catastrophes. (Knickerbocker, 1939, pp. 134–135)

Jung's reticence to view large groups of people as having a superior collective intelligence began to develop after World War I when he first explored the herd mentality concept. Writing at that time, he noted that individuals infused with an especially potent amount of charisma which he referred to as *mana*—reflecting Frazer's views of community leaders endowed with potent life energies originating in the natural world—could infect millions if allowed a platform to express their views. This is because such individuals have become possessed by an influx of life energies from the unconscious. Since Jung (1943/1972) believed the unconscious reflected the powers of the natural world, he considered people with a strong, charismatic power to be possessed by the "*mana-personality* [which] which evolves into the hero and the godlike being" (p. 233). Ego possessed by such an archetype becomes a collective rather than an individual personality. Such a person can influence masses of people, which, if one is Jesus or Martin Luther King, Jr., can have a positive effect. However, both Jesus and King knew where their power originated: in God, the source of all power. Someone like Hitler took all the credit when in fact, according to Jung (Knickerbocker, 1939), Hitler was possessed by a god-power; in this instance, Jung considered the Norse god Wotan, the god of storm and frenzy, as the type of archetypal god-power possessing Hitler: " ... you take the widespread revival in the Third Reich of the cult of Wotan ... .[All] these symbols together of a Third Reich led by its prophet under the banners of wind and storm [i.e. Nazi Storm Troops] and whirling vortices [i.e. the swastika symbol] point to a mass movement which is to sweep the German people in a hurricane of unreasoning emotion on and on ... " (p. 118).

Although Jung referred to the rapid acceptance of a point of view coming from a charismatic figure as having the ability to spread within minutes to a large population and then "several millions of human beings may be smitten with a new madness," Jung probably could not have imagined the Internet as having a similar influence as someone like Hitler or any other charismatic figure possessed by an archetype expressing the god-like power of the Self. However, members of contemporary societies are highly aware of this new form of communication and attempt to harness its power, some to benefit the world, and others to destroy it with misinformation. And, of course, there are others who use this tremendous power to escape from the madness by posting lots of cat memes.

Scapegoats

According to Frazer, when something goes wrong within a traditional community, it's because someone within the community has sinned. To sin means to go against the laws of the natural world which could result in extreme weather conditions or natural disasters that threaten the livelihood of the community. A sacrifice of some sort is necessary to restore the purity of the community.

Frazer presented legions of examples of sacrifice, illustrating how critical it was for certain cultures to maintain a harmonious relationship with the powers inherent in the natural world. In certain instances, a supreme gift to the gods from humans—ritual human sacrifice—was deemed necessary to appease their wrath, restore order, and ensure productivity and fertility within the community. In other instances, an annual ritual of sacrifice was performed to rid the community of sin or other contaminating elements affecting the community's welfare, a practice reflected in modern New Year's celebrations when the Old Year—usually depicted as a worn-out old man—is replaced by a peppy baby.

In *The Golden Bough* (1900 & 1906-15/2018), the scapegoat concept is embedded in one of the book's main themes: the leader of the community embodies the powers of nature; therefore, maintaining the health and potency of a community leader by preventing him from becoming contaminated by outside forces is of supreme importance. Otherwise, if the leader shows signs of contamination that affects his vitality, he could be removed from his position and either banished or killed ritually or symbolically. In addition, if the community was plagued by unusual weather conditions, poor hunting or poor crops, or other extraordinary occurrences that threatened the community's wellbeing, the king was considered responsible and became a scapegoat for the community's hardships and done away with in some manner.

Numerous rites were created to keep the king or community leader from becoming contaminated in some way and either decrease his potency or create disharmony. In some cases, a king was not allowed to touch the earth with his bare feet for any extended time period, nor was he allowed to remain outdoors in the sun for too long since both the earth and the sun are supreme power sources and could drain away the king's own inherent life powers. This type of nonrational logic also applied to community leaders crossing large bodies of waters: if at all possible, such crossings had to be avoided since, like the earth and the sun, large lakes, rivers, and oceans are power sources threatening to compromise the king's potency since his own powers originate in these natural elements and, therefore, are in danger of returning to their sources.

The tribal leader, therefore, was subjected to many restrictions in his behavior and contact with the natural world and other communities. Taboos against touching certain objects, eating certain foods, uttering certain words and phrases, meeting with foreigners, visiting certain places—all of these restrictions applied to leaders.

Community members also had their own taboos, many similar to those of their leader. A major taboo in numerous cultures, for example, centered around menstruating women; in certain cases, they had even more restrictions than the king. This is because during menstruation, a woman is in a liminal state, between sexual potency and self-pollution. Numerous cultures practice isolating menstruating women to protect their ability to bring forth new life and also to protect the community from their impure state. In some cultures, even looking at a menstruating woman could cause a person to become physically ill. Women in this condition have the power to blight crops, make sharp knives dull, and cause miscarriages in livestock. According to Frazer, in certain parts of modern-day Europe, people believe that if a menstruating woman enters a pub or brewery, she risks turning the beer sour (p. 725).

Naturally, with all of these restrictions, it was hard for community members, as well as the king, to keep from breaking at least a few of them. Therefore, an annual purification rite with the use of a scapegoat became a common practice within these communities. The word scapegoat comes from the ancient Jewish tradition of annually transferring "the sins of the people to the beast [i.e. a goat] and sending it "away into the wilderness" (p. 599).

Frazer referred to scapegoat practices as "the transference of evil:"

> The notion that we can transfer our guilt and sufferings to some other being [or object] who will bear them for us is familiar to the savage mind. It arises from a very obvious confusion between … the material and the immaterial … . [The] savage fancies that it is … possible to shift the burden of his pains and sorrows to another who will suffer them in his stead. Upon this idea he acts, and the result is an endless number of very unamiable devices for palming off upon someone else the trouble which a man shrinks from bearing himself. (p. 575)

Frazer refers to savages as "palming off" their guilt upon someone else, but it's hardly a practice exclusive to indigenous cultures. If you grew up with a younger sibling, you know who took the blame for most of your own screw ups.

Former president Trump was famous for not taking responsibility for any questionable practices or policy failures during his presidency when, in fact, as the leader of his nation, he should have taken responsibility for all the sins of his administration. For example, when there was a major problem at the beginning of the pandemic with making COVID-19 tests available to the general public, Trump stated: "No, I don't take responsibility at all" (Voytko, 2020, n.p.). The main trouble in this situation turned out to be Trump himself; he held up testing because he didn't want new cases reported and thus make the United States look bad with high numbers of reported infections and deaths. Ultimately, with the delay in testing and with the administration's sometimes confusing messages about practicing safety measures such as wearing masks, frequently sanitizing hands, and maintaining a safe distance from others while in public, the United States ended up reporting more cases and deaths than any other country. In this example, it was the community, not the king, who became scapegoats and were sacrificed so the king could remain blameless and free of sin.

Taboo

Restrictions and safety measures put into place by traditional cultures to avoid contamination and ensure the wellbeing of the community are so voluminous, it took Frazer twelve volumes to compile them. In modern cultures, there are probably less restrictive practices but ultimately no society is free from acts, thoughts, and beliefs considered to be off-limits, unhealthy, evil—in a word, taboo.

Frazer's investigation of taboo included examples of practices that can only be performed under special circumstances. In other words, an act can remain taboo, considered impure, but during a certain time of the year, the taboo is lifted and everyone partakes of the act. This is because taboo refers to something holy. As Frazer stated: " ... some of the [practices] we should call holy, others we might pronounce unclean and polluted. But the savage makes no such moral distinction between them; the conceptions of holiness and pollution are not yet differentiated in his mind ... . These taboos act ... as electrical insulators to preserve the spiritual force ... ." (p. 186).

In one example of a conflict between what is thought to be unclean and what is sacred, Frazer used the pig as an animal considered impure by some cultures, holy by others, and both by still others. Although modern practitioners of Judaism refrain from eating pig's flesh, according to Frazer, the ancient Jews at one time did consume pork, as well as the flesh of mice, and did so:

> ... as a religious rite. Doubtless this was a very ancient ceremony, dating from a time when both the pig and the mouse were venerated as divine, and when their flesh was partaken of sacramentally on rare and solemn occasions as the body and blood of gods. And in general it may perhaps be said that all so-called unclean animals were originally sacred; the reason for not eating them was that they were divine. (p. 502)

As Frazer stated, taboo practices "act as electrical insulators to preserve the spiritual force;" in other words, they are infused with an electric charge of numen, or archetypal energy, giving these concepts a sense of the uncanny, resulting in a fascination that both attracts and repels the individual. This can lead to obsessive thoughts about the forbidden act.

We all know what happens when something is considered to be off-limits or unspeakable. The folklore motif of the forbidden room that should never be entered, or the act that should never be performed, or the name that should never be uttered, almost universally results in the room entered, the act performed, and the word said. There is a psychological term for this type of behavior: *psychological reactance*: " ... when we are told what to do and what not to do, we react by wanting to do exactly what is forbidden to us" (Gazzaniga, Heatherton, & Halpern, 2011, p. 337).

In the United States, which prides itself as a nation that offers its citizens a wide range of freedoms, it's interesting that the year 2021 saw more restrictions put on reading material for young people than ever before. According to a report released in April 2022 by the literary organization PEN America, many school districts across the United States seemed eager to ban entire subjects from curricula, especially books that explored the topics of race, sexuality, and gender identity. The bans were so aggressive and widespread that Jonathan Friedman, Director of PEN America's Free Expression and Education program, voiced his concerns about students having their First Amendment rights infringed upon (Sarstedt & DeSantis, 2022, n.p.).

Book challenges in schools have always been an issue, since some books are not appropriate reading for children and adolescents. Imagine a high school carrying the complete works of the Marquis de Sade. There have to be guidelines for age-appropriate reading material. However, as Jonathan Friedman pointed out, the censoring of entire topics indicated a reversal in progress made toward a better understanding and acceptance of these topics.

Once again, it appears that scapegoats are being created to blame those who, apparently, would make America less great. According to this reasoning, if such books are removed from the school library, students will not dwell upon such topics as racism, gender identity, and sex. It is the same type of attitude many parents have toward teaching safe sex practices in schools: if educators teach it, the kids will want to indulge in premarital sex out of curiosity. In the present situation, reading about transgenderism might encourage a teen to start saving up for a sex change, or reading about the history racial inequality and ethnic discrimination will make students question America's greatness. But, that's when psychological reactance could tempt students to dare look inside the covers of a banned book. And, like Eve, their eyes could end up being opened while feelings of guilt and shame compromise their acceptance of this new perspective, for they now have knowledge about what is forbidden, and it is a terrible responsibility to bear, requiring a person to think about the unspeakable and wrestle with the consequences. However, such a psychological conflict is exactly what Jung recommended each individual must experience in order to become someone with a distinct personality: we must be tempted by what at first appears to be evil, and then resist becoming overwhelmed by this new information in order to determine whether it truly is evil or something that benefits conscious growth.

The Incest Taboo

We are all familiar with the power of words, and efforts to keep certain books off limits to impressionable minds reflect their power to effect change in consciousness. However, some words remain taboo for adults as well as for children. For example, a leading candidate for the most obscene word in the English language is a twelve-letter word referring to a person who has sexual intercourse with his or her mother. I personally respect the word's power to shock, outrage, and disgust, and therefore rarely use it, especially since it is most commonly used to denigrate someone or to express extreme outrage over a situation which serves to distort its intended meaning and significance; however, its offensive power does relate to the taboo to which it refers: the incest taboo.

The power of the incest taboo, one of the most universal of all taboo acts, triggers thoughts of shame and repulsion while stirring up volatile emotions, even rage, especially in those subjected to sexual abuse at a young age from a family member.

Frazer (1900 & 1906-15/2018) provided voluminous examples of the perceived effects of incest and other sexual acts considered taboo within indigenous cultures, emphasizing how such acts are considered to have detrimental effects on the natural world due to the "invisible ether" that links all human acts with the cycles of nature:

> Again, the sympathetic relation supposed to exist between the commerce of the sexes and the fertility of the earth manifests itself in the belief that illicit love tends, directly or indirectly, to mar that fertility and to blight the crops … . The Battas of Sumatra [for example] think that … [the] crime of incest … would blast the whole harvest if the wrong were not speedily repaired. Epidemics and other calamities that affect the whole people are almost always traced by them to incest. [In addition, the indigenous peoples of] Loango [in Africa] suppose that the intercourse of a man with an immature girl is punished by God with drought and consequent famine, until the culprits atone for their sin by dancing naked before the king and an assembly of people, who throw hot gravel and bits of glass … . Conceived as an unnatural union of the sexes, incest might be thought to subvert the regular processes of reproduction, and so to prevent the earth from yielding its fruits and to hinder animals and men from propagating their kinds. (pp. 104–107)

Frazer's examples emphasize how human actions that seem to have no direct impact on the cycles of nature nevertheless have a profound effect that can result in contaminating the natural world with "unproductive" energies leading to infertility in both animals and plants. The connection between these incestuous actions and their detrimental effects on the natural world is completely nonrational, and yet due to the instinctual reaction of abomination over such acts, and the fact that incest is nearly universally condemned, incest must be considered an archetypal motif that compels certain people to impulsively act it out. Jung, however, considered the motif to have a profound symbolic meaning.

Jung's views of incest contrast radically with Freud's and to some degree with Frazer's. In *Psychology of the Unconscious* (1916/2001) and its revised version, *Symbols of Transformation* (1956/1967), Jung first praised Freud for his insights into one of Freud's most famous theories—the Oedipus complex, which refers to a young boy's growing affection for his mother and the desire to have an exclusive intimate relationship with her, reflective of the Greek myth featuring Oedipus who inadvertently ended up killing his father and marrying his mother:

> We did not know then—and who knows even today?—that a man can have an unconscious, all-consuming passion for his mother which may undermine and tragically complicate his whole life, so that the monstrous fate of Oedipus seems not one whit overdrawn ... .We cannot, to begin with, admit such possibilities in ourselves without a feeling of moral revulsion, and without resistances which are only too likely to blind the intellect and render self-knowledge impossible. But if we can succeed in discriminating between objective knowledge and emotional value-judgments, then the gulf that separates our age from antiquity is bridged over, and we realize with astonishment that Oedipus is still alive for us. The importance of this realization should not be underestimated for it reaches us that there is an identity of fundamental human conflicts which is independent of time and place. What aroused a feeling of horror in the Greeks still remains true ... . That, at least, is the hope we draw from [Freud's] rediscovery of the immortality of Oedipus. (pp. 4–5)

Jung's positive reaction to Freud's insights into the incest taboo, however, turned to doubt about the taboo's true intent. Freud actually remained ambivalent about the origins of the incest taboo. Although he was an atheist, Freud (1913/1950) used religious and supernatural terms to describe incest, referring to it as a "holy dread" (pp. 24–25), and having a "demonic power" (p. 31). After investigating various theories about the intent of the incest taboo, Freud ultimately embraced Frazer's view, from which Freud quoted extensively in his book, *Totem and Taboo*, inspired by Frazer's in-vestigation into taboos surrounding marriage rites. According to Frazer:

> ... we may always safely assume that crimes forbidden by law are crimes which many men have a natural propensity to commit. If there was no such propensity, there would be no such crimes, and if no such crimes are committed, what need to forbid them? Instead of assuming, therefore, from the legal prohibition of incest that there is a natural aversion to incest, we ought rather to assume that there is a natural instinct in favor of it, and that if the law represses it, as it represses other natural instincts, it does so because civilized men have come to the conclusion that the satisfaction of these natural instincts is detrimental to the general interests of society. (quoted in Freud, 1913/1950, p. 153)

Freud followed Frazer's comments with praise:

> I may add to these excellent arguments of Frazer's that the findings of psychoanalysis make the hypothesis of an innate aversion to incestuous intercourse totally untenable. They have shown, on the contrary, that the earliest sexual excitations of youthful human beings are invariably of an incestuous character and that such impulses when repressed play a part that can scarcely be over-estimated as motive forces for neuroses in later life. (pp. 153–154)

What this view of incest promotes is how the incest taboo inspired certain cultures to incorporate the practice of exogamy, marriage outside immediate and extended family relationships. In other words, the Freudian id, which is dominated by sexual and aggressive urges, was tamed in this instance by the Freudian superego, the latter an aspect of the psyche influenced by a culture's moral and ethical practices.

The Freudian view of incest dominated psychology for decades. In a convoluted example of scapegoating, some Freudians blamed the mother for encouraging their young sons to succumb to the incest taboo. For example, N.K. Rickles (1950), writing from a mid-20th-century Freudian perspective, blamed the mother's unconscious obsession with penis envy which encouraged a boy to develop an incestuous attitude toward her; fighting off the urge to sexually dominate the mother resulted in a young man's impulsive acts of public exhibitionism as a way to satisfy the urge (pp. 53–57). According to this view, young girls are also to blame for stirring up incestuous desires in their fathers, again because of penis envy; however, unlike boys, young girls have no desire to engage in exhibitionism to defuse the urge because, according to Rickles, they have nothing to exhibit (pp. 49–50), certainly one of the most nonrational—or, to be more accurate, nonsensical—views associated with the incest taboo ever presented.

As I mentioned, Jung, had a radically different view of incest. He considered it one of the crucial archetypal motifs that challenge ego to wrestle with its implications, which could ultimately lead to an expansion of consciousness. Jung went even further in this view of incest, stating that the motif is an expression of the impulse for a return to the womb in order to experience a rebirth from the mother, in this instance, the Great Mother, the source of all life:

> "It is not cohabitation that is desired, but rebirth … . The effect of the incest taboo … is to stimulate the creative imagination, which gradually opens up possible avenues for the perceptibly spiritualized. The [unconscious] power which 'always desires evil' thus creates the spiritual life" (p. 244).

For children, Jung considered the incest taboo irrelevant since they already enjoy a life dependent on parental figures and are "in that state of unconscious identity with the mother, [and] still one with the animal [i.e. instinctual] psyche ... . Yet, the longing for this [infantile] world continues and, when difficult adaptations are demanded, is forever tempting one to make evasions and retreats, to regress to the infantile past, which [the unconscious] then starts throwing up incestuous symbolism [as a compensatory reaction]" (pp. 235–236).

Jung pointed out that in mythology, heroes and god figures are the ones who can attain rebirth through incestuous union with the Great Mother by performing a Sacred Marriage rite—union between masculine and feminine god powers, or humans and a god power (p. 256). An example from Greek mythology featured the god Hermes who secretly spied upon a mother goddess figure as she rested naked one evening beside Lake Phoebus in northern Greece, with the lake deriving its name from the premier symbol of the feminine principle in nature, the moon. As Hermes continued to spy on the goddess, he became sexually aroused and approached her in anticipation of performing a Sacred Marriage rite. According to Hungarian mythologist Carl Kerenyi 1951/1995), the mother goddess in this instance was not only Hermes' lover but also his mother (pp. 143, 171).

The myth is relevant to the mystery religion tradition that flourished throughout the ancient Mediterranean area, with one of these spiritual centers located in northern Greece where this mythic Sacred Marriage encounter between Hermes and a Great Mother figure occurred.

The ancient mystery rites were held in initiation temples and remain shrouded in mystery; however, it is generally accepted that the culminating rite of these secret ceremonies was the Sacred Marriage rite involving a type of holy union between participants and a Great Mother Goddess figure. The most well-known mystery religion ceremony was held annually in the Greek town of Eleusis, approximately twenty miles from Athens. Participants were required to walk from Athens to Eleusis before preparing to enter the Eleusinian initiation temple. As they walked the road to Eleusis, nonparticipants in the rites lined up along the road and yelled obscenities and made obscene gestures at the initiate candidates, in this instance breaking taboos about the proper type of language and behavior allowed in public. The mystery rite participants reacted to these verbal and gestural assaults by doing the same. The purpose was to arouse the life energies within the participants by using words and gestures considered both sacred and profane, demonstrating the power of these words and acts to stimulate both outrage and erotic desires.

How the initiates participated in the Sacred Marriage rite, or what form this rite took, remains a mystery. What is not disputed is that, by participating in this sacred rite, they experienced a type of symbolic resurrection and rebirth from the land of the dead, meaning that they had achieved a transformation of consciousness likened to the achievement of hero status through the initiation process which was essentially a purification process that prepared them for union with the Great Mother. And after achieving hero status through this sacred union, all participants embraced and embodied the true meaning of the most obscene word in the English language.

Jung (1956/1967) also commented that a potential hero was considered a "mere mortal" until he or she achieved hero status and then "can do that which is forbidden and superhuman: he commits the magical incest and thus obtains immortality." In other words, through union with the Great Mother—the source of all life—a hero figure experiences a god power that is immortal, eternal, and inexhaustible, what Carl Kerényi (1976/1996) called *zoe*: "the experience of infinite life" (p. xxxvi). Jung (1956/1967) called this experience the mortal ego's encounter with the immortal Self, essentially a reminder that "man does not change at death into his immortal part, but is mortal and immortal even in life, being both ego and Self" (p. 384).

Both the Freudian and Jungian view of the incest taboo fail to deal with its traumatic, violent, and destructive repercussions. The urge to commit incest has nothing to do with penis envy, nor does it have much to do with the longing for rebirth. It is more closely associated with aggressive dominance and violent assault perpetrated by an adult sexual predator upon an innocent child. In this light, it does reflect Freud's concept of the id which is largely associated with sex and aggressive tendencies; it is also related to Jung's "evil intent" of the unconscious that, if fully given into, will result in catastrophe. In this case, the catastrophe envelops and contaminates not only the child, but the family, the community, and the society.

Frazer's comments about how traditional cultures view the incest taboo as a violation against the natural order leading to blight, sterility, and natural disasters as well as compromising the health and well-being of the community, seems to be a more accurate view. The sexual abuse scandals involving priests and other religious leaders preying upon the children of their congregations have underscored the psychic epidemics unleased by such predatory acts. Although not explicitly considered acts of incest, such major scandals underscore how sexual violation against a child can contaminate the child's sense of self-identity, leading sometimes to severe bouts of depression that could culminate in suicide; if a person survives such an experience, the individual can be plagued with a life-long struggle in regards to his or her own sexual desires. In other words, a sexual predator who gives into the incest taboo violates the relationship a survivor of such abuse has with life itself, reflecting the true nature of this brutal act of contagion and contamination.

Hope for Humanity

During the worst times of the pandemic when it appeared people would remain in lockdown for the rest of the decade and wear surgical masks to their graves and no one would be allowed to hug anyone else ever again, reports of people feeling depressed, isolated, anxious, and hopeless reached levels that many in the therapeutic profession referred to as an epidemic of despair. As I mentioned previously, the pandemic added to the struggles many middle-aged Americans were experiencing with addictive pain medications, leading to an upsurge in "deaths of despair," or overdoses. Another segment of the population was also experiencing high rates of depression and suicide: teenagers. The increase in reports of depression and suicide in teens compelled the US surgeon general in December 2021 to warn the nation of a mental health crisis overwhelming the adolescent population (Richtel, 2022, n.p.).

Because I'm surrounded by adolescents and young adults on practically a daily basis in my profession, and also because my position as a psychology professor means I must know something about psychological disorders, I make the attempt to ensure that students are mentally healthy enough to engage with the material in order to complete their courses successfully. However, as the pandemic continued to impact how classes were taught—remotely via Zoom—and students struggled to stay engaged while sitting in their bedrooms in front of their computers as siblings, parents, and pets tramped through their work space, I could see how the pandemic was wearing them down.

During fall semester 2021, more students than ever before either failed to complete my classes, asked for extensions to complete work, or just dropped out and disappeared. I worked with counselors to help some of the more troubled students remain focused or avoid succumbing to despair, and was successful to a certain degree. What I also attempted to do was to try to help them remain hopeful by attempting to create assignments that gave them an opportunity to express hope for the future.

To be honest, one key assignment was more for my benefit than theirs. I knew my own sense of hope for the future was fading. The world seemed to be hell bent on destroying itself by creating an endless, destructive debate over what is true and what is bonkers about a major pandemic as COVID death rates rose and legions of people downed ivermectin while accusing Microsoft founder Bill Gates of including tiny microchips in the COVID-19 vaccine in order to manipulate their minds. It appeared the world was descending into madness as an invisible enemy destroyed us all.

I needed help to break out of the despairing mind set, so I created an assignment called "Hope for Humanity." I asked students to share something that gave them a sense of hope when their lives seemed to be out of their control: a favorite song, a favorite poem, book, movie, image, person, or experience.

I must admit, the responses I received saved my life by restoring hope. Here is perhaps my favorite response, a photo (see Figure 3.4) followed by a

Figure 3.4 Men from a rural community in the Philippines work together to move a person's house, an example of the *bayanihan* tradition.

Source: Creative Commons.

description of its significance, shared by a student who grew up in the Philippines:

> This image is called *bayanihan*. Bayanihan is positive Filipino values that inspire the community to help fellow countrymen in times of need without expecting anything in return. The word bayanihan is derived from the word "bayani" which means someone who loves his bayan (community or nation) and is a hero. In other words, bayanihan means "being heroes" to the community. This image gives me hope since it shows unity, solidarity and cooperation. (R. Penaroyro, 2022, personal correspondence with the author)

It was the lack of "unity, solidarity, and cooperation" during one of the worst crises of the 21st century that drove rates of depression, anxiety, and suicide to epidemic levels. In this one amazing example, however, hope for the future of humanity was vividly on display, demonstrating what was needed to best deal with a world crisis. The joy inherent in the expressions of some of the men in the photo as they worked together to help another member of their community was infectious. And so was their act of heroism.

According to Greek myth, after being told not to open a secret box, the silly girl Pandora was gripped by psychological reactance and opened it anyway, releasing all the diseases, plagues, and miseries of humanity, with only a sliver of "hope" stuck in the lid of the box. However, according to another version of this myth, Pandora was not a silly, curious girl but a goddess, a Great Mother figure whose name translates to "mother of all life," and who "bestows all things necessary for life" (Harrison, 1903/1955, pp. 283, 285).

All god figures have dual roles as creators and destroyers of life. Pandora's gift was life itself in all of its horrors and delights. The myth of Pandora as Mother of All Life reminds us that if the world can survive a pandemic—one of Pandora's gifts—then perhaps it can also survive something as destructively perverse and supremely inspiring as "the psyche of man."

Note

1 A Native American traditional belief.

References

Adereyko, O. (2021, August 12). Polio vaccine history: Timeline of poliomyelitis discovery and vaccine invention. *Flo.health*. Retrieved from https://flo.health/health-articles/diseases/infectious-diseases/polio-vaccine-history.

Armfield, J.M. (2007). When public action undermines public health: A critical examination of antifluroidationist literature. *Australia and New Zealand Health Policy*, 4(25). Doi: 10.1186/1743-8462-4-25. Retrieved from https://www.ncbi.nlm.nih.gov/pmc/articles/PMC2222595/

Budson, A.E. (2021, March 4). The hidden, long-term cognitive effects of COVID-19. *Harvard Health Publishing-Harvard Medical School*. Retrieved from https://www.health.harvard.edu/blog/the-hidden-long-term-cognitive-effects-of-covid-2020100821133.

Bryan, R. (2020, May 21). What is atomic theory timeline? *Handlebar-Online.com*. Retrieved from https://www.handlebar-online.com/writing-tips/what-is-atomic-theory-timeline/.

Chan, K., Dupuy, B., & Lajka, A. (2020, April 21). Conspiracy theorists burn 5G towers claiming link to virus. *ABCNews.com*. Retrieved from https://abcnews.go.com/Health/wireStory/conspiracy-theorists-burn-5g-towers-claiming-link-virus-70258811.

Cheng, M. (2022, May 5). WHO: Nearly 15 million deaths associated with COVID-19. *AssociatedPress.com*. Retrieved from https://www.msn.com/en-us/health/medical/who-nearly-15-million-deaths-associated-with-covid-19/ar-AAWWQBu?ocid=msedgntp&cvid=1038c9c5b83d48fcbe20703440a9d40a.

Clarke, I. (2021, February 24). Complacency, convenience, confidence: The history of vaccine hesitancy. *ScienceMuseumBlog.org*. Retrieved from https://blog.sciencemuseum.org.uk/complacency-convenience-confidence-the-history-of-vaccine-hesitancy/.

Dawkins, R. (1976/2016). *The selfish gene: 40th anniversary edition*. Oxford, UK: Oxford University Press.

Dwoskin, E. (2021, February 16). On social media, vaccine misinformation mixes with extreme faith. *WashingtonPost.com*. Retrieved from https://www.washingtonpost.com/technology/2021/02/16/covid-vaccine-misinformation-evangelical-mark-beast/.

Fauzia, M. (2021, April 14). Fact check: COVID-19 vaccines won't create a zombie apocalypse. *USAToday.com*. Retrieved from https://www.usatoday.com/story/news/factcheck/2021/04/14/fact-check-covid-19-vaccines-wont-lead-zombie-apocalypse/7126542002/.

FDA (Food and Drug Administration) (2020, August 21). You are not a horse. You are not a cow. Seriously, y'all. Stop it. *Twitter.com*. Retrieved from https://twitter.com/US_FDA/status/1429050070243192839

Frazer, J. (1900 & 1906-15/2018). *The golden bough: A study in magic and religion, an abridgment from the 2nd and 3rd editions* (R. Fraser, Ed.). London, UK: Folio Society.

Freud, S. (1913/1950). *Totem and taboo*. New York, NY: Norton.

Fu, A. (2021, May 11). United facts of America: Fauci reflects on the pandemic's misinformation. *Politifact.com*. Retrieved from https://www.politifact.com/article/2021/may/12/united-facts-america-fauci-reflects-pandemics-misi/.

Gazzaniga, M., Heatherton, T., & Halpern, D. (2011). *Psychological Science* (4th ed.). New York, NY: W.W. Norton.

Harrison, J.E. (1903/1955). *Prolegomena to the study of Greek religion*. New York, NY: Meridian.

Hillman, J. (1975/1994). Towards the archetypal model for the masturbation inhibition. In J. Hillman (Ed.),*Loose Ends: Primary papers in archetypal psychology*, pp. 105–125. Dallas, TX: Spring Publications.

Hillman, J., & Ventura, M. (1992). *We've had a hundred years of psychotherapy and the world's getting worse*. New York, NY: HarperCollins.

Jung, C.G. (1916/2001). *Psychology of the unconscious: A study of the transformations and symbolisms of the libido*. W. Mcguire (Ed.). Princeton, NJ: Princeton University Press.

Jung, C.G. (1933/1955). The spiritual problem of modern man. In *Modern man in search of a soul*, pp. 196–220. New York, NY: Harcourt Brace.

Jung, C.G. (1934/1981). The development of personality. In H. Read, M. Fordham, G. Adler (Eds.), W. McGuire (Senior ed.)*The development of personality. Collected Works, volume 17*, pp. 165–186. Princeton, NJ: Princeton University Press.

Jung, C.G. (1943/1972). *Two essays on analytical psychology. Collected Works, volume 7*. H. Read, M. Fordham, G. Adler (Eds.), W. McGuire (Senior ed.). Princeton, NJ: Princeton University Press.

Jung, C.G. (1956/1967). *Symbols of transformation. Collected Works, volume 5*. H. Read, M. Fordham, G. Adler (Eds.), W. McGuire (Senior ed.). Princeton, NJ: Princeton University Press.

Kasprak, A. (2020, April 1). Origins and scientific failings of the COVID-19 conspiracy theory. *Snopes.com*. Retrieved from https://www.snopes.com/news/2020/04/01/covid-19-bioweapon/

Kendi, I.X. (2019, January 13). The day *shithole* entered the presidential lexicon. *The Atlantic.com*. Retrieved from https://www.theatlantic.com/politics/archive/2019/01/shithole-countries/580054/.

Kerenyi, C. (1951/1995). *The gods of the Greeks*. New York, NY: Thames & Hudson.

Kerényi, C. (1976/1996). *Dionysos: Archetypal image of indestructible life*. Princeton, NJ: Princeton University Press.

Knickerbocker, H.R. (1939, January). Diagnosing the dictators. *Hearst International-Cosmopolitan*. In McGuire, W., & Hull, R.F.C. (1977), *Jung speaking: Interviews and encounters*, pp. 115–135. Princeton, N.J.: Princeton University Press.

Kubrick, S. (Director). (1964). *Dr. Strangelove, or: How I learned to stop worrying and love the bomb*. [Film]. United Kingdom: Columbia.

Levinson, B. (Director). (2012). *The Bay* [Film]. United States: Lionsgate.

Neuman, S. (2020, September 22). In U.N. speech, Trump blasts China and WHO, blaming them for spread of COVID-19. *NPR.org*. Retrieved from https://www.npr.org/sections/coronavirus-live-updates/2020/09/22/915630892/in-u-n-speech-trump-blasts-china-and-who-blaming-them-for-spread-of-covid-19.

Rickles, N.K. (1950). *Exhibitionism*. Philadelphia: J.B. Lippincott.

Rehder, K., Lusk, J., & Chen, J. (2021, February). Deaths of despair: Conceptual and clinical implications. *Cognitive Behavioral Practices*, 28(1), 40–52. Doi: 10.101 6/j.cbpra.2019.10.002. Retrieved from https://www.ncbi.nlm.nih.gov/pmc/articles/PMC8221228.

Rice, D., & Pulver, D.V. (2022, April 4). 'It's now or never:' UN climate report shows globe is on 'track toward an unlivable world." *USAToday.com*. Retrieved from https://www.ncbi.nlm.nih.gov/pmc/articles/PMC8221228/

Richtel, M. (2022, April 23). 'It's life or death:' The mental health crisis among U.S. teens. *New York Times.com*. Retrieved from https://www.nytimes.com/2022/04/23/health/mental-health-crisis-teens.html.

Sarstedt, J., & DeSantis, N. (2022, April 7). Report: 1,586 school book bans and restrictions in 86 school districts across 26 states. *PEN.org*. Retrieved from https://pen.org/press-release/report-1586-school-book-bans-and-restrictions-in-86-school-districts-across-26-states/.

Smith, A. (2021, August 22). Trump booed at Alabama rally after telling supporters to get vaccinated. *NBCNews.com*. Retrieved from https://www.nbcnews.com/politics/donald-trump/trump-booed-alabama-rally-after-telling-supporters-get-vaccinated-n1277404.

Trump, D.J. (2020, March 18). We are at war with an invisible enemy. *Twitter @realDonaldTrump*.

Voytko, L. (2020, March 13). Trump: 'No, I don't take responsibility' for botched coronavirus testing rollout. *Forbes.com*. Retrieved from https://www.forbes.com/sites/lisettevoytko/2020/03/13/trump-no-i-dont-take-responsibility-for-botched-coronavirus-testing-rollout/?sh=786629da46f0.

Weiland, M., & Sanger-Katz, M. (2022, May 11). Overdose deaths continue rising, with fentanyl and meth key culprits. *New York Times.com*. Retrieved from https://www.nytimes.com/2022/05/11/us/politics/overdose-deaths-fentanyl-meth.html?searchResultPosition=1.

Weiten, W. (2011). *Psychology: Themes and variations* (8th ed.). Belmont, CA: Wadsworth/Cengage.

Chapter 4

Totemism—The Golden Bough, Toilet, Dildo, and Gun

The Birth of a Totem

In addition to teaching General Psychology, I also teach a class in Human Growth and Development. One of the assignments for this class was inspired by "show and tell" activities normally reserved for elementary school-level children. For my students, I ask them to share with the class an object they have held onto since childhood and explain why this object continues to be of some importance to them.

In many cases, a young adult will bring into class a well-worn teddy bear, or a faded pillow emblazoned with a cartoon character, or a piece of cloth that was once a baby blanket. One student brought in her entire collection of Barbie movies all on VHS tape format. Another student shared his collection of Mario video game cartridges from the first computer game console he'd owned. A surprising number of students shared jewelry they received at birth from a parent or close relative—a necklace or earrings for example—that they have worn ever since.

An impressive example of a jewelry item came from a Chinese student:

> I have a [jade] necklace which [has the figure of] a dog … . You can see this is not a normal dog, he is standing on a cloud. This dog figure is from our Chinese myth. And the dog has its own name: Xiao Tianquan, who was a guardian from a Chinese God's second son. This powerful dog protects the owner and fights for the owner. This was a birthday gift from my dad when I was in elementary school (I was born in the year of the dog, and dog is my Zodiac sign). And I have [had] this necklace for over 15 years. I believe this dog is my guardian. He can protect me from sickness and brings me good luck … . Also in Chinese culture, wearing jade relates to health. They benefit each other, and the color of jade will turn darker as you wearing it for a longer time. In China jade is considered to be a living stone. Jade is one of the most treasured stones in China … . This highly valued and beautiful stone represents strength, luck, and invites good health. (M. Chen, 2021, personal correspondence with author)

DOI: 10.4324/9781003271482-5

In this example, the jade stone is much more than a green rock. It has a history tied up with the student's relationship with her father. It also expresses cultural beliefs associated with a great Chinese myth featuring a dog as protective spirit. The student now believes the dog has become her own guardian spirit. In addition, according to Chinese culture, the stone itself is a living entity.

One can see how this example and numerous other "show and tell" examples embody the belief in animism along with the belief in contagious magic; in regard to the jade necklace, for example, its inherent powers keep the student healthy and safe as long as it remains in contact with her. Jade, therefore, could be considered a type of totem, a representation of the Chinese belief in protective spirits that essentially inhabit this type of mineral.

A more formal definition of totem is that it is an object associated with a culture and can stand as a representation of that culture's beliefs as well as its ancestral heritage. According to James Frazer, a totem is:

> ... a class of material objects which a savage regards with superstitious respect, believing that there exists between him and every member of the class an intimate and altogether special relation ... . [The] totem protects the man, and the man shows his respect for the totem in various ways, by not killing it if it is an animal, and not cutting or gathering it if it be a plant ... . The clan totem is reverenced by a body of men and women who call themselves by the name of the totem, believe themselves to be of one blood, descendants of a common ancestor, and are bound together by common obligations to each other and by a common faith in the totem. (quoted in Freud, 1913/1989, pp. 128–129)

With this definition of totem, many of the student examples probably wouldn't qualify as a totem object since they are hardly representative of their ancestral heritage. However, the examples do qualify as early beliefs in animism, which developmental psychologist Jean Piaget considered a belief that all of us embrace at a young age until we learn better from much wiser, reasoning adults that rocks, teddy bears, and old video games are not endowed with any sort of life spirit. And yet, the students still hold onto these so-called lifeless objects. And in many instances and many ways, so do their much wiser, rational-thinking adults.

In my case, I still have my collection of Tarzan novels that I bought when I was 12. I could blame my obsessive clinging to these books as proof that I am a hopeless bookaholic, but I do know how many hundreds of other books I have discarded over the years, so why do I refuse to part with Tarzan? Even though I know the author, Edgar Rice Burroughs, was a racist, and many passages from the series are blatant in their depiction of African natives as inferior to the Great White Ape Man, nevertheless, I am afraid I will have these books in my collection for the rest of my life. And I know why: Tarzan ignited the untamed, instinct-driven "feral child" that lives within me and everyone else. Tarzan is a modern, archetypal representation of the god of nature with a wealth of natural intelligence, an ability to communicate with animals, and who acts as a guardian and protector of the natural world in which he lives and thrives. He could be considered the embodiment of a kid's view of an ancestral spirit infused with a blending of human and superhuman power, and who still speaks to me as I live on an island surrounded by thick jungle and an infinite expanse of ocean.

Like the Tarzan I relate to, totems were all originally embodiments of a culture's ancestral spirit, usually represented in animal form. A good example of an ancestral spirit that is both human and animal is the Greek's Cecrops who was depicted as a human with a serpent's tail. Cecrops was considered to be the founder of Greek norms centered in the area where Athens is now located. The Greeks honored their founding serpentine father by creating numerous icons featuring giant serpents along with rituals in which serpents were part of the ceremony. Many Greek gods appeared in serpent form: Zeus, Dionysus, and Apollo, to name a few. And Greek goddesses such as Demeter, Athena, and Hera had serpent companions (Harrison, 1912/1962, pp. 261–263).

Religious scholar Mircea Eliade (1954/2005) noted that serpents are the premier earth-bound animal, considered autochthonic, having been born spontaneously out of the Earth and, therefore, the first inhabitants of the land. In order to claim the land and tame it from its wild, primitive origins, a hero figure or community leader had to conquer the serpent (p. 40). This tradition of a hero battling a serpent is one of the most common of all archetypal motifs. In fact, so many hero figures from myriad cultural traditions battle serpents or other large reptiles such as dragons and three-headed serpentine monsters, that one can't really consider the serpent as the ancient Greek's totem animal. It seems to be a purely archetypal motif acted out by individuals considered hero figures or potential kings whose heritage is bound up with the land upon which they historically rule and must, therefore, establish their claim to the land over the original inhabitants: serpents.

However, the Greeks did consider certain clans as having an autochthonic origin from serpents. For example, in addition to the Cecrops clan, there was as the Erechthonius clan, the latter taking its name from the second hero/king of Athens who, like Cecrops, was born out of the Earth and later became Athena's consort (Harrison, 1912/1962, pp. 263–267).

Jung had much to say about serpent symbolism (for example, see Jung, 1989/2012, pp. 102–107), and in this case would have agreed with Eliade that the hero-serpent battle motif is archetypal, found all over the world, and the inspiration for many myths and legends about heroes and potential king figures battling serpents to claim the land for their clan. Jung considered the serpent as a symbol of instinctual wisdom from the unconscious, and the battle between a hero figure and a serpentine entity is an archetypal motif symbolizing the battle all of us go through when we are confronted by so-called "evil" inclinations from the unconscious and must wrestle with this alleged evil to effect conscious growth.

Jung's attitude regarding serpent symbolism sheds light on how an animal might become a totem for a particular clan or community: the animal appears as a revelation from the unconscious. As Jung (1928/1969) explained:

> ... the idea of the totem ... is closely bound up with the beginnings of tribal life and leads straight to the idea of the palladium, the tutelary tribal deity, and to the idea of an organized human community in general. The transformation of libido through the symbol is a process that has been going on ever since the beginnings of humanity and continues still. Symbols were never devised consciously, but were always produced out of the unconscious by way of revelation or intuition. In view of the close connection between mythological symbols and dream-symbols ... it is more than probable that most of the historical symbols derive directly from dreams. We know that this is true of the choice of totem, and there is similar evidence regarding the choice of gods. (pp. 48–49)

Jung's ideas about the origins of totems relate to the origin of the word totem which comes from the Native American tradition, specifically the Ojibwa tribe of the northern United States and parts of Canada. The word is derived from *ototeman*, and refers to an Ojibwa tribe's "brother-sister kin" (Haekel, n.p.). How a tribe creates different totems—also called crests—for the various clans within a tribal community is through mystical revelation:

> ... families traced their origins to encounters with spirits and could tell of many instances in which supernatural powers had come to the aid of their ancestors and strengthened their lineage. Such guiding spirits were portrayed on many of the objects people used and admired.... . The ... figures ... were in fact crest designs—stylized representations of the spiritual patrons of a particular family, some of whom appeared as animals and others as humans, hybrids, or natural phenomena like the sun and moon ... . They embodied the sacred history of the family ... .Thus the crest figures constituted an expression of the family's unique heritage as well as a way of transmitting that tradition to future generations. (Debelius & Lewis, 1993, pp. 55–56).

As the above quote indicates, and as Frazer pointed out, totems eventually included objects other than animals. In the Northern Mariana Islands, for example, totem objects are trees, specifically the banyan tree which still causes many islanders to pause and pay respect; otherwise an ancestral spirit might be offended and end up causing illness or even possession as they almost did in the example from Chapter 2. Totems of the Marianas are also man-made objects that can only have come in a revelation of some sort long ago since they are unique in structure: giant latte stones that once held up the huge communal lodges of the first inhabitants of the islands, the Chamorros. According to legend, the first latte stone pillars held up the first lodge, considered the house of their ancestral spirit, the giant known as Taga.

If one visits the Marianas these days, one can easily find latte stones represented upon official items such as the Marianas seal and flag. But, it can also be found on key chains, T-shirts, hats, bottle openers, nail clippers, and other touristy items. When I first arrived in the Marianas in 2009, I was puzzled by the iconic image since it seemed to be everywhere, marking school bus stops and entrances into various stores, and appearing on sides of buildings as part of a mural. Because of its overuse, and because the original stone structures are now rare with many toppled and in pieces, this symbol of Chamorro heritage has lost much of its ability to stir a sense of communal tribal spirit. There is a movement to revivify Chamorro cultural pride, but it seems that the commercialization of the once sacred symbol has somewhat compromised the movement.

As I mentioned, many of the student examples shared during the "show and tell" assignment would not be considered a totem object for a community. However, the origins of a totem indicate that such objects were first personal since they came from a vision, a dream, or other altered state of consciousness experienced by an individual. After this revelatory experience, no doubt deriving from a shamanic trance, the object from the vision became related to the clan associated with the shaman or whomever experienced the vision. Here are not only the possible origins of totems but, as Jung stated, the origins of gods.

With the trivialization of totem objects in modern times, it becomes necessary to create one's own totems. This necessity is, in fact, one of the key intentions of Jung's psychological philosophy. Since the icons and religious figures associated with certain organized religions have lost much of their numinous power—a state similar to the totems of the Marianas and many other cultures—individuals must now rely on their own experiential revelations regarding totems as a way to express their inherent spiritual inclinations.

In this light, the student examples could become totem objects if the object itself is supercharged with numinous energy, as the example of the jade necklace illustrates. The jade necklace also has relevance to a culture's ancestral heritage, reflecting myths and legends about the culture, one of which relates to the mineral itself as being "alive," with the ability to change hues as it ages along with the individual wearing the jade.

Other examples of modern totems and crests illustrate their ability to inspire strong devotion to a clan's belief system despite their sometimes trivial nature and their having originated from sources other than visionary experiences; in fact, many of these modern totems and crest designs come from popular culture.

Vivid examples of modern crests were on display during the January 6, 2021 riot that occurred at the US Capitol Building when loyal fans of former president Trump attempted to stop the certification process for the election results of the 2020 presidential election since, according to their leader, an obvious plot to steal the election away from a Trump victory had been perpetrated by Satan-worshipping Democrats. Many of Trump's most loyal fans were members of various far-right leaning organizations with strong beliefs in white supremacy and easy access to military-style weaponry. Each group came with its own crests emblazoned on T-shirts, hats, battle gear, and flags.

Journalists from the *New York Times* covering the riot noted the range of symbols and provided details about the numerous examples of "clan" symbols on display. Many referenced Trump as the uniter of all these "clans," a type of ancestral father figure who, in one flag, was depicted riding astride a Tyrannosaurus rex as if he were part of the ancient hero/king tradition and had personally fought and subdued a giant reptile in order to ride it into battle and wage war with enemy tribes. Additional examples of clans and their crests included certain groups with white supremacist agendas dressed in gear or carrying flags with anti-Semitic and pro-Nazi slogans and imagery. One of these groups, known as Kek, featured a frog as its totem animal, and claimed that the clan's origins was "Kekistan," a fictional country with a fictional green and white flag modeled after the Nazi swastika. Like the traditional beliefs associated with totem animals, Kek the frog was the god-like source of the clan's power, one devoted to the powers of destruction. (Rosenberg & Tiefenthaler, 2021, n.p.)

As indicated, some of the emblems and flags displayed by the rioters had underlying mythic and religious references, reflecting the power of these images to express the religious function which Jung considered inherent in all humans and could be projected upon secular causes and charismatic political figures. This underlying religious fervor associated with "klanish" emblems included the most recognizable and infuriating symbol on display that day, one with a long US history: the Confederate flag. During the riot, one of the participants managed to carry the flag into the US Capitol building, the first time it had ever appeared inside the building. Many of us know the history of this flag, what it stands for, and therefore understand why so many Americans who weren't storming the Capitol that day were outraged over this symbol now appearing in the Capitol building, a symbol that represents an earlier attempt by white supremacists to destroy the United States. Its appearance clearly demonstrated the power of totemic symbols to arouse great emotional fervor, outrage, and reverence. It also illustrated how people sometimes go to war over totems.

The Palladium and the Taime

Thankfully, a full-fledged war did not break out during the Capital riot. However, it seems that was the intent. Many of the rioters were armed with guns and knives and were convinced in their righteous cause of overturning the election results to keep their tribal father figure in power. They even insisted that he was a virile leader, far from being a worn-out king in need of replacement like the kings and leaders of certain traditional communities who were either killed symbolically or literally, and replaced by more potent leaders after the current leader showed signs of ill health. As mentioned in the *New York Times* article, Trump appeared on a flag astride a Tyrannosaurus rex and also on a flag as Rambo, the fictional Vietnam War veteran featured in many testosterone-fueled films starring Sylvester Stallone. Trump himself encouraged such an identification with Stallone when, during his time as president, he re-Tweeted an image of Stallone as the muscle-bulging cinematic boxing champ, Rocky Balboa; the tweeted image featured Stallone as Rocky showing off his bulges, except Stallone's head was gone, replaced by Trump's own (Palma, 2019, n.p.).

In some cases, a totem was so revered and crucial to a clan's identification with its ancestral heritage that wars did break out if a totem was disfigured, destroyed, or stolen from one clan by a hostile outsider clan. Certain references to one of the most famous of all wars from ancient history could be interpreted as the war having been fought over the theft of a totem, or even totems stolen from both warring clans. This was the Trojan War.

In the earlier quote by Jung regarding totems, he referred to the Palladium, one of the most mysterious icons from ancient myth. According to accounts of its origins, the Palladium was allegedly a carved figure of the goddess Athena as a youth or "pallas." The figure was referred to as a *xoanon*, usually considered to be a cult object. It originated in heavenly Olympus where it was carved out of wood and dedicated to a companion of Athena whom she accidentally killed during a mock battle between the two. Zeus ultimately threw the Palladium down from Olympus where it landed in Ilium, the ancient name for Troy. It was immediately recognized as a sacred object sent from the gods and ultimately revered as the symbol of the newly established Trojan culture (Graves, 1955/1992, pp. 623–624).

Those familiar with the details of the Trojan War know that the Trojan hero Paris was responsible for starting the war with the Greeks after he abducted the Spartan queen Helen who was also a moon goddess figure (p. 638). What many might not know is that Helen had also been abducted as a child by the Greek hero figure Theseus and his companion Peirithoos, indicating that the abduction motif was an archetypal element associated with the figure of Helen. A very telling image, the earliest known image of the abduction or "rape" of Helen, appeared on a Greek vase circa 7th century BC. The image depicts Theseus and Peirithoos as Theseus grabs Helen by one of her upraised

Figure 4.1 Greek vase image, circa 7th century BC, featuring the abduction of Helen by Theseus and Peirithoos, with Helen's brothers Castor and Polydeuces riding horses in an attempt to rescue her.

Source: *Prolegomena to the Study of Greek Religion (Harrison, 1903/1955, Figure 94, p. 323).*

arms and Peirithoos stands behind him brandishing a sword; the two brothers of Helen, Castor and Polydeuces—also known as the Dioscuri—are also present, attempting to come to their sister's aid while on horseback (see Figure 4.1).

Classical scholar Jane Harrison (1903/1955) pointed out something obvious and very significant about this image: Helen appears nearly twice as large as the other figures, indicating she is a goddess or, more likely, a statue or totem object. Her pose with both arms held up is an ecstatic gesture associated with gods and priests (p. 323).

According to Harrison: "It is important to note that Helen is here more image than living woman ... . This early 7th century document suggests that the 'rape of Helen' was originally perhaps the rape [or theft] of a *xoanon* from a sanctuary rather than of a wife from her husband" (p. 323).

As Harrison mentioned, the cult figure of Helen was prized because of its sacred status as a totem object of the Spartans; if stolen, the Spartans would lose their connection with their goddess.

It is also interesting to note that the motif of two Greek hero figures abducting Helen, with one hero figure clutching her as another hero figure stands behind his companion brandishing a sword, is replicated with the details of the story of the abduction of the Palladium from Troy during the Trojan War. In the latter story, the Greek hero figures are Odysseus and Diomedes who steal the Palladium from the Trojans, a theft that led to the Trojans' defeat. According to the details of the theft, Odysseus disguised himself as a beggar and snuck into the Trojan confines looking for the Palladium. None other than Helen herself helped him find it—indicating that she was the Palladium or a similar totem object—after which Odysseus carried the Palladium out of the Trojan confines with Diomedes brandishing a sword behind him, thus replicating the motif from the Greek vase featuring the abduction of Helen by Theseus and Peirithoos (Graves, 1955/ 1992, pp. 690–691).

The ancient vase image of Helen's abduction, therefore, has relevance to both of her alleged abductions by two sets of Greek hero figures, indicating a relationship between the Spartan xoanon and the Trojan Palladium which, coincidentally, was also referred to as a xoanon in the context of its being a carved idol. In any event, the vase image and the story of the defeat of the Trojans after the loss of their totem underscore the crucial importance of such objects to a clan, and to a nation: the clan receives mana, life energy, from the totem, since the totem is linked to the spirit of their ancestors and to their gods.

To muddle matters even further about the Palladium, there is evidence that the Palladium was a meteorite and not a xoanon or carved wooden object in the form of Pallas Athena. The clue is the reference to Zeus hurling the Palladium from Olympus as if it were one of his lightning bolts or some other natural object falling from the sky rather than a carved object. Other references to meteorites as sacred objects descending from the realm of the gods are found in accounts of the founding of religious centers in various areas of ancient Greece and surrounding countries, usually associated with the mystery religion tradition that flourished throughout the ancient Mediterranean area. For example, there was a sacred stone associated with the mystery religion located on the Aegean island of Samothrace (Cole, 1984, p. 30), the mystery cult associated with the Phrygian goddess Cybele of eastern Turkey (Kerenyi, 1951/1995 pp. 88–89), and the Theban cult of the Cabiri located in northern Greece. The latter is described by Harrison (1903/1955):

> One day while [the ancient Greek poet] Pindar was teaching a pupil on a mountain, possibly Cithaeron [in north-central Greece] ... there was heard a great noise, and a flame of lightning was seen descending, and Pindar saw that a stone image of the Mother [of the Gods] had come down at their feet, and the oracle ordained that he should set up a shrine to the Mother. (p. 410)

The description is nearly the same as the details surrounding the founding of Troy, indicating that, like this sacred object associated with the Mother of the Gods, the Trojan Palladium was a type of meteorite or aerolite, the latter referring to a black meteorite stone. As a modern comparison with these ancient stone objects, the most sacred object of Islam is the ka'aba stone, housed in the Grand Mosque in Mecca, Saudi Arabia, and visited by millions of faithful Muslims each year. The ka'aba stone is black in color, indicating that it is an aerolite (Hill, 2020, n.p.).

Another example of a sacred stone that descended from above and was set up by a clan as its totem was the *taime* of the Native American Kiowas. Like the Palladium, the taime was considered to be the image of a young girl.

According to legend, long ago a young woman from the tribe "climbed a tree to heaven and married the son of the sun, only to perish when she fell back to earth" (Wooldridge, 1995, p. 60). The taime then became the Kiowa's link to the life energies of the sun. Like the ka'aba stone of Islam, it was kept hidden from public view except during the most sacred of all ceremonies, the sun dance, when the tribe reaffirmed its link to the sun through ecstatic dances that would result in trances and visionary experiences later shared with the rest of the tribe (see Figure 4.2).

An uncanny replication of the Trojan War occurred in 1833 when a rival tribe, the Osage, raided the Kiowas and stole the taime, leading to one of the most volatile wars ever waged between two rival tribes. The war waged on and off for nearly a year and became so fierce that the US Calvary intervened and attempted to settle the conflict. It took nearly another year of negotiations between the tribes before the Osage agreed to return the taime to the Kiowas (pp. 104–105).

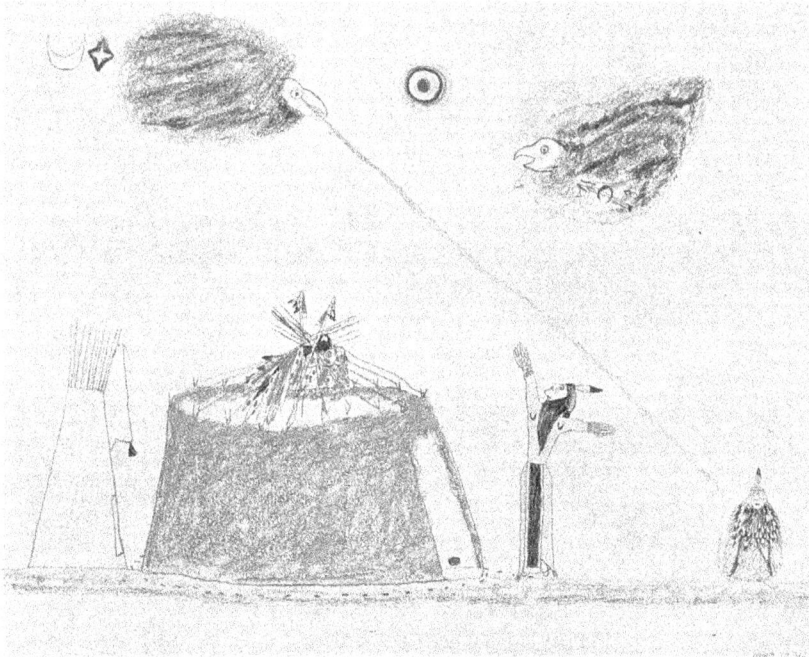

Figure 4.2 The taime of the Kiowa tribe (far right), from a drawing by tribal member Wo-Haw, circa 1875. The taime acted as the tribe's link to the sun's life energies and their gods, depicted here as mythical thunderbirds.

Source: *Missouri Historical Society.*

Psyche and Totem

The worship of meteorites as totem objects illustrates the contagious connection we all have with certain material objects with unique characteristics. Stones seem to be one of the most common of all types of objects that people are generally attracted to, as one of Jung's closest colleagues, Marie-Louise von Franz (1964) explained:

> Many people cannot refrain from picking up stones of a slightly unusual color or shape and keeping them, without knowing why they do this. It is as if the stones held a living mystery that fascinates them. Men have collected stones since the beginning of time and have apparently assumed that certain ones were the containers of the life-force with all its mystery. The ancient Germans, for instance, believed that the spirits of the dead continued to live in their tombstones. The custom of placing stones on graves may spring partly from the symbolic idea that something eternal of the dead person remains, which can be most fittingly represented by a stone ... . In this sense, the stone symbolizes what is perhaps the simplest and deepest experience—the experience of something eternal .... (p. 209)

Von Franz included additional references to famous sacred stones, one of which was the stone upon which the Biblical Jacob used as a pillow while sleeping in an open field and later dreamed of angels descending and ascending a great ladder that reached up to heaven where Yahweh sat on a royal throne and blessed him. After he had his amazing dream, Jacob built a small shrine and set up the stone pillow within it, then anointed it, and referred to it as a manifestation of the ancestral spirit of his people.

Von Franz also referred to the philosopher's stone of the alchemists, mentioned previously in Chapter 2. As von Franz explained, the philosopher's stone was considered to be "a symbol of something that can be found only within the psyche of man ... . The philosopher's stone (the *lapis*) symbolizes something that can never be dissolved, something eternal that some alchemists compared to the mystical experience of God within one's own soul" (p. 210).

With her examples, von Franz emphasized the relationship the psyche has with matter; in fact, Jung considered psyche and matter different aspects of the same phenomenon, "one observed from 'within,' and the other from 'without'" (p. 210). This link between psyche and matter, and how certain basic material objects such as stones have an enduring fascination, underscores the longing many people have for spiritual fulfillment. As von Franz insisted, stones are symbols of the Self, inorganic substances that express a sense of the eternal. The relationship humanity has with inorganic substances seems to be related to the fact that all living things emerged from inorganic matter.

In his autobiography, Jung (1961/1989) recounted an unusual incident from his childhood that illustrated the archetypal relationship all of us have with inorganic substances, that they are somehow connected with an eternal source from which all material life emerged. At age ten, Jung felt compelled to carve a small manikin out of a wooden ruler which he then dressed in a tiny black coat and housed it in a pencil box. He then found "a smooth, oblong, blackish stone" (p. 21), and put it inside the box with the manikin. Later, he wrote notes to this figure which he also stored in the box. In an uncanny way, Jung was creating his own ark of the covenant, the most sacred totem object of the ancient Israelites, which housed the stone tablets inscribed with the Ten Commandments.

Jung realized much later that his nonrational actions as a ten-year-old were spontaneous attempts to acknowledge his own connection with his ancestral past through the performance of ritualistic actions that replicated the actions of people from numerous other traditional cultures. Jung specifically mentioned the Australian native custom of rubbing sacred stones to get in touch with ancestral spirits. Commenting on the significance of his youthful experience, Jung concluded: "Ultimately, the manikin was a *kabir* [i.e. a Cabirian dwarf from the mystery religion tradition], wrapped in his little cloak, hidden in the *kista* [i.e. a basket used in the mystery religion rites to carry sacred objects], and provided with a supply of life force, the oblong black stone" (p. 23).

Talismans, Trophies, and Toys

This brief look at sacred stones as totem objects has obvious relevance to the jade stone necklace of my Chinese student. I called the jade necklace a potential totem since it was associated with Chinese legends featuring ancestral figures and beliefs about jade as a living substance with the power to heal, similar to the alchemical philosopher's stone. Perhaps better names for the jade necklace would be talisman and amulet, both of which include objects made from precious stones and metals as well as from animal teeth, bones, and claws. The amulets and talismans are infused with life power from the natural world and therefore act as protectors of those who wear them or set them up as a revered object (Britannica, 2020, n.p.).

My Chinese student had a sincere belief in her jade necklace as having special powers that would protect her from harm. One can see how similar objects, most especially crosses, rosaries, and figurines of saints and other holy figures are considered to be talismans or amulets. The gold ring and gold-plated pocket watch my father left me after he died, both of which belonged to his own father, could be considered talismans or even totem objects since they are connected with my ancestral heritage.

In a modern, materialistic society, certain material objects are coveted more than others and, in some cases, considered to be an expression of the owner's essence. However, because there are so many objects out there that tantalize and tempt a material girl or boy to possess, a gotta-have-it-now bauble can quickly lose its mana.

Two interesting *New York Times* articles from March, 2005, appearing within a week from one another, struck me at the time as a potent illustration of the difference between a talisman and a toy. One article appeared in the "Styles" section, the other in the main news section. The Styles article was about the latest so-called totem object of the Hollywood elite, which had previously been shiny sports cars. Now, the must-have object was watches: "They have function, they convey status, and, like cars ... watches have power in a way that other toys don't" (Hirschberg, 2005, p. S6, 88).

I was attracted to this description of watches as totem/toys of the Hollywood power boys no doubt because of the watch my father had given to me after he died in 2003. It was obvious that these toys of the Hollywood elite were all associated with power, virility, and status, unlike my father's watch which was associated with my ancestral heritage. The article did make an attempt to address how a watch could convey "personal history, real or imagined" (p. S6, 88), but in this case the emphasis was upon an imaginary, Hollywood-produced personal history rather than a documented, flesh, and blood history.

One week earlier, a *Times* news article appeared about the serial killer known as BTK (Bind, Kill, Torture) who had recently been captured after having terrorized a suburban community in Wichita, Kansas for decades. The article detailed the killer's first-known attack, occurring on January 15, 1974, and perpetrated upon an entire family. According to the article, before he left the family bound, tortured, and dead, he took "at least one souvenir of the day: a watch" (Davey, 2005, p. S1, 1).

In both examples, the watch is endowed with a special power coveted by its possessor. However, in the Styles article, the watch is essentially the latest toy-bauble of the Hollywood elite, soon replaced by another shiny bauble signifying personal power and prestige. The watch referred to in the other article is something else. It certainly signifies power, but this power is associated with ritual torture and death.

The watch in this instance is not an amulet, talisman, or toy. It has nothing to do with endowing BTK with good luck, or good health. It is something a hunter would keep after he killed and dismembered his prey and mounted the head or horns of the animal on one of the walls of his man cave, signifying the power the hunter displayed and his victory over the untamed elements, reflecting the archetypal motif of a king/hero battling a serpent and claiming the land it once inhabited. In other words, the watch in this instance is a kill-trophy of a serial predator.

While the Style article is about faddish toys, the BTK article expresses an unfathomable mystery: out of all the objects he could have taken as a trophy-reminder of his despicable deed, why did he take a watch? In this example, the watch becomes an object symbolizing the life energies of BTK's victims which he covets and feeds upon like a vampire or zombie until the hunger to kill and covet the life energy from other victims overtakes him again.

In turn, there are numerous examples of objects associated with demonic deeds perpetrated by criminals that are coveted by collectors of such objects. In the 1930s, for example, the car in which gangsters Bonnie and Clyde were gunned down toured America for decades and currently remains on display in a Nevada casino (Blazeski, 2017, n.p.). After gangster John Dillinger was shot to death in 1934 by FBI agents outside of a Chicago movie theater, bystanders dipped handkerchiefs into pools of Dillinger's blood to keep for souvenirs (History.com editors, 2018, n.p.), their actions mirroring those from traditional cultures who consider blood to be a sacred substance infused with the life essence of the individual.

In addition, Dillinger was allegedly endowed with an especially large penis which was severed from his body during an autopsy performed shortly after his death; currently, it's on display at the Smithsonian. And if you believe that, I'd like to sell you some of the foreskin from Jesus' circumcision at the limited one-time offer of … .

This urban legend of Dillinger's alleged giant penis being severed from him and displayed in a prestigious museum expresses the gangster as a potent force of unbridled power, with the FBI as a collective hero figure in battle with this destructive force; the organization's triumph is equivalent to the powers of civilizing justice and order claiming victory over the forces of chaos. It also illustrates the actions of a hunter or serial killer taking body parts from his kill as a trophy-representation of his link with this power. Just as the theft of a traditional culture's totem object severed the connection the culture had with the powers of nature, the legend of the severing of Dillinger's penis from his body illustrates how this body part was considered the source of his inherent demonic powers.

The Totem Gold Standard

The phallus remains an obvious masculine power symbol, and Dillinger's legendary penis imagined as one of the millions of unique historical items housed in the Smithsonian is a type of modern phallus worship, with the primeval power associated with Dilllinger having a numinous effect on those who imagine its prestigious display in America's most renowned museum.

This urban legend about the potency of a gangster's severed phallus raises a question that I'm sure many others have raised as well: can a dildo made of 24-carat gold embody that same power? According to the modern folk devil Gwyneth Paltrow, yes it can. And she can sell it to you for a limited one-time offer of $1,249.00 as part of her line of ultra-elite products known as Goop.

Paltrow, one of the most accomplished and respected film actresses, apparently had an epiphany in 2008 and became a seller of New Age health, cooking, and beauty products. Her credentials for selling these products were essentially her respected reputation as an actress.

Paltrow offers a variety of sex toys, primarily for her target audience: rich women, some of whom must hold the belief that, by purchasing a product associated with Paltrow, they can experience via contagious magic the life essence of this glamorous and respected actress, especially if they're burning one of Paltrow's designer candles called "This Smells Like My Vagina."

The golden dildo, also known as the gold wand, is one of Paltrow's most exclusive and elegant products, described as: "A gorgeous, smooth, impossibly luxurious dildo wrapped in twenty-four karat gold. Because it's made entirely of metal—under the gold, it's heavy stainless steel—it has a firmer touch than a typical dildo and runs cool to the touch" (de Montparnasse, 2022, n.p.). With a description like that, it's hard to resist just buying one. Perhaps by purchasing two, women can attempt to replicate an ancient dance performed by Greek courtesans or hetaerai with the use of two dildos. Instead of being made of gold, the dildos were made of leather; some were decorated with eyes painted at the tip and wings carved at its base as if it were a fabulous phallic bird infused with both masculine and feminine life energies that the dancer then embodied, achieving a type of ecstatic reverie considered to be associated with the androgynous god Dionysus (see Keuls, 1993, pp. 82–84).

What makes Paltrow's glittering product especially appealing is that it is made of one of the most sought-after minerals on the planet. Gold has been prized by cultures throughout human history for its glittering elegance and enduring permanence. Countless millions over millennia have become possessed by the lust for gold, either as raw mineral or as material objects fashioned from it. The search for gold has led to wars, mass murder, and feverish gold rush outbreaks, resulting in invasive mining operations that have left wilderness areas decimated and uninhabitable.

The fascination with gold is one of the most explicit examples of a material object endowed with numinous energy. Those who flaunt their gold objects do so to signal their sense of being endowed with a superior power. An ancient example from Eastern Europe not only underscores the prestige associated with gold, but also its reputation as a numinous mineral able to endow its owner with god-like powers. In 1970, a series of graves from 5th century BC were found near the modern city of Varna in Bulgaria, one of which contained the remains of a man adorned with an abundance of gold objects, so many that it was obvious that he was a figure of great importance. Along with numerous golden necklaces and bracelets adorning the remains of "Varna Man" was a golden scepter. There was also a golden sheath adorning his penis (Gillan, 2020 , n.p.).

Interpreting the presence of the golden scepter in the man's grave is relatively easy. The scepter is a totem object symbolizing the power of a king or leader. James Frazer (1900/1906-15/2018) might call such an object a physical representation of the leader's soul essence, or "external soul," having a similar symbolic significance to the king as the lightning bolt has to Zeus.

Frazer named his multivolume masterpiece after the Golden Bough, a totem object which he interpreted as mistletoe growing upon a sacred oak tree that was considered to be the representation of a king's relationship with the forces of the natural world. If, for example, mistletoe was plucked from a sacred oak tree and then destroyed, the king would die. In other words, Frazer interpreted certain totem objects as "the receptacle in which a man keeps his life ..." (p. 811). I will explore the concept of the external soul further in Chapter 6.

At first, it might appear that the significance of Varna man's golden penis sheath is a more difficult object to interpret, unless it's interpreted from Frazer's point of view as an icon associated with the leader's sexual potency. Surrounding the penis with a covering of a precious mineral could symbolize its connection with the inexhaustible, fructifying power inherent in the natural world. Far from being merely a fashionable piece of golden jewelry worn by a rich elite figure or used as a toy for sexual stimulation, the golden penis sheath had a similar significance as John Dillinger's legendary penis, symbolizing the Varna man's supreme masculine potency and his ability to keep his kingdom fruitful and abundant with life.

In modern consumer cultures, gold remains the high standard of elegance and importance. Like the Varna man, the more golden adornments one has, the more prestige. This explains why someone might install a golden toilet in his bathroom: it's a symbol of a great seat of power and superior status. However, I can't help thinking that someone who installs a golden toilet must also have an affinity for his or her own bodily fluids. This is actually an archetypal impulse. Numerous traditional cultures have strong taboos regarding the treatment of bodily fluids, most notably blood and semen, echoing the idea of the dangers of contamination and disruption of the flow of fluids within the body, explored in Chapter 3. Jung (1964) also referred to spittle as especially revered by certain African tribes (p. 81). Excrement and urine are also byproducts associated with the purging of a person's body of contaminating elements.

Someone who reveres excrement might, therefore, insist upon doing his waste elimination business while sitting on a golden toilet, illustrating an early Freudian developmental stage where a preoccupation with defecation becomes especially pleasurable. Also according to Freud, such a person might be into hoarding precious material objects, such as gold. A telling figure from German folklore reminds all of us of a close association between hoarding precious objects and finding pleasure sitting on a golden toilet to defecate. This is the figure of the *Dukatenscheisser*, or the "money shitter."

There are numerous variations of the Dukatenscheisser's act of shitting coins, and some of these variations refer to him relieving himself of a pile of gold coins (see Figure 4.3), no doubt inspired by the Aesop fable featuring a very talented goose that lays eggs of solid gold for its master. According to this tale, the master ends up with a case of gold fever, growing impatient over the goose's habit of laying only one gold egg per day. So he kills and disembowels the goose, looking for the source of its gold, but since the source is the goose itself, the greedy man ends up with no more golden eggs. The moral of this tale is somewhat obvious but worth repeating: "Those who have plenty want more and so lose all they have" (Daboss, 2013, n.p.).

Figure 4.3 The Dukatenscheisser (money shitter) as he appears on the façade of the Hotel Kaiserworth in Goslar, Germany.

Source: *Creative Commons.*

An icon from Dusseldorf featuring the Dukatenscheisser squatting and excreting a pile of gold coins includes an inscription that relates to the Aesop tale: "This [gold-shitting] fairy tale will never come true. Life teaches us, be wise and frugal." The Dukatenscheisser, however, appears in this icon to be more interested in fulfilling his own anal-stage desires and being supremely rewarded for laying a pile of golden turds. What a silly goose.

The Second Amendment Totem

One might be hard pressed to name a contemporary object in US society with the god-like power of a totem and its significance as a representation of a culture's ancestral heritage. Unfortunately, for some, it's relatively easy to name. It's the gun.

No other country in the world has more guns than the United States, and no other country has less restrictions put upon gun purchasing and gun ownership, indicating a reverence and respect for this object of power. In addition, no other country has more gun-related deaths. And no other country has more active shooter incidents in which a young man with a load of guns and ammunition opens fire in a public setting and slaughters innocent bystanders (Kristof, 2021, n.p.).

Two incidents related to plane travel offer a dramatic contrast to the attitude the United States has regarding the safety of the public whenever a mass shooting occurs. On December 22, 2001, a man flying from London to Miami attempted to ignite a bomb stuffed in his shoes. Fortunately, he failed and was arrested. The other incident occurred on December 29, 2009, involving a man flying from the Netherlands to Detroit who attempted to blow up a plane with a bomb hidden in his underwear. Fortunately, he also failed to ignite his bomb (Dan, 2022, n.p.).

It's interesting to note that, as a response to the first incident, the Federal Aviation Administration (FAA) now requires everyone boarding a commercial plane to remove his or her shoes to check for shoe bombs. I'm still waiting for the FAA to require the removal of underwear before boarding a plane. In any event, the first incident illustrates how one very disturbing potential act of global terrorism led to major changes in safety regulations for all commercial flights in order to prevent such an incident from ever occurring again. So far, it's been a successful requirement since no subsequent shoe bomb incidents have occurred.

Compare the shoe bomb incident with the following.

On December 14, 2012, a 20-year-old man from Newtown, Connecticut, shot and killed his mother before driving to nearby Sandy Hook Elementary School, loaded down with an AR-15 assault rifle, two semiautomatic pistols, and a shotgun along with hundreds of rounds of ammunition. Upon arriving at the elementary school, which holds classes for children in grades kindergarten to the fourth grade, the young man proceeded to open fire in various classrooms, killing 20 children and 6 adults before killing himself.

The massacre was one of the worst active shooter incidents in US history and resulted in feverish cries of outrage and fervid demands for regulating the sale of guns. President Obama at the time was adamant about Congress coming up with some plan to regulate gun purchases, specifically on assault rifles and semiautomatic pistols. However, no action resulted from this massacre of children. Instead, the incident resulted in the birth of one of the most despicable of all conspiracy theories.

Not long after the massacre, the public call for more gun purchasing restrictions triggered a response from gun owners fearful that the mass shooting would lead to the government demanding that certain guns be banned and that those who were in possession of them would be required to turn them in. Conspiracy theorists were quick to see a connection between the shocking slaughter of children and the feverish call for gun regulation and confiscation of certain types of military-style weaponry by the Obama administration. The call this time for some sort of way to limit the public availability of lethal weaponry traditionally reserved for the military inspired the conspiracy theorists to reach an obvious conclusion, or at least one obvious to them: the Sandy Hook Elementary School massacre had been faked. In an attempt to force Congress to pass gun regulation laws, and to justify the confiscation of certain types of guns, the Obama administration had hired "crisis actors" to play the victims and grieving parents of the Sandy Hook shooting in order to stage the entire massacre.

Ever since the Sandy Hook massacre, the "false flag," or faked government ploy to stir up the public so it can justify banning certain guns, has been used to discredit the slaughter of innocent citizens. Apparently, the false flag strategy seems to be working, or at least has helped justify the conflicted attitudes some conspiracy theorists have toward active shooter incidents. One telling example involves a father whose son survived the school shooting that occurred on February 14, 2018, at the Marjory Stoneman Douglas High School in Parkland, Florida where a former student opened fire and killed 17 people and wounded 17 others. The father whose son survived the tragedy later accused his son of being a crisis actor who had helped fake the shooting.

In an interview with *Vice* Magazine, the son, referred to with the pseudonym of "Bill," explained the situation:

> "It started a couple months into the [COVID-19] pandemic with the whole anti-lockdown protests," Bill said. "[My father's] feelings were so strong it turned into facts for him. So if he didn't like having to wear masks it wouldn't matter what doctors or scientists said. Anything that contradicted his feelings was wrong. So he turned to the internet to find like-minded people which led him to QAnon." (Gilbert, 2021, n.p.)

According to "Bill," his father's immersion into the QAnon conspiracy community led him to accept the false flag conspiracy theory and to accuse his son of being a part of it; the father also referred to the shooter as a "radical commie actor," expressing the link QAnon and other conspiracy theory advocates believe exists between Satanic forces within the government and the decades-old Red Scare communist plot to take over America, referred to in Chapter 2.

Bill concluded the interview with the following:

> "[My father will] never stop on his own, because there are always new theories and goalposts being moved," Bill said. "I don't know how to help someone that far gone. My guess is restricted access to the internet and lots of therapy. But even if there was hope he'd eventually snap out of it, it wouldn't change my mind on never wanting to see him again. So it doesn't really matter anymore." (Gilbert, 2021, n.p.)

Bill also mentioned that he continues to struggle with survivor's guilt as his father continues to embrace multiple conspiracy theories and further alienate himself from his family members. But, as tragic as this personal account is, it does help shed light on why people embrace these types of conspiracy theories: they are just as outraged and troubled by these tragedies, but in order to channel the rage and fear stirred up by these horrific events, they project their rage upon perceived "sinister forces," over which they have no control. Thus, they can yell paranoid-fueled plots from the sidelines and demonize those who have made them feel vulnerable and powerless.

The Second Amendment to the US Constitution, written by our ancestral founding fathers giving citizens the "right to bear arms," is the one Constitutional amendment that false flag believers and other conspiracy theorists wholeheartedly support. Guns give those who feel vulnerable and constrained by society's rules a sense of control, comfort, security, and great power. Their totem object also receives support from the National Rifle Association which remains one of the most powerful special interest groups lobbying Congress to do nothing when it comes to gun regulation. So far, they have succeeded.

After the Sandy Hook massacre, any hope for regulating the sale of certain lethal weapons to keep them out of the hands of rage-fueled young men possessed by the archetypal figure of the great hunter or kill-trophy predator have vanished. Not long after the massacre, historian Gary Wills (2012) wrote a response which appeared in the *New York Review of Books*. The article inspired my own attitude toward the gun as America's totem object with a god-like reverence as Wills described the attitude some gun owners have for their weapons, comparing this reverence to those who willingly offer up children to the god most closely associated with human sacrifice, specifically the sacrifice of children: the ancient Middle Eastern cannibal god Moloch (referred to in the Introduction. Also, see Figure 4.4).

Figure 4.4 A man at the 2022 National Rifle Association convention held in Houston, Texas, raffles off a golden AK-47 assault rifle with an estimated worth of $10,000. The convention was held less than one week after an 18-year-old adolescent killed 19 children and 2 adults at the Robb Elementary School in Uvalde, Texas, with a similar military-style assault weapon, the worst massacre of school children since the Sandy Hook Elementary School shooting in 2012.

Source: *Mark Abramson/The New York Times/Redux.*

Totemism and Idolatry

With Wills' disturbing assertion that the gun is America's totem object used by Americans to honor and connect with the god most often associated with certain ancient cultures offering sacrificed children to honor its unbridled power and appease its wrath, it becomes obvious how dangerous it can be to worship an object and consider it beyond any human moral constraints. Here is evil that must be challenged; otherwise, those who continue to revere the gun as a symbol of power likened to a god fall into idol worship.

According to psychologist Erich Fromm, idol worship, or idolatry, is rampant in modern society and is a type of alienation from one's self-identity. As Fromm explained: " … instead of experiencing his own human powers—for example, love or wisdom, thought or reason, acting justly—a person transfers these powers to some idol, to force or forces outside himself. In order, then, to get in touch with his own human power, he must submit completely to this idol" (Evans, 1966, p. 88).

Fromm offered an imaginary inner dialogue of someone in the grips of idolatry: "I get in touch with myself by submitting to the idol. That's why I have to submit to the idol; if I don't, I'm completely empty. I have delivered myself to the idol. I [feel] dead inside because I identify with a dead thing, the idol" (p. 88).

Although Fromm referred to an idol as "a dead thing," this is far from the case when the idol is a gun. In this context, a person is nothing, has no inherent powers, no sense of justice or dignity, without first getting in touch with the idol. Those who idolize guns are empty vessels until they strap on their pistol and parade around in public, or shoot up a wilderness area with their AR-15's, or even worse, shoot up an elementary school full of children under the age of ten.

The gun as totem dramatically illustrates how isolated many of us have become from our own inherent powers. Freud considered the gun to be a symbol of the phallus (1900/2010, p. 335), and in this context, gun worship is a type of modern phallus worship as it was in the case of gun-toting gangster John Dillinger and his legendary super penis. Guns also offer a way for men to embrace the hunter or predator motif of taming the wilderness with their sophisticated, man-made thunder toys. That's why a good number of gun enthusiasts in general advocate for no restraints on any type of weaponry. To put any restrictions is to deny their right to hold onto their external source of power.

Gun manufacturers recognize the relationship between a man's virility and the products they promote; for example, an ad for an AR-15 assault rifle manufactured by Bushmaster that appeared in the men's magazine *Maxim* proclaimed: "Consider your man card reissued" (McIntire, Thrush, & Lipton, 2022, p. SA1). In addition:

> At the [2022] National Rifle Association convention in Houston ... a Missouri-based gun maker, Black Rain Ordnance, featured a line of "BRO" semiautomatics, punning on the company's acronym: AR-15-style guns with names like BRO-Tyrant and BRO-Predator. Dozens of other vendors had similar messages. (p. SA1)

The gun as totem is also a supremely potent example of the concept of nonrational logic. Gary Wills (2012) in his "Moloch worship" article further commented on how guns have wreaked havoc on the reasoning capabilities of not only those who idolize guns but also those in Congress who refuse to make a correlation between the United States having more guns per capita than any other country and more gun-related deaths as a result.

As so many of us struggle to achieve a sense of self-respect and integrity in our lives, as well as a sense of purpose and meaning, we can't afford to look outside of us and project our own inherent powers upon an object. We need to reclaim our "external soul" and realize all over again that it was never outside of us. We must all be good alchemists and plumb the unconscious depths as we search for the gold within. However, what makes this so difficult is the unsettling fact that many of us living in modern, sophisticated, technologically-advanced societies have projected our soul essences upon toys, gadgets, and gold-plated toilets. And this has led to what Jung considered to be the true crisis of modern humanity: loss of soul.

References

Blazeski, G. (2017, May 23). Bonnie and Clyde's bullet riddled death car is on display at Whiskey Pete's casino in Primm, Nevada. *TheVintageNews.com*. Retrieved from https://www.thevintagenews.com/2017/05/23/bonnie-and-clydes-bullet-riddled-death-car-is-on-display-at-whiskey-petes-casino-in-primm-nevada/?edg-c=1.

Britannica, The Editors of Encyclopaedia (2020, February 23). Amulet. Encyclopaedia Britannica.com. Retrieved from https://www.britannica.com/topic/amulet.

Cole, S. (1984). *Theoi megaloi: The cult of the great gods at Samothrace*. Leiden, The Netherlands: E. J. Brill.

Daboss (2013, December 1). The goose with the golden eggs. *FablesofAesop.com*. Retrieved from https://fablesofaesop.com/the-goose-with-the-golden-eggs.html.

Dan, M. (2022, April 21). December 22, 2011: Who was the shoe bomber? *Historyandheadlines.com*. Retrieved from https://www.historyandheadlines.com/december-22-2001-shoe-bomber/.

Davey, M. (2005, March 6). Suspect in 10 murders lived an intensely ordinary life. *New York Times*, p. S1, 1.

Debelius, M., & Lewis, S. (1993). *The American Indians: Keepers of the totem*. Alexandria, VA: Time-Life Books.

De Montparnasse, K. (2022). The gold wand. *Goop.com*. Retrieved from https://goop.com/kiki-de-montparnasse-the-gold-wand/p/?taxon_id=1292&variant_id=96982.

Eliade, M. (1954/2005). *The myth of the eternal return*. Princeton, NJ: Princeton University Press.

Evans, R.I. (1966). *Dialogue with Erich Fromm*. New York: Harper & Row.

Frazer, J. (1900/1906-15/2018). *The golden bough: A study in magic and religion, an abridgment from the 2nd and 3rd editions* (R. Fraser, Ed.). London, UK: Folio Society.

Freud, S. (1900/2010). *The interpretation of dreams. The definitive edition*. J. Strachey (Trans.). Philadelphia, PA: Basic Books.

Freud, S. (1913/1989). *Totem and taboo*. New York: Norton.

Gilbert, D. (2021, July 6). I'm a Parkland shooting survivor. QAnon convinced my dad that it was all a hoax. Retrieved from https://www.vice.com/en/article/epnq84/im-a-parkland-shooting-survivor-qanon-convinced-my-dad-it-was-all-a--hoax?utm_source=vicenewstwitter.

Graves, R. (1955/1992). *The Greek myths: Complete edition*. New York: Penguin Books.

Gillan, J. (2020, July 20). Varna man and the richest grave of the 5th millennium B.C. Retrieved from https://www.ancient-origins.net/ancient-places-europe/varna-man-002798.

Harrison, J.E. (1903/1955). *Prolegomena to the study of Greek religion*. New York: Meridian.

Harrison, J.E. (1912/1962). *Themis: A study of the social origins of Greek religion*. New York: Meridian.

Hill, B. (2020, April 3). The Kaaba black stone: A holy stone from outer space? *AncientOrigins.net*. Retrieved from https://www.ancient-origins.net/artifacts-other-artifacts/kaaba-black-stone-holy-stone-outer-space-003661?msclkid=aba144 d4cf0111ecb8b3d507f4a9be44.

Hirschberg, L. (2005, March 13). Face time: Among L.A.'s go-to guys, the watch replaces the Ferrari as the new favorite toy. *New York Times*, p. S6, 88.

History.com editors (2018, August 21). John Dillinger. *History.com*. Retrieved from https://www.history.com/topics/crime/john-dillinger.

Jung, C.G. (1928/1969). On psychic energy. In H. Read, M. Fordham, G. Adler (Eds.), W. McGuire (Senior ed.). *The structure and dynamics of the psyche. Collected works, volume 8*, pp. 3–66. Princeton, NJ: Princeton University Press.

Jung, C.G. (1961/1989). *Memories, dreams, reflections* (A. Jaffe, Ed.). New York: Vintage Books.

Jung, C.G. (1964). Approaching the unconscious. In C.G. Jung (Senior ed.), *Man and his symbols*, pp. 18–103. New York: Doubleday.

Jung, C.G. (1989/2012). *Introduction to Jungian psychology: Notes of the seminar on analytical psychology, given in 1925* (W. McGuire & S. Shamdasani, Eds.). Princeton, NJ: Princeton University Press.

Kerenyi, C. (1951/1995). *The gods of the Greeks*. New York: Thames & Hudson.

Keuls, E.C. (1991993). *The reign of the phallus: Sexual politics in ancient Athens*. Berkeley, CA: University of California Press.

Kristof, N. (2021, March 23). How to reduce shootings. *NewYorkTimes.com*. Retrieved from https://www.nytimes.com/interactive/2017/11/06/opinion/how-to-reduce-shootings.html?action=click&module=Opinion&pgtype=Homepage.

McIntire, M., Thrush, G., & Lipton, E. (2022, June 18). Gun sellers' message to Americans: Man up. *New York Times*, SA1.

Palma, B. (2019, November 29). Did Trump tweet a picture of himself as Rocky Balboa? *Snopes.com*. Retrieved from https://www.snopes.com/fact-check/trump-rocky-tweet/.

Rosenberg, M., & Tiefenthaler, A. (2021, January 13). Decoding the far-right symbols of the Capitol riot. *NewYorkTimes.com*. Retrieved from https://www.nytimes.com/2021/01/13/video/extremist-signs-symbols-capitol-riot.html?action=click&module=RelatedLinks&pgtype=Article.

von Franz, M-L. (1964). The process of individuation. In C.G. Jung, ed., *Man and his symbols*, pp.158–229. New York: Doubleday.

Wills, G. (2012, December 15). Our Moloch. *NewYorkReviewofBooks.com*. Retrieved from https://www.nybooks.com/daily/2012/12/15/our-moloch/.

Wooldridge, Jr. R. (1995). *The American Indians: Tribes of the southern plains*. Alexandria, VA: Time-Life Books.

Chapter 5

Soulful and Soulless

The Rise of "Extreme Boredom"

On May 14, 2022, Buffalo, New York was the site of a white supremacist's attack on a supermarket with a predominantly African American clientele. The perpetrator was an 18-year-old adolescent who showed up at the supermarket laden down with weaponry and ammunition which included the gun of choice for mass shooters, an AR-15 assault rifle. The adolescent opened fire first in the parking lot, killing several shoppers before entering the market and killing and wounding numerous others before being subdued by arriving police. Ten individuals ended up dead and three wounded, with all but two of the victims African American.

The carnage that day was livestreamed on social media, compliments of the mass killer who filmed himself during his attack with a small video camera attached to his forehead. Although efforts were made by social media content monitors to delete the footage, too many viewers had already made copies and distributed it to other social media platforms, ensuring the event's posterity (Stanley-Becker & Harwell, 2022, n.p.).

The Buffalo killer was not the first to livestream his mass shooting, nor was he the first to kill as many people as possible with non-white ethnic or racial heritages, or religious beliefs other than Christian. In fact, the Buffalo killer was copying the acts and justifying them in the same manner as an earlier mass shooter had done in Christchurch, New Zealand on March 21, 2019, when a young man livestreamed his attack on two Muslim mosques killing 51 people.

In addition to the Buffalo killer copying the Christchurch shooter by livestreaming the atrocity, he also posted a manifesto on social media that was a heavily plagiarized version of the New Zealand shooter's own online nonrational justification for his acts. Both individuals had embraced an antisemitic racist conspiracy theory about how Jews were behind a plot to have non-Christians and people of color replace God-fearing white Christians by overpopulating the world with their inferior genetic codes (Stanley-Becker & Harwell, 2022, n.p.; Myers & Thompson, 2022, n.p.).

DOI: 10.4324/9781003271482-6

This conspiracy theory, embraced by people such as Hitler, has roots as far back as the early Christian era when Jews were accused of killing Christian children and using their blood and flesh for meals prepared for their religious holidays (see Cohn, 1977).

The Buffalo massacre indicates that there is a type of online active shooter support group (Stanley-Becker & Harwell, 2022, n.p.; Myers & Thompson, 2022, n.p.), where like-minded boys and young men gather to share their "twisted world" views. The implication here is that there are lots of young men tempted to stage a livestream mass murder event and have the world's attention for fleeting moments as they attempt to kill as many people as possible before they hopefully die a spectacularly gruesome suicide-by-cop death as if they were the star of a first-person shooter video game.

Little or no response has been the standard reaction in the United States since these types of events began to occur with increasing rapidity after the 1999 mass shooting at Columbine High School in Littleton, Colorado, where two students shot up their school and took the lives of 13 fellow students before killing themselves. There was a time when I became enraged over every mass shooting that occurred after the Columbine event due to the inaction of the government to do anything except fuss over what our forefathers meant when they wrote the Second Amendment. A well-regulated militia's right to bear arms? How did this lead to teens slaughtering other teens at the local high school with military-style assault weaponry?

When Columbine occurred, my son was around the same age as the two high school-age shooters, and because nobody at that time had a clue about why young people would willfully choose to plan and execute an attack on their own high school and then kill themselves afterwards, I was worried that my son might be influenced by their acts. Although I knew my son was a compassionate, well-adjusted young man with a great passion for a variety of interests, I remained concerned over his mental state since I knew he loved playing violent first-person shooter video games, the same type of games that the Columbine shooters reportedly played for hours each day.

One of the Columbine shooters kept a diary and wrote about his love for the first-person shooter game called Doom: "I wish I lived in Doom … . Doom is so burned into my head my thoughts usually have something to do with the game … . I have a goal to destroy as much as possible so I must not be sidetracked by my feelings of sympathy, mercy, or any of that, so I will force myself to believe that everyone is just a monster from Doom" (Langman, 2009, p. 151).

In the aftermath of Columbine, I couldn't help thinking about the influence these types of games might be having on the developing minds of impressionable young men, including my own son, especially since I knew that the reasoning center of the brain, located in the prefrontal cortex, is still in the process of development for teens and young adults. The concerns I had were shared by millions of other parents struggling to understand why kids would want to either borrow guns from Mom and Dad or order a load of weapons online through both legal and illegal channels and use them to destroy as many lives as they could before committing suicide.

Since Columbine, we have learned more about the causes of such atrocities, and the causes are only marginally associated with the effects of playing violent video games for hours each day since these games are widely popular with billions of people around the world playing them daily. The easy availability of guns in the United States is certainly a major factor since the United States has, by far, more active shooting incidents than any other country. But, that still doesn't explain why boys use them to kill their peers and themselves and, in some cases, post manifestos, livestream their carnage, or make YouTube videos flaunting their weaponry before going on their self-destructive rampages.

After Columbine, students from elementary school through college began practicing lockdown drills on a regular basis which train students, instructors, and administrators to respond to an active shooting incident in one of the following ways: hide in a locked classroom, run like hell, or pick up a chair and attack the perpetrator wielding the AR-15. As a college instructor, I have participated in such drills along with my students, huddling behind a locked classroom door while sirens blare and a recorded voice demands we all take cover or risk being mowed down by the perpetrator. I'm sure I'm not the only person who believes that this approach to dealing with these types of events might need some re-evaluation since the lockdown response doesn't seem to be having any effect on those who perpetrate such events.

As I mentioned, since the Columbine mass shooting, there has been a steady increase in such incidents in the United States with no significant plan to do anything about how to prevent these incidents. In 2021, for example, there was a 52% increase in active shooter incidents over the previous year, and a 96% increase between 2017 and 2020 (Sganga, 2022, n.p.). Although debate continues over why such events occur with such regularity in the United States, the easy availability to lethal, military-style assault weaponry remains an obvious factor, but because the gun is a totem object for America (see Chapter 4), the idea of attempting to regulate the sale of such weaponry to the public doesn't seem to be a popular option. While the debate over the regulation of guns continues to go next to nowhere, what needs to happen is to better understand why a kid would want to aspire to become a mass murderer.

Too many kids are the perpetrators of these acts. My own theory about why adolescent boys and young-adult men feel compelled to kill their fellow students before killing themselves can be summed up by one word: *nihilism*, the belief that life is meaningless. To be more accurate, nihilism is the attitude of, "I am worthless because life is meaningless," or conversely, "Life is meaningless, therefore, I nor anyone else has a reason to exist." Such a view of the world and oneself implies that someone has either projected a nihilistic view of life upon his society or that society has, in some way, encouraged a person to develop such a world view. Or a combination of both.

I would suggest that, in some individuals, there is an internal predisposition to respond to a nihilistic view of life, and such a person with this tendency finds elements within a society's belief system that encourage the development of a nihilistic world view. This is where the influence of first-person shooter video games could inspire a person with a nihilistic tendency to find affirmation for his world view. Such games could resonate with someone who might have a predator, stalker, or "great hunter" tendency, referred to in Chapter 4, and be inspired by these games to develop strategies for staging an active shooter incident. The easy access to guns can also inspire him to act out his nihilistic world view which emphasizes not only how life is meaningless, but that the world would be better off if it were destroyed by someone who embraces this anti-life philosophy.

What is it about a modern, technologically sophisticated society such as the United States that would encourage a teenager to embrace such a view of life? Nihilism was certainly the philosophy embraced by the Columbine mass shooters whose goal was "to destroy as much as possible," as well as Elliot Rodger, whose mass shooting near the campus of UC Santa Barbara in 2014 was explored in Chapter 2. Rodger at one point in his autobiographical manifesto proclaimed, "I will never be a creator, but I could be a destroyer." Rodger was fully immersed in a nihilistic world view, which began to develop while he was in middle school and he realized how much he hated the cool kids—essentially the skateboarding crowd—because they attracted all the cute girls.

As I attempted to illustrate with modern examples of totemism in Chapter 4, there is too much emphasis in modern consumer cultures upon viewing one's self-worth in the same manner that makers of material objects would determine the worth of their latest bauble. In such consumer-driven societies, too often we determine the worth of people by their ability to successfully market their talents, as if they were commodities put up for sale to the highest bidder. Erich Fromm (1955/1965) called this attitude the *marketing orientation:*

> … man experiences himself as a thing to be employed successfully on the market … . His sense of value depends on … whether he can sell himself favorably … . His body, his mind, his soul are his capital, and his task in life is to invest it favorably, to make a profit of himself. Human qualities like friendliness, courtesy, kindness, are transformed into commodities, into assets of the "personality package," conducive to a higher price on the personality market … . Clearly, [a person's] sense of his own value always depends on factors extraneous to himself, on the fickle judgment of the market which decides about his value as it decides the value of commodities. (pp. 129–130)

Fromm's comments about alienation and idolatry, referred to in Chapter 4, applies to his ideas about the marketing orientation concept that drives modern consumer cultures; the marketing mentality alienates us from our own talents since any inherent talents are worthless unless they can be exploited for profit. This exploitation of talents includes marketing one's capacity to display empathy and other social-emotional intelligence skills (SEL) currently being promoted in certain K-12 schools:

> "The overwhelming majority of educators and parents acknowledge that teaching children SEL skills is critical," [stated] Marc Brackett, director of the Yale Center for Emotional Intelligence … . "At the other end, in corporate America, employers are looking for people who have these skills." But the colorful classroom posters and the drive for data through "social-emotional competencies" student assessments—not necessarily bad things in themselves—risk reducing our idea of empathy to yet another job skill (Worthen, 2020, p. SR 4).

One can see how the marketing orientation dominates social media. Too many people (including yours truly) try to impress social media friends by narcissistic attempts at self-promotion. We want to make a striking, skin-deep impression online, so we post information about our latest promotion, our latest fabulous purchases, the latest accomplishments of our fabulous kids, and share loads of fabulous selfies from our latest fabulous vacation in perfectly composed settings that ultimately distort our own sense of self-identity. By attempting to present ourselves as living the perfect life and achieving spectacular things in all facets of our lives, we alienate ourselves from our core self-identity, one that is linked to and regulated by the Self.

As Fromm pointed out, making a good impression by successfully selling one's "personality package" is what can lead to success, and failing to do so leaves a person feeling like a failure. As Fromm clarified:

> This idea is based on the concept of life as an enterprise which should show a profit. The failure is like the bankruptcy of a business in which the losses are greater than the gains … . [However, there] is no sensible balance which could show whether life is worthwhile living. Maybe from a standpoint of a balance [between pleasurable and unpleasurable events] life is never worth living. It ends necessarily with death [with] many of our hopes … disappointed; it involves suffering and effort; from the standpoint of the balance, it would seem to make more sense not to have been born at all … . (p. 136)

Fromm followed these statements, written in 1955, with this theory about the effects of the marketing orientation: "The interpretation of life as a [business] enterprise seems to be the basis for a typical modern phenomenon about which a great deal of speculation exists: the increase of suicide in modern Western society" (p. 136). Although suicide rates declined for decades after Fromm made this statement, they have risen once again since the 1990s. As mentioned in Chapter 3, "deaths of despair" became the number one cause of deaths for middle-aged white Americans during the late 1990s and have continued to plague the United States since then due to a large degree by the opioid addiction crisis; the COVID-19 pandemic exacerbated the problem, leading to increased suicide rates among adolescents and young adults.

In this context, it becomes easier to determine one of the root causes of kids developing a nihilistic view of life. They are encouraged to view objects as more important than humans. Because objects have more worth, possessing the ones considered to be the most valuable is the key to happiness and a sense of self-worth. So, if a kid can't afford to buy the coolest skateboard or most recently released video game console, he's a loser. The only way to make up for being such a loser is to post perfect selfies and offer them to social media friends with the hope that they'll reward the person with lots of "likes." In other words, what is most important is to look good and have the right toys rather than accomplish anything that gives a person a sense of accomplishment and self-esteem.

The early adolescent stage is one of the most crucial of all life stages. It is during this stage when puberty kicks in and destroys a young person's childhood by engorging a kid with an overdose of raging hormones. It's also during this stage when a young person becomes obsessed with establishing a social identity, of wanting to fit in with his or her peers, share like-minded interests, and engage in mutually satisfying activities. It's interesting that a desire to establish a social identity is more important at this stage than establishing a self-identity: we need to be seen by others as worthy before we can begin to see it in ourselves and believe it.

Social media is a formidable tool when it comes to creating a social identity. However, when it comes to determining one's self-identity, maintaining a perfect social media persona and collecting "likes" when successful are more important.

Those with money can invest it in creating a perfect persona and then selling it for profit in some manner. Some of the most successful individuals who have achieved great financial success marketing themselves to the public via social media are the Kardashians whose long-running reality TV show, *Keeping Up with the Kardashians*, featured a family of rich, statuesque women showing off their statuesque physiques for 20 seasons—from 2007 to 2021—while making millions of dollars promoting their lines of clothing and beauty products.

The emphasis put upon marketing oneself as if one were a consumer product up for sale begins at an early age when all of us learn which baubles have the most value in a consumer culture. Because of the importance modern societies put upon technologically sophisticated baubles, the demands kids make to own the latest tech gadgetry such as a smartphone start earlier than ever before. This is due to a large degree by the habits of their parents whose smartphone use is, in some cases, a borderline addiction.

Parents who are worried about kids abusing smartphone privileges have a good reason for being concerned since there is evidence that the tech industry giants purposely design them to become addictive (McCarthy, 2022, n.p.).

There is an organization called "Wait Until the 8th" (McCarthy, 2022, n.p.), which helps parents deal with their children's demands for a smartphone by encouraging parents to wait until the last year of middle school before allowing their children to have one. However, because children at that age are obsessed with fitting in with their peers, a kid without a smartphone could end up ostracized and left out of chats, texts, and event planning. Giving a child a basic cellular phone that can only text and make and receive calls also is an insult to the child who craves the latest glitzy, mega-G phone.

Obviously, this is a distorted view of childhood, but it is unfortunately becoming a more common view. As one of the mothers who voiced concern over her children having smartphones explained: "… it just feels like there's no choice … . Because everyone feels like the world is just going this way" (McCarthy, 2022, n.p.).

The woman's statement about "having no choice" because "the world is just going this way" is disturbing on many levels, most especially since it implies we have no control over the way one's culture is trending. We are just passive consumers doing our best to keep up with the latest trends in a tech-dominated world.

Bonding with an object that promises social acceptance rather than ensuring a child develop a sense of self-esteem helps keep a consumer culture in the black. However, even when parents are encouraging their kids to become involved in extracurricular activities, sometimes the emphasis is on the parent's achievement of status through the success of their children rather than how the child's success affects his or her sense of self-esteem.

I cannot list the number of times students have voiced frustration, anger, and despair over a parent's constant pressure to succeed. The drive to excel even when there is a lack of interest in whatever the goal or challenge is puts undue pressure on young people still struggling to understand what they like rather than what makes their friends give them a "like" on social media. Here is the influence of the marketing orientation: endless promotion of one's talents in order to be approved of by one's peers, by authority figures such as caregivers, and by one's culture.

There is a significant spike in children experiencing psychological issues at around age fourteen (Kearney & Trull, 2018b). The pressure to fit in and to excel at everything they attempt while experiencing major changes in physical, psychological, and behavioral growth, and all the time desiring the right kind of baubles to feel accepted by their peers, takes a toll on the maturing minds of young people. In some cases, these pressures result in feelings of never doing enough to ensure their success by meeting the expectations of their caregivers and their culture. Some kids give up trying. And some kids never even try because they feel they don't have the right talents to succeed at anything. And this self-conception of one's lack of worth leads to nihilism.

An interesting aspect about nihilism is that it is a common attitude that all of us experience at some time to some degree. It is essentially a state of mind in which nothing seems to make sense, and nothing seems interesting enough to explore with any enthusiasm. In other words, nihilism is a transitional state between inactivity and pursuit of something engaging enough to lift oneself out of a state of inertia. However, with some young people, because they feel they have no worthwhile talents, or the wrong interests, or that they are not good enough to succeed if they ever try, they remain stuck in a nihilistic state of "extreme boredom."

A sense of "extreme boredom" was allegedly the inspiration for the 18-year-old Buffalo mass shooter to check out radical right-leaning chat rooms when he was sixteen. It was at one of these chat sites that he found a version of the livestream video of the Christchurch massacre as well as the shooter's manifesto. The Buffalo shooter felt an immediate connection with the gruesome video footage and the hate-fueled passages from the manifesto (Stanley-Becker & Harwell, 2022, n.p.). After watching this livestream version of a first-person shooter video game with real victims and real blood, complemented with a violent, anti-human philosophy, a 16-year-old kid with underdeveloped reasoning abilities and in a nihilistic state of "extreme boredom" had an epiphany: he too could become a media star and get likes from his online mass murderer support group by having "no loyalties, and no purpose other than, perhaps, an impulse to destroy." In other words, his teenage psyche was overwhelmed by pure evil and he succumbed.

According to philosopher Friedrich Nietzsche, who wrote extensively about nihilism: "Inevitably, nihilism will expose all cherished beliefs and sacrosanct truths as symptoms of a defective Western mythos. This collapse of meaning, relevance, and purpose will be the most destructive force in history, constituting a total assault on reality and nothing less than the greatest crisis of humanity" (Pratt, 1995, n.p.). Writing at the end of the 19th century, it appears that Nietzsche predicted a trend in human history that continues to unfold: two world wars, the development of a weapon with the power to destroy the world, and, of course, the influence of astonishing achievements in communication that at one time were thought to be breakthroughs in uniting the world through technology—all come together to shed doubts upon the future of the planet.

In Search of Humanity's Lost Soul

In the Introduction, I mentioned that many people living in technologically advanced societies sometimes struggle with the sense that something is missing from their lives, resulting in feelings of restlessness, anxiety, and envy for others who seem to have it all. In the previous passages, I have tried to point out why such feelings arise: by attempting to achieve fulfillment through the creation of a perfect persona to promote themselves and impress social media friends, many people have become alienated from their core sense of self-identity. People have also succumbed to a type of idol worship as they lust after the latest trendy toy, believing that after possessing it, the feeling that something is missing from life will be replaced by a satisfying sense of completeness.

Jung (1933/1955) commented on the ungrounded restlessness inherent in those living in modern societies while describing an influential meeting he had with an elder member of the Hopi tribe in New Mexico which he visited in 1925. While speaking with the tribal elder about the characteristics of mainstream Americans, the Hopi elder told Jung: "We don't understand the whites; they are always wanting something—always restless—always looking for something. What is it? We don't know ... . We think they're all crazy" (p. 213).

Jung agreed. Modern man acts like a tourist, looking upon his environment as a backdrop for a selfie rather than something to which he is connected on a deeply unconscious, archetypal level of understanding.

Fromm (1955/1965), writing from the perspective of 1955, made comments about the "tourist view" of life when he stated: "The 'tourist' with his camera is an outstanding symbol of an alienated relationship with the world. Being constantly occupied with taking pictures, actually he does not see anything at all ... . The camera [i.e. technology] sees for him, and the outcome of his pleasure trip is a collection of snapshots which are the substitute for the experience ..." (p. 125). The rise of the smartphone selfie as art form is in danger of turning too many of us into modern versions of the beautiful boy Narcissus who fell in love with his reflection in a pool of water and ended up drowning himself as he tried to embrace his perfect persona reflection. Narcissism is encouraged in a marketing orientation society as so many of us attempt to promote ourselves through selfie art.

Ironically, the way in which we can connect with the world around us is to put down the smartphone with the built-in, ultra-sophisticated, high-resolution camera and make the attempt to look deeply within in order to better understand the elements in life that perplex, fascinate, and even terrify you. A quote from a favorite film, *Joe Versus the Volcano* (Shanley, 1990), comes to mind that expresses the necessity of exploring what is both a person's most hidden and haunting desire: "If you had the choice between killing yourself and doing something you're scared of doing, why not take the leap and do the thing you're scared of doing."

As I mentioned in Chapter 1, Jung's own initial experiments upon himself during his "Red Book" period beginning in 1913, ultimately formed the essence of his psychological philosophy. After he began experiencing apocalyptic visions of mass destruction during this period, Jung made the decision to encourage such visions even though he was afraid of losing his mind; in doing so, he descended into the dark realm of his psyche where he found horrors beyond his imagination, but also found what he had been missing: his revitalized soul.

Through his actions, Jung realized the necessity of maintaining a strong, enduring relationship with the nonrational elements of the unconscious, even though it required confrontations with demons and gods, as if the descent were mirroring those taken by mystery religion initiates who simulated a descent into the underworld to confront the dark gods associated with this realm in the hope of experiencing a rebirth from the land of the dead. As Jung (1953/1968) explained: "The dread and resistance which every natural human being experiences when it comes to delving too deeply into himself is, at bottom, the fear of the journey to Hades" (p. 336).

It's obvious that Jung had the mystery religion tradition in mind with this statement. He might also have had traditional puberty rites in mind since these rituals also simulate a journey to the land of the dead during which boys are put through brutal, death-simulation rites by elders with the intent of marking the end of the boys' childhood and the beginning of their adulthood. In both traditions, the symbolic descent is to confront the god powers of this realm in order for a participant to experience a renewal of his or her soul essence. This is exactly what Jung had in mind: we must make the effort to know our deepest, darkest selves, our core sense of self-identity, because this deep self is the soul. When we understand aspects of our soul essence, we experience a broadening and deepening of our relationship with the god within, the Self.

Perhaps what is needed at this point is to ask the question: "What are we talking about when we talk about soul?"

A Brief History of the Soul

On the first day of the General Psychology classes I teach, I ask students, "What comes to mind when you think of soul?" I like asking the question because I know that, although soul is a common word, it remains one of the most nonrational terms in existence.

The main reason for asking the question is because the word soul is derived from the ancient Greek word "psyche," upon which the word psychology is derived. However, modern psychology now interprets the word psyche as mind, or mental processes. Does this mean the soul is within the mind? Or that soul is, in fact, the mind? Or that the concept of soul has been replaced by the concept of the mind? To a certain degree, it appears that modern psychology has lost its soul, replacing it with intellect, and in doing so, has put into question the soul's existence.

Because modern psychology does not deal effectively with the concept of the soul, after students have wrestled with the concept, I ask, "Do you have a soul?" Normally, all of them believe they have a soul, but when I ask where it is, few can say where it might be located, although after telling them about the link between soul, psyche, and mind, they are tempted to believe it is somewhere in their brains. This actually makes sense for students whose ancestry is linked to the ancient Chamorros who inhabited the Mariana Islands for thousands of years before the Spanish showed up in the 16th century; during those early years, Chamorros honored their ancestors by keeping their skulls preserved as totem objects.

Certain traditional ideas about the location of the soul do, in fact, point to a part of the brain where many cultures believe it's housed: cultural traditions speak of the soul existing in the pineal gland, located in the central area of the brain. I learned this from a student presentation about the pineal gland, which is actually responsible for maintaining the secretion of melatonin in the body to regulate the body's sleep cycle. The student's presentation included this factual information about the pineal gland along with a YouTube video featuring a New Age-type personality warning of the dangers of fluoride in drinking water because it destroys the pineal gland and, in doing so, kills one's soul. General Ripper from *Dr. Strangelove* (see Chapter 3) no doubt would exclaim, "That's the way those hard-core commies work!"

James Frazer in *The Golden Bough* (1900/1906-15/2018) provided additional traditional views about the concept of the soul and its location within the body. Generally speaking, those in traditional cultures believe that:

> If an animal lives and moves, it can only be … because there is a little animal inside which moves it; if a man lives and moves, it can only be because he has a little man or animal inside who moves him. The animal inside the animal, the man inside the man, is the soul. And as the activity of an animal is explained by the presence of the soul, so the repose of sleep or death is explained by its absence; sleep or trance being the temporary, death being the permanent, absence of the soul. Hence if death be the permanent absence of the soul, the way to guard against it is either to prevent the soul from leaving the body, or, if does depart, to ensure that it shall return. (p. 158)

Frazer included examples from various cultures that illustrate the idea of the soul taking animal form, or imagined as an animal, usually as a bird or insect such as a butterfly or bee. In fact, the ancient Greek word "psyche" referred not only to soul but to butterfly: when a person dies, his or her soul leaves the body as a butterfly and flies back to its original source. The implication is that while alive on Earth, humans remain in a larval or mortal state, and at death achieve the immortal state symbolized by the butterfly.

Frazer's comments about how the soul of a person can leave the body during sleep or trance includes "the ability [of a soul] to wander away from the body and actually to visit the places, to see the persons, and to perform the acts of which he dreams" (p. 161). This idea relates to a controversial concept known as remote viewing. During the height of the Cold War, the CIA sponsored programs in the mid-20th century to determine whether or not remote viewing was possible, testing hundreds of participants who were given the challenge of finding someone hiding somewhere not by going out and looking for the person but by envisioning the location of the hiding person (Hiltz, 2021). Such an individual with remote viewing ability would be incredibly valuable for spying on enemies without the use of expensive and highly sophisticated surveillance technology.

As I mentioned, remote viewing remains controversial, but also illustrates the mind–brain controversy that has existed for millennia, with some believing that the mind can exist and endure without the brain—and thus travel away from the body and remotely view events far removed from the person's physical self—while others insisting that the mind is the result of brain activity and therefore couldn't exist without a functioning brain responsible for all mental processes. The controversy, therefore, relates to the original ideas about the word psyche and how it morphed from referring from soul to mind.

As Frazer indicated, losing one's soul leads to mortal death. Keeping the soul within the body, therefore, was necessary, and many practices came about to ensure the soul didn't fly away too soon or get lost, leading to a premature death. One of the ways a soul could accidentally be expelled from the body is through yawning, coughing, or sneezing. This idea remains with us: we say "Bless you," after someone sneezes, meaning, "Get back in there, soul."

Now that we have a better understanding about how difficult it is to locate the soul within the body, it is necessary to make an attempt to define what soul actually is. Some ideas about the soul describe it as not so much an animal or homunculus-type entity inside the body but "an invisible substance that animates the physical body, [or] as an unseen presence separate from the body and surviving physical death, [or] as consciousness, as mind, as personality ..." (Delano, 1989, p. 12).

Wherever or whatever the soul is, its existence or nonexistence is directly related to the concept of nihilism. The belief that there is a part of one's make-up that expresses one's core essence, and that this core essence is, like the rest of the universe, derived from an inexhaustible force of creation, gives many people a sense that they are part of something far greater than themselves and thus are here on Earth for a purpose. This was the attitude of Isaac Newton, referred to in Chapter 2, which inspired him to embrace the concept of animism, essentially the animating soul of physical reality linked to God, the divine source of this animating spirit. People with a similar attitude insist there must be a reason for existence; otherwise, life is an accidental result of random chemical activity and has no meaning, so nothing that a person does has any significance.

Jung championed the existence of the soul. However, like many people who have made references to the soul, Jung was someone who overused the word without clearly defining it since the meaning and significance he gave to it sometimes varied depending upon the context of its use. A favorite example of Jung's attempt at a definition of soul appeared in Alchemical Studies (1967/1983), in a section where Jung defined the archetype of the *anima* or soul guide, personified as a feminine figure:

> The anima belongs to those borderline phenomena which chiefly occurs in special psychic situations. They are characterized by the more or less sudden collapse of a form of style of life which till then seemed the indispensable foundation of the individual's whole career. When such a catastrophe occurs, not only are all bridges back into the past broken, but there seems to be no way forward into the future. One is confronted with a hopeless and impenetrable darkness, an abysmal void that is now suddenly filled with an alluring vision, the palpably real presence of a strange yet helpful being in the same way that, when one lives for a long time in great solitude, the silence or the darkness becomes visibly, audibly, and tangibly alive, and the unknown in oneself steps up in an unknown guise. (p. 177)

What Jung was essentially describing is the action of the anima which is linked to the action of the Self since all archetypal energies are manifestations of the Self. When trauma, or the "collapse of a form of a style of life" deemed to be the standard way of behavior for an individual occurs—in other words, when one is engulfed by nihilistic tendencies—the Self acts to heal the psychological trauma through the release of archetypal energies that, in a dream or visionary experience, can take human form; in this case, it's the form of a woman who, in a dream scenario, guides the individual's dream persona out of darkness to a new vision or potential perspective of one's life.

For Jung (2009), the anima appeared during his Red Book period numerous times in the form of a seductive femme fatale figure which he interpreted as a variation of the enticing Salome from the New Testament. In his visions, Salome was usually accompanied by a masculine soul guide figure, or *animus*, in the guise of a wise old man or prophet. Both archetypal figures aided him in discovering his revitalized soul.

Perhaps one of Jung's most successful attempts at a definition of soul appeared in *Psychological Types* (1921/1976), in the section where he defined numerous terms relating to his psychological philosophy. Jung defined soul in this context as one's personality which is made up of an outer image or ego identification which he called *persona* that can change according to one's social situation, as if one were putting on and taking off various masks for each specific social occasion. One's inner personality was the anima: "the inner attitude, the characteristic face, that is turned toward the unconscious" (p. 467). Like all archetypal energies, the anima can change appearance but its function is always the same: to guide a person to the Self in order to experience a sense of revitalized wholeness.[1]

In the General Psychology classes, after we have discussed the concept of the soul, I have students attempt to define soul. The following is one of the best definitions of soul I have received from a student which reflects Jung's own definition:

> I think that the soul is just the essence of oneself. It is a pure thing that encapsulates our existence, the experiences, character, values, and everything else that makes us who we are. It is who we are at our core, the person we are when nobody else is around to see us and when there is nobody to fake an appearance for … . When the idea of the soul was mentioned in class, I immediately thought of the Christian and Egyptian depictions of the soul. In both Christianity and Egyptian myths, the soul is the metric by which the gods judge one's purity and fate after life. Christianity has the idea that one must … [maintain] the purity of one's soul to enter heaven … . If you are insincere about your kindness, then you're probably not going to make it into heaven as that insincerity is thought to reflect in your soul. The sins you commit in private would reflect on your soul as much as the ones you commit in front of others, both are equally reflected … . The same goes for the Egyptian myths. The quality of your soul is weighed on a scale to see if you deserved a good or bad afterlife, and the things that tipped the scales in or out of your favor would be the deeds you did and the kind of life you led. The soul is very much tied to life and the act of living. That is why we say that objects, vampires, and zombies do not have souls, because there is no life lived in those things. (J. Gomez, 2021, personal correspondence with author)

As Jung did, the student emphasizes personality as being related to an individual's soul concept. As he mentions, an individual's core personality is his soul essence which remains the same in any circumstance, and becomes more noticeable to an individual during times of solitude, also as Jung indicated. His references to different religious interpretations of soul underscore the importance of never deceiving oneself about who one really is since to deceive oneself about one's core sense of self-identity is essentially lying to the Self, the god within.

Certain research studies have indicated a tendency for individuals today to avoid solitude, or at least to be sure to have a tech gadget if spending time alone, in order to avoid "the fear of the journey to Hades," or having to look inwardly and be confronted by a personality that has little relationship with one's perfect social persona (Murphy, 2014, p. SR3).

To illustrate how the concept of soul is related to a core identity that becomes more apparent when one is alone, one can look at Anne Frank and the approach she took to writing her famous diary. During World War II, as she hid from Nazis in the backroom area of her father's business establishment along with her family members and other acquaintances of her father's, Anne conceived of a way to reveal her core identity to herself: each diary entry was written as a letter to an imaginary best friend she called Kitty. However, in the final entry of the diary, Anne (2003) revealed the true identity of Kitty:

> I'm awfully scared that everyone who knows me as I always am will discover that I have another side, a finer and better side ... . I'm used to be not taken seriously but it's only the lighthearted Anne that's used to it and can bear it; the deeper Anne is too frail for it. Therefore, the nice Anne is never present in company, has not appeared one single time so far, but almost always predominates when we're alone. I know exactly how I'd like to be, how I am too ... inside. But, alas, I'm only like that for myself. And perhaps that's why, no I'm sure it's the reason why I've got a happy nature within and why other people think I've got a happy nature without. I'm guided by the pure Anne within ... . (p. 720)

Writing in her personal diary and directing her entries to an entity called Kitty helped Anne reveal to herself the "deeper Anne." This "finer and better" aspect of her personality, her anima, guided her to the "pure Anne within," her soul, and the result was an experience of inner and outer happiness and wholeness.

The Two Marias

The definition of soul from one of my students made mention of how zombies, vampires, and inanimate objects are soulless. The two types of traditional monsters referred to here are called the "living dead:" they are animated and look like humans, yet they are lacking something crucial about them, acting more like programmed robots with one goal in mind: consume life from the living. For the modern zombie, the life essence they need is in a living human's brain, expressing the idea that the soul or animating spirit is located there; for a vampire, it's in the blood. In order to remain animated, these dead beings must kill and consume other living humans. To a very large degree, these creatures are caricatures of the modern consumer, which explains to a large degree why zombies and vampires with a rich legendary and mythic history remain so popular in contemporary society.

What is especially disturbing about these creatures is that, in the case of vampires, there is an attempt in popular culture to make them appear like role models. They're sexy, they dress really cool, and, even though they're dead, they can mate with humans and have babies. Or, at least that's the lesson we learn from the extremely popular *Twilight Saga* series of books and films, the latter series released from 2008 to 2012, featuring a community of buff and beautiful vampires living in the Pacific Northwest.

Erich Fromm used a common word to describe this type of glorification of the living dead within certain societies: necrophilia. Fromm considered certain cultures having a necrophilious tendency, glorifying lifeless, inanimate objects at the expense of neglecting flesh and blood humans. Societies that have more of a tendency to champion life-affirming rather than death-affirming aspects of their cultural value system are considered biophilious.

Fromm (1973/1992) also explored the necrophilious personality, characterized as "... the passion to transform that which is alive into something unalive; to destroy for the sake of destruction; the exclusive interest in all that is mechanical. It is the passion to tear apart living structures" (p. 369). One can see how Fromm's definition of the necrophilious personality relates to those who have embraced nihilism, as well as the tendency in the United States to provide more protection for objects such as guns rather than to find ways to protect humans from mass shooters who, in many cases, bought their military assault-style weaponry through perfectly legal channels rather than through black market methods.

Fromm's mentioning that a necrophilious personality is attracted to "all that is mechanical" obviously applies to consumer cultures and the glorification of guns, tech toys and golden toilets (see Chapter 4). Although Fromm was highly critical of such cultures that have major necrophilious tendencies, he was also extremely cognizant of the fact that all of us are a blending of biophilious and necrophilious characteristics with some people having more of an affinity to embrace one of these tendencies. As I pointed out when referring to mass shooters who develop a nihilist view of life, these individuals might have more of a necrophilious personality tendency.

Echoing Jung's ideas about the importance of confronting what is at first interpreted as evil in order to deepen one's understanding of one's view of reality and values, Fromm stated that, "the conflict between the two [tendencies] is often the source of a productive development" (p. 367). However, if a person never questions a necrophilious orientation, a society's own necrophilious characteristics can encourage a person to further develop and justify such a view of life, such as embracing racist and other anti-human attitudes while idolizing assault rifles and other military-style weaponry.

A vivid comparison between a soulful or biophilious personality and a soulless or necrophilious personality, and how both can be part of the same individual, is provided in director Fritz Lang's *Metropolis* (1926), referred to in the Introduction. The film features the character of Maria as both soulful and soulless. The soulful Maria acts as a spiritual leader for the exploited workers of the glittering metropolitan marvel they built and maintain for the rich elite. She gives hope-filled sermons to these downtrodden workers which are held in ancient subterranean caverns located under the city. She also comforts and watches over the children of the workers while the parents are tending the machines.

Freder, the elite son of the ruler of Metropolis, becomes entranced by Maria after she invades the exquisite lounging areas reserved for the rich; suddenly appearing with a group of starving children, Maria looks around at the luxurious surroundings populated by the elite, and tells the children, "See? These are your brothers and sisters."

After she and the children are quickly escorted out of the elite's play-ground, Freder follows her and learns about the secret sermons she gives to the downtrodden. He attends one of her meetings dressed as a worker, and when she speaks of a mediator who will one day appear and unite the workers with the elite, he meets with Maria after the meeting and declares his loyalty to her cause.

Unfortunately, his overlord father, Joh Frederson, after learning about Maria's sermons, turns to the mad genius-architect Rotwang and orders him to give the strangely alluring robot he created in honor of his dead wife the physical appearance of Maria. Frederson's reason for having Rotwang

Figure 5.1 The soulful Maria from *Metropolis*, comforting the destitute children of the city as their exploited parents work to keep the city's machines functioning.

Source: *Creative Commons.*

create a robot-doppelganger of Maria is to use the robot to manipulate the workers in order to keep them in line. Rotwang obeys Frederson's order and kidnaps Maria; then, through his innovative blending of technology and sorcery, he creates the false Maria (see Figure I.2) who has the features of the real Maria but is missing one crucial aspect: her soul.

Joh Frederson then has the false Maria speak to the working masses to keep them under his control and destroy their hope for the appearance of a mediator to heal the rift between the elite and the workers. Because of her inability to feel anything about the fate of the workers or the fate of the glittering city above them, the soulless Maria preaches hate, destruction, envy, and revenge. The result is a riot among the workers. Later, Maria appears to the rich young men of Metropolis dressed in a provocative outfit and performs a lustful dance that stirs up their desires (see Figure I.3). Fistfights and duels to the death break out among the rich young men, much to the false Maria's delight.

While the false Maria continues to create havoc among the elite, the workers begin to destroy the machines until most of Metropolis is in ruins. Fortunately, the real Maria escapes from her confines while the rioting workers are capturing the false Maria, tying her to a stake and lighting her on fire, as if she were a medieval witch. Then, with the soulful Maria acting as a mediating guide for Freder to heal the rift between rich and poor, Freder takes the hands of his father and the leader of the workers, and unites them.

The contrast between the soulful and soulless Marias is vividly dynamic, most notably in the scenes where the real and the false Marias speak to the exploited workers. The real Maria has an ethereal, compassionate aura about her, while the false Maria is the epitome of evil tempting those to succumb to her nihilist rants and lustful dance moves in order to partake in the destruction of their society.

The two Marias, representing the conflict between biophilious and ne-crophilious tendencies that all of us struggle with, could be interpreted as the anima of Freder. Both Marias create what Jung and Fromm considered a necessary tension of opposite forces within an individual, with the potential for psychic growth.

Freder is first depicted as completely isolated from his own biophilious tendencies as he romps with the rest of his elite friends in an Eden-like garden setting located in one of the top floors of Metropolis' tallest sky-scrapers. The appearance of Maria surrounded by starving children triggers an immediate response from his core essence: Freder's reaction is *pathos,* an instinctual response to the suffering of others with the desire to stop the suffering. Pathos is another nonrational concept; it is linked to the hero archetype, the universal response to come to the aid of a person whose life is threatened in some manner. The hero impulse is sometimes so powerful, someone in the grips of its dynamic energy can neglect his or her own safety in order to provide assistance to the individual in danger.

After his first encounter with Maria, Freder becomes obsessed with finding out more about her, leading him to willfully descend deeply into the dark, underground caverns of Metropolis. When he does, he kneels in reverence with other workers as they all listen to Maria preach sermons of love, compassion, and hope.

It's significant that, before he met Maria, Freder had no idea that the underground chambers existed, nor even that there was a working class, illustrating how alienated Freder is to this underground realm which symbolizes the relationship he has with his unconscious. It's also significant that when Freder descends and first sees Maria, he instinctively bows down in reverence to her, as if he has immediately recognized Maria as an anima figure ruling this subterranean realm, reflective of his own inner psyche. Here is Freder's own "finer and better" side, the "pure" Freder within. He also has an immediate response to Maria's references to a mediator; in other words, by following his soul guide down into the depths of his psyche, Freder finds his core sense of self-identity.

Maria refers to the mediator as someone who will unite the head and heart of Metropolis, essentially the intellect with the soul. In order to infuse Metropolis with more heart—or soul—the city must go through an apocalyptic transformation of its soulless qualities. The old way of life must be destroyed in order for a new way of life to emerge from the rubble, the same process involved in traditional initiatory rites that are performed to trigger a transformation of consciousness through the destruction of the old conscious attitude. This transformation happens in the film with the assistance of both Marias who create the horrible tension between life-affirming and death-loving tendencies within the hero figure Freder who represents these same elements in his society. In this case, the conflict between what is soulful and what is soulless within a society leads to a revitalized affirmation of life.

The Immortal Dimension of the Psyche

In Chapter 3, I included a quote from Jung in which he expressed his attitude toward the psyche as a whole, that it has both mortal and immortal dimensions to it, with the Self as the psyche's immortal aspect. Obviously, the concept of immortality is yet another nonrational concept seemingly beyond the scope of science and philosophy to determine its existence. Since we failed to find the soul's existence within the physical body, the implication is that the soul is like the mind, existing without any physical form. However, at least with the mind, the majority of scientists are in agreement, that it is a product of brain activity. As for the soul, scientists are more doubtful, which leads to the conclusion that there is no soul: nothing remains after physical death except a rotting corpse.

However, in recent decades, there has been a resurgence of interest in exploring the dimensions of consciousness, due to a large degree by the availability of advanced technological breakthroughs in the use of fMRI brain imaging to observe and measure brain activity. Still, even with these brain-scanning machines, it remains impossible to determine what a person is actually thinking or dreaming about; that requires input from the individual under study, which could lead to faulty interpretations since there is no way to determine whether the person's subjective observations are accurate.

The subjective factor of consciousness has always been a problem for psychologists and scientists interested in the study of brain activity. Some of the conclusions they have made about whether the mind is a product of brain activity or exists as a separate entity from the brain remain conflicting and contradictory, a point dramatically illustrated by still another nonrational concept: near-death experiences, in which a person in a death crisis due to a heart attack, stroke, or major accident, is declared brain dead by medical experts, but then recovers and reports seeing visions that many who have had such experiences interpret as proof of an afterlife existence.

Such experiences have been reported for millennia, but have been criticized for being influenced by a person's already strong beliefs in an afterlife, or that the person's visions are a neurologically-based reaction caused by the lack of blood flow to the brain. Both of these explanations are valid, but they could also support the idea that, in a death crisis, the brain reacts to the lack of blood flow by preparing the person for the next stage of existence with visions of this next stage before the brain begins to recover from its trauma.

To illustrate the conflicting attitudes regarding near-death experiences, one could compare the conclusions of two neurologists who have studied these types of experiences for decades. In his book, *Spiritual Doorway in the Brain* (2012), Dr. Kevin Nelson theorized that the near-death experience is a product of REM intrusion, meaning that a person's brain in a death crisis switches to the REM stage of sleep when dreams are most vivid; it is also a stage of sleep that mirrors waking consciousness when viewed on an electroencephalograph that records the brain's various sleep and wake cycles.

Nelson's theory obviously hinges on the brain having some activity during the death crisis. However, because of the similarities over the centuries in the descriptions of individuals reporting these types of experiences, Nelson concluded that the experience is a type of hard-wired, neurological narrative pattern: "At its very core and center, the near-death experience is a *story* ... [about] a journey and a return, an old story that stretches back at least as far as the ancient civilizations of Mesopotamia, Egypt, and Greece, where corpses were ritualistically prepared for their journey into an afterlife" (pp. 112–113).

The journey and return motif Nelson referred to in regards to people reporting near-death experiences is a variation of the archetypal motif of journeying to the celestial sphere to experience an encounter with the *empyrean*. The empyrean is considered to be the highest heaven where God dwells. In many traditions that refer to the empyrean, such as the one featured in the final passages of Dante's epic poem, *The Divine Comedy*, the empyrean is described as a brilliant light that triggers extreme feelings of awe and tranquility. As Nelson implied, with REM stage intruding upon the person's traumatized brain, the individual suffering from a death crisis has an intensely vivid vision of what they interpret as a glimpse of the afterlife before recovering and returning to waking consciousness.

Figure 5.2 Detail from "Ascent into the Empyrean," 16th-century painting by Hieronymus Bosch depicting the empyrean as a brilliant circle of light where angels guide the souls of the recently dead. Numerous individuals who have had a near-death experience report similar visions which some interpret as a glimpse of the afterlife before they recover from the near-death trauma.

Source: *Creative Commons*.

The other book, appropriately titled *After* (2021), was written by Dr. Bruce Greyson, a professor of psychiatry and neurobehavioral sciences. Like Nelson, Greyson studied near-death experiences for decades, after which he came to a very unscientific conclusion about the controversy surrounding the brain-mind connection: the mind is separate from the brain, and can endure after physical death. He made this conclusion after dealing with numerous patients who suffered severe brain trauma and fell into a near-death state which triggered visions relating to the concept of the empyrean. Greyson realized that, because the brain is primarily focused on keeping a person alive, if it is damaged or suffers trauma, the mind becomes freed from the brain's survival focus and expands, resulting in an experience of being connected with infinite life, or a universal source of life. As Greyson commented: "NDEs [near-death experiences] may be the ultimate example of elaborate experiences associated with not only reduced, but practically absent brain activity. All this evidence is consistent with the idea that the brain is a filter of our thoughts and feelings, and that the range of our thoughts and feelings expands as the filtering activity of the brain decreases" (p. 129).

Greyson ultimately concluded that:

> It seems plausible to me that NDEs may be triggered by electrochemical or chemical changes in the brain that permit the mind to experience separating from the body at the moment of death ... . [People] who have had NDEs consistently say that their experience of being awake and aware while their brains are impaired convinces them that their minds act independently of their brains at times, and are not just the product of their physical brains. And that leads them to believe that their mind or consciousness may continue after the physical body dies. (pp. 211–212)

Although both neuroscientists agree that people in a near-death crisis are experiencing powerful visions dominated by the archetypal motif expressing the concept of the empyrean, they disagree about the mind–brain connection. And yet, both subscribe to the idea that these people are seeing and experiencing something that seems impossible, or at least nonrational: a vision of what many interpret to be an alternate reality existing beyond physical death (see Kline, 2019).

An example of such an experience involves a clinical academic psychiatrist who described himself as antireligious prior to suffering severe trauma to his body which resulted in him being hospitalized for treatment. While he was under anesthetics and drifting in and out of waking consciousness, he had a perception of a ladder "where I am on a certain rung or level, moving upwards" (Singh, 2022, p. 1). As he progressed up the ladder:

> ... [I] gradually become aware of a peaceful and inviting bright white light at the top of the "ladder." The light has an ethereal quality and an

undefinable personhood. I feel the light as a sacred being and experience immense peace and calm as I get closer. As I approach the light, I "visualize" a massive explosion with widespread dispersion of "material." Illuminations spread across my awareness, followed by coalescence of everything back into nothingness. A cascade of explosions and collapses follow each other. I feel a sense of wonder and splendor. I have a profound and deep sense of understanding that these are cycles of creation and destruction. This awareness arises fully formed, is utterly convincing, and has a complete certainty of knowing. It has a noetic quality—a direct and immediate apprehension of knowledge and understanding. I know something completely and wholly, which I had never known before. I do not know how I know, but I know that I know ... . As I approach the light, I continue to experience a profound sense of peace and understanding. I feel I understand the cosmos, not in a cognitive sense of knowing but in an experiential manner, which is difficult to articulate. I near the light, am turned away, and fall asleep. (p. 2)

The individual reporting the experience, Dr. Swaran P. Singh, commented on its impact:

I was not primed, prepared for, or seeking the experience, and it has left me with nothing but peace and equanimity. Regardless of its causation, it has been life affirming and positive in its impact. (p. 4)

After the experience, Singh began to delve into religious belief systems and realized similarities in doctrines that speak of the beginning, ending, and cyclical reformulation of the cosmos, what religious scholar Mircea Eliade (1949/2005) called the eternal return motif found in numerous cultures throughout human history. As Singh further described his experience:

In the aftermath of the experience, I started believing that I understood the cosmos—its beginning from a single point, the emergence of matter and energy within the fabric of time and space, the creation and transformation of life forms, and the collapse of the universe into itself, its annihilation, and recreation ... . I also felt a deep sense of understanding of the meaning and purpose of existence. (p. 2)

Note how Singh, despite his antireligious perspective, felt this experience, in which a "single point" of concentrated energy gave birth to the cosmos, underscored how all forms of matter have a common origin and are thus interconnected, reflecting the concept of animism, the most primal expression of religious belief as Frazer and others have pointed out. There is also an obvious relationship that Singh's experience has with the famous dream from Genesis, referred to in Chapter 4, featuring Jacob having a dream of a ladder reaching up to heaven with angels traversing up and down the ladder while God speaks to Jacob from the ladder's pinnacle, a variation of the concept of the empyrean. Although Singh referred to the bright light at the top of his ladder as a "sacred being," having "an ethereal quality and an undefinable personhood," he ultimately questioned this "personhood" as the originator of the cosmos. Nevertheless, the similarities between Jacob's reported dream and Singh's description are evident. It's also interesting to note the title Singh gave to the article describing his experience: "Stairway to Heaven."

Singh was fully aware of the unscientific dimension of his and other similar experiences reported through the ages, and as someone trained in scientific discipline, he struggled to accept the experience as having a relationship with others who have interpreted their experiences as an affirmation of a type of spiritual dimension existing beyond waking reality. Although he continued to question the experience as having a divine origin, he could not interpret it as having been the result of a malfunction of the brain. It was too unsettling, too real, and too transformational, inspiring him to delve into avenues of philosophical and religious doctrines that he normally would have never considered a valid interpretation of how the world works. Like others who have an animistic view of life, the experience ultimately gave Singh "a deep sense of understanding of the meaning and purpose of existence."

My own interpretation of such experiences emphasizes the relationship they have with preparing individuals for the next phase of life, thus linking them with the mystery religion tradition that simulated a journey into the dark land of the dead to experience rebirth through an encounter with god powers which, in some instances, were referred to as appearing to initiates in the form of a brilliant light or great fire (Kerenyi, 1967/1991, pp. 92–93). Jung would agree that some aspect of the psyche endures after physical death. He came to this conclusion after hearing numerous reports of the dreams of individuals in the final stages of life and realizing that the psyche disregards linear or historical time in preference for emphasizing cyclical and eternal time: "... from the needs of his own heart, or in accordance with the ancient lessons of human wisdom ... anyone should draw the conclusion that the psyche, in its deepest reaches, participates in a form of existence beyond space and time, and thus partakes of what is inadequately and symbolically described as 'eternity ...'" (p. 414).

Perhaps the aspect of the psyche that "partakes of what is inadequately and symbolically described as 'eternity,'" is the soul.

Possessed by an Archetype

Jung's definition of soul as he defined it in *Psychological Types* considered the soul an expression of personality, with two dimensions of personality:

persona and anima. Persona has many dimensions since it can change according to the social situation; one adapts to a business environment, for example, by putting on one's professional business mask and embracing that role within that environment before taking off that mask and assuming a "family and friends" persona.

Jung also put a major emphasis upon how the persona dimension of personality can be influenced by personal complexes which he described as volatile concentrations of psychic energy that can take over a person's ego consciousness and dominate his or her personality as if ego had no control over the sudden appearance of this personality characteristic. The emotional factor of complexes is linked to personal experiences that trigger the emergence of this personality. This is where such terms as father or mother complex apply to certain types of spontaneous emotional outbursts when, for example, a current experience triggers a memory of Mom or Dad aggressively reprimanding the person; such an experience can take the person by surprise as the volatile power of the complex suddenly and momentarily dominates his or her actions beyond the person's control.

Jung (1934/1969b) considered complexes splinter factions of the persona: "… complexes are in fact 'splinter psyches.' The etiology of their origin is frequently a so-called trauma, an emotional shock or some such thing that splits off a bit of the psyche" (p. 98). Jung's description of complexes relates to those who have experienced PTSD or post-traumatic stress disorder, in which a current situation triggers a volatile memory of a traumatic experience and the person reacts to the current situation as if he or she were reliving the trauma associated with the experience.

Another psychological disorder is also associated with complexes, as Jung explained when he stated that, in some cases, "… their powers of assimilation become especially pronounced, since unconsciousness helps the complex to assimilate even the ego, the result being a momentary and unconscious alteration of personality known as identification with the complex. In the Middle Ages it went by another name: it was called possession" (p. 98).

Jung's reference to possession by a complex that dominates ego consciousness relates to the psychological disorder known as dissociative identity disorder (DID), also known as multiple personality disorder. Someone suffering from DID can experience a hostile takeover of one's ego persona by a personality that dominates ego to the point where ego loses its hold on reality while this splinter personality expresses itself. The sudden switch to another personality for those with DID is a coping mechanism to help the person disassociate from the traumatic memories.

As Jung indicated, sudden fluctuations in personality resulting in emotional outbursts and uncontrollable behavior were once considered indications of possession by a spirit, demon, or some other foreign entity. This ancient view of DID now has a specific dissociative disorder sub-category: dissociative trance disorder (DTD), also known as possession disorder

(Kearney and Trull, 2018a, p. 163). This variation of DID is quite prominent in certain cultures; in the Marianas Islands, for example, it is not unusual for someone to report these types of dissociative experiences.

In the General Psychology class, I have an assignment in which students are required to pick a psychological disorder and comment on its characteristics and then explain why this disorder is of interest to them in preparation for conducting further research into the disorder. One student responded with the following:

> Dissociative identity disorder is the disorder that interests me; it is defined as the occurrence of two or more identities that lives in one individual. It used to be called multiple personality disorder until 1994. This disorder caught my eye because I have an aunt who has another identity that lives in her. However, it is not from being abused as a child, it is from a supernatural phenomenon. Just like those who have dissociative identity disorder, she also has personality switches. These two different things share the same characteristic of switches. These personalities can be very different in gender, sexual orientation, physiological profiles, and more. In my auntie's case, according to a witch doctor [i.e. a traditional healer called a siruhuano], her spirit that possesses her is a man, of Asian descent, and is extremely strong. I have seen this phenomenon happen in real life. It is true that the spirit is very strong, it takes many of my strong uncles to hold her down when the possession is triggered. My family and I also notice the changes in her personality when it happens; that is how my family knows that the possession is happening. It is also interesting to me that before people really learned about mental disorders, they believed that dissociative identity disorder was actually possession. It is the same switches in both of these things that made me interested in this specific type of disorder. (K. Camacho, 2021, personal correspondence with author)

As the student indicates, these types of experiences result in a dynamic change in personality with great displays of power and emotion as well as a distinct foreign personality dominating the person's behavior and demeanor. Some students who have had similar experiences with possession have heard the possessed person talk in a different language or speak of events completely foreign to the possessed individual. As the student mentions, at one-time possession was considered the cause of all psychological disorders. A traditional healer—a witch doctor, or exorcist—was required to perform a ritual or recite a prayer or liturgy to disrupt the possession and restore the person's ego personality. It is significant to note that traditional healers consider possession as "loss of soul." It was up to the healer to restore a person's lost soul, essentially restoring a person's core sense of self-identity (Ellenberger, 1970, pp. 6–9).

Possession of this type indicates an impersonal rather than a personal complex as the cause of a disruption in one's ego identity or persona. The rogue personality in the majority of student examples I'm familiar with is linked to the possessed person's ancestral heritage; insulting or disrespecting one's ancestral spirits in these instances can lead to the behavior described by the student's possessed auntie. In other words, culture plays a major role in cases of dissociative trance disorder, specifically cultures that have a tradition of ancestral worship which is the case for the Marianas.

The student example of possession also relates to Jung's statement about how personal complexes have "powers of assimilation [that] become especially pronounced, since unconsciousness helps the complex to assimilate even the ego." Because the unconscious is the realm of archetypal energies, a personal complex can gain additional psychic volatility if the complex is linked to an archetypal power; the Great Mother archetype, for example, can influence a personal mother complex, resulting in a person possessed by this god-like archetypal power. When this occurs, one is in danger of becoming possessed by an archetype, referred to previously in Chapter 3 in the context of Jung's comments on the mana-personality. According to Jung (1953/1972), there is no more dangerous type of possession since ego has assimilated a power beyond its ability to control it: "… possession of the conscious personality entails a psychic danger … by inflating the conscious mind … . The ego has appropriated something that does not belong to it" (pp. 228–229).

Obviously, possession of this sort can lead to a state of egomania in which the ego takes on characteristics of the Self. However, such incidents can also be an indication that trauma is a factor in triggering this type of possession; if this is the case, then possession by an archetypal energy is what the Self intends in order to heal the trauma. Possession by an archetype, therefore, can be possession by the anima or animus, soul guide archetypal powers, in order for the soul to guide the individual to a state of homeostasis or even to reveal a new, emerging sense of self-identity.

An example of possession by an archetype to heal trauma and allow a new splinter of personal identity to emerge comes from another student. Unlike the other student examples, this was a graduate student enrolled in a depth psychology program with Pacifica Graduate Institute. Pacifica specializes in offering graduate programs in psychology emphasizing Jung's approach to depth psychology. Programs include courses devoted to mythological studies, art therapy and creativity, dream interpretation, and amplification of dream imagery—all methods of investigation of the unconscious influences on personality and behavior developed by Jung during his Red Book period.

The student, in this case, Tracy Ferron, enrolled in one of the depth psychology programs when she was in the grips of a midlife crisis. As she described it, Ferron felt stuck wearing the persona mask of a mother of five in a marriage that was on the verge of dissolution. Her intent in enrolling in the program was to earn a degree that would help her pursue her interest in writing historical fiction. Instead, during the program, she had a dream that essentially destroyed her previous life.

The dream was influenced by trauma she experienced as a child growing up in a family that included two brothers suffering from schizophrenia. One of the brothers had murdered a girlfriend of his and spent many years in a mental institution. Living in this family environment with two unstable brothers caused much turmoil and anxiety with a lot of repressed anger and fear.

The Pacifica environment encouraged exploration of trauma and its influence upon personality, behavior, and dreams. One night while in the midst of her studies, Ferron dreamed of being back home with her father and the one brother who had committed murder, although her home in this dream looked more like a medieval castle. The following is Ferron's (2017) summary of the dream:

> I am standing in front of a vast, grey stone castle, which is covered in rust spots. A man is making his young son power wash these spots but it is not working. The son refuses to continue, so the father proclaims, "There must be a sacrifice." And suddenly we are in the basement of the castle—where the father has created a small theater set, with candles and photos on an antique dresser. A young naïve woman comes in, expecting to audition. But she is the sacrifice. The scene changes: She has been murdered and her body plastered into the basement wall of the castle. I can see the scattered outline of her broken body under the plaster, her limbs askew like a Picasso painting. The only thing exposed is her right eye. The scene shifts again and now I am directly in front of her. I am the murderer and the woman is emerging from the wall. I pull off her eye and begin stabbing her in the chest but she is unstoppable. She is coming out from the wall. (p. 2)

This incredibly vivid and savage dream of ritual sacrifice through a brutal murder, followed by a startling rebirth of the murdered victim, could have easily been interpreted as demonic. If someone unfamiliar with archetypal symbolism had experienced a similar dream, the person could have easily interpreted the dream as a nightmare with figures from a person's past acting like sadistic demons and inspiring the dreamer to join their orgy of murder and dismemberment. However, because Ferron was familiar with Jung's own brutal Red Book dreams and the methods he had devised to interpret archetypal symbolism, Ferron embraced the dream, knowing immediately from its emotional impact that it was significant. She became determined to investigate its central image of a young woman ritually sacrificed and entombed in a wall, leading to an amazing resurrection. The dream's violent, necrophilious content demonstrates the alleged evil of the unconscious that, when investigated further, becomes a powerful force of transformation.

As Ferron later discovered, the motif of the "walled woman" is archetypal, with numerous examples in legend, tradition, and history in which a woman was either sacrificed and then her body used as part of a building's foundation, or walled up while still alive and left to die. In Ferron's dream, the motif becomes a commentary on her feelings of being stuck or "walled up." It's extremely significant that it's Ferron's own dream persona who pulls out the woman's one staring eye peering out of the wall, then tries to keep her walled up by stabbing her repeatedly. But, as she states, "... she is unstoppable. She is coming out from the wall." In this scene, Ferron embodies a necrophilious power and participates in the ritual death of her old persona so that it can be reborn and emerge with renewed, "unstoppable" vitality.

After having this dream and realizing that the walled woman motif was archetypal, Ferron became obsessed with researching the walled woman archetypal pattern by applying Jung's amplification method. Ferron uncovered legions of examples of the motif with various expressions and interpretations. One of the examples she found was the tradition of religious women, or anchoresses, in Spain who volunteered to be walled up or immured into a corner of the church with items and provisions in order to better devote themselves to their religious studies. Ferron (2017) commented on this tradition: "By sacrificing their lives in the world, the anchoresses were thought to be bringing life to and purifying their towns. Their space, the anchorhold, was often referred to as a tomb but also a return to the womb, indicating the paradoxical liminal place held by these women in the cycle of death and rebirth within their communities" (pp. 4–5).

After realizing the profound, archetypal significance of the dream, Ferron felt compelled to honor the dream's universal motif from a collective perspective: "I feel my Walled Woman dream illustrates a collective archetypal story erupting to the surface, that of divine feminine consciousness, which has been suppressed and suspended over millennia, and is now so desperately needed to balance, partner with the masculine, and heal our planet. Walled Woman evokes this new story" (pp. 5–6). Ferron also wanted to pay homage to the dream's impact on her from a personal perspective, how the dream was an expression of her longing for a way to throw off a stagnated and outdated persona as mother and wife in order to allow the emergence of a new dimension of her personality: an artist.

In order to do justice to the dream's profound impact and bring it to life for others, she conceptualized the dream as an art project. Ferron then began prowling through antique shops and swap meets looking for items to include in her project while teaching herself skills in bricklaying, metallurgy, and sculpting. At one point, in order to better understand the experience of being walled up, Ferron settled into the family's bathtub, covered herself with a layer of bricks save for her head and arms, and lay there for hours. The session ended when Ferron's husband helped her release a paper mache winged heart, symbol of her soul being released from confinement and allowed to fly free of all restraints (Bright, 2018, n.p.).

Ferron's own experience with the dream expressing the walled woman archetypal motif underscores Jung's comments on what he called big dreams dominated by archetypal patterns and how they differ from little dreams:

> How is [a person] to know whether his dream is a "big" or "little" one? He knows it by an instinctive feeling of significance. He feels so overwhelmed by the impression it makes that he would never think of keeping the dream to himself. He has to tell it, on the psychologically correct assumption that is it of general [i.e. collective] significance ... . The processes of the collective unconscious are concerned not only with the more or less personal relations of an individual to his family or to a wider social group, but with his relations to society and to the human community in general ... . [A big dream therefore] impels not just private communication, but drives people to revelations and confessions, and even to dramatic representations of their fantasies. (1953/ 1972, pp. 178–179)

Figure 5.3 Tracy Ferron as the Walled Woman releasing a winged heart, symbol of her liberated soul.

Source: *Lori A. Cheung.*

Jung's comments relate directly to Ferron's experience. The dream was an expression of her static, frustrated state and longing for transformation. The Self responded to this desire for transformation by fashioning a dream scenario incorporating the walled woman archetype to illustrate her psychological state, then provided a solution to it: through a symbolic, ritualistic death, the sacrificed woman emerges from a confined existence and she is unstoppable.

When I met Ferron as a student in one of the Pacifica classes I was teaching, she was in the culminating stages of her graduate program, finalizing the details of her walled woman project in both art and written form. What immediately impressed me about her was that she remained agitatedly astonished by the dream's powerful grip upon her. She felt the dream was demanding her to explore and expand upon the archetypal motif as it had been expressed and interpreted by other cultures; it was also driving her to delve into avenues of artistic expression that she never would have considered if the dream had not demanded it from her.

Ferron at the time was preparing to deliver a presentation to a Jungian organization about her walled woman experience as she also prepared her final assignment for the class. She became fixated on her presentation, revising it so many times that she nearly missed the deadline to submit it for review in my class. To be honest, I have never seen someone so obsessed over a dream experience, compelled to give creative expression to this dream that she believed was a comment on how her personal life reflected the lives of women in general who have been immured by their societies, pigeonholed into a persona that allows no expression of the anima.

From my perspective, there was no doubt that she was possessed by this archetypal motif which demanded that she share it with the world since it was not only an expression of her core essence, but a universal expression of the necessity to sacrifice oneself—one's old persona—in order to give birth to a new, revitalized soul-self.

Ultimately, Ferron was able to share her walled woman project with her community by establishing a non-profit organization, Life On Earth, which concentrates on creating hands-on art projects that emphasize art as a way to heal trauma and conflict while infusing wonder and awe within "life on Earth." The organization's CFO is her husband who has embraced her experience to the point where the rift that threatened their marriage has been healed. One of her public presentations inspired by the walled woman project, was called "Unbound." As Ferron described it:

> Unbound [is] an 80 foot sculpture of hope and liberation. This artwork was inspired by my brother, Bob, who lived in a world of paranoid schizophrenia and was lost in this world. In this sculpture, 769 paper mache winged hearts fly free of the cage of darkness. This artwork was co-created with over 500 psychiatric patients and 200 staff at one of

California's largest public psychiatric hospitals and over 800 community volunteers. (Ferron, 2022, n.p.).

Ferron's example profoundly illustrates the validity of Jung's approach to psychology. By emphasizing the necessity of recognizing one's soul essence through willful acts of descent into the unconscious through the use of techniques Jung developed through his own terrifying descents into the dark depths of soul, Ferron underscored how a society stuck in an unconscious obsession with necrophilious tendencies can renew itself by incorporating actions and traditions that encourage self-discovery through self-reflection rather than identifying with material objects that promise wholeness but ultimately distort one's connection with the "pure" and "deeper" concept of self as it relates to the Self.

Skepticism remains about the existence of the soul due to its nonrational character. However, those who have made the effort to embrace solitude and look inward, or have experienced near death and seen the empyrean, or experienced a big dream and had their psyche invaded and held hostage by an archetype that demanded not only recognition but expression, have little doubt about its existence.

Note

1 I am aware that anima is usually associated with a man's contrasexual identity and animus is a woman's contrasexual identity. However, as indicated here, Jung also referred to the anima as a representation of a person's inner attitude that reflects the relationship a person has with the Self, regardless of a person's sex. Jung also referred to the anima as "the personification of the collective unconscious" (1956/ 1967, p. 324).

References

Bright, B. (2018). Depth psychology, art, and the archetype of the walled woman: An interview with conceptual artist Tracy Ferron. *Pacifica.edu*. Retrieved from https://www.pacificapost.com/depth-psychology-art-and-the-archetype-of-the-walled-woman.

Cohn, N. (1977). *Europe's inner demons: An enquiry inspired by the great witch-hunt*. New York: New American Library.

Delano, M.F. (1989). *Mysteries of the unknown: Search for the soul*. Alexandria, VA: Time-Life Books.

Eliade, M. (1949/2005). *The myth of the eternal return*. Princeton, NJ: Princeton University Press.

Ellenberger, H. (1970). *The discovery of the unconscious: A history and evolution of dynamic psychiatry*. New York: Basic Books.

Ferron, T. (2017, May 31). Walled woman demands sacrifice: Archetypal art and the emergence of divine feminine consciousness [Unpublished manuscript]. Pacifica Graduate Institute.

Ferron, T. (2022, June 1). Unbound. *Facebook.com*. Retrieved from https://www.facebook.com/tracy.ferron.

Frank, A. (2003). *The diary of Anne Frank: The revised critical edition* (D. Narnouw & G. van der Stroom, eds.). New York: Doubleday.

Frazer, J. (1900 & 1906-15/2018). *The golden bough: A study in magic and religion, an abridgment from the 2nd and 3rd editions* (R. Fraser, ed.). London, UK: Folio Society.

Fromm, E. (1955/1965). *The sane society*. New York: Fawcett.

Fromm, E. (1973/1992). *The anatomy of human destructiveness*. New York: Owl/Henry Holt.

Greyson, B. (2021). *After: A doctor explores what near-death experiences reveal about life and beyond*. New York: St. Martin's Press.

Hiltz, M. (2021, June 9). Project star gate: The CIA's human experiments with mind control. *Warhistoryonline.com*. Retrieved from https://www.warhistoryonline.com/war-articles/project-stargate.html?edg-c=1.

Jung, C.G. (1921/1971). *Psychological types. Collected Works, volume 6*. H. Read, M. Fordham, G. Adler (Eds.), W. McGuire (Senior ed.). Princeton University Press.

Jung, C.G. (1933/1955). The spiritual problem of modern man. In *Modern man in search of a soul*, pp. 198–244. New York: Harcourt Brace.

Jung, C.G. (1934/1969a). The soul and death. In H. Read, M. Fordham, G. Adler (Eds.), W. McGuire (Senior ed.). *The structure and dynamics of the psyche. Collected works, 2nd edition, volume 8*, pp. 404–415. Princeton, NJ: Princeton University Press.

Jung, C.G. (1934/1969b). A review of complex theory. In H. Read, M. Fordham, G. Adler (Eds.), W. McGuire (Senior ed.). *The structure and dynamics of the psyche. Collected works, 2nd ed., Volume 8*, pp. 92–106. Princeton, NJ: Princeton University Press.

Jung, C.G. (1953/1968). *Psychology and alchemy, 2nd ed. Collected works, volume 12*. H. Read, M. Fordham, G. Adler (Eds.), W. McGuire (Senior ed.). Princeton, NJ: Princeton University Press.

Jung, C.G. (1953/1972). *Two essays on analytical psychology. Collected works, volume 7*. H. Read, M. Fordham, G. Adler (Eds.), W. McGuire (Senior ed.). Princeton, NJ: Princeton University Press.

Jung, C.G. (1956/1967). *Symbols of transformation. Collected works, volume 5, 2nd ed.* H. Read, M. Fordham, G. Adler (Eds.), W. McGuire (Senior ed.). Princeton, NJ: Princeton University Press.

Jung, C.G. (1967/1983). *Alchemical studies. Collected works, volume 13*. H. Read, M. Fordham, G. Adler (Eds.), W. McGuire (Senior ed.). Princeton, NJ: Princeton University Press.

Jung, C.G. (2009). *The red book: Liber novus* (S. Shamdasani, Ed.). New York: W.W. Norton.

Kearney, C., & Trull, T. (2018a). *Abnormal psychology and life*, 3rd ed. Boston, MA: Cengage Learning.

Kearney, C., & Trull, T. (2018b). Risk and prevention of mental disorders [Chapter Three PowerPoint slides]. In *Abnormal Psychology and Life*, 3rd ed. Boston, MA: Cengage Learning.

Kerenyi, C. (1967/1991). *Eleusis: Archetypal image of mother and daughter.* Princeton, NJ: Princeton University Press.

Kline, J. (2019). *The otherworld in myth, folklore, cinema, and brain science.* United Kingdom: Cambridge Scholars Publishing.

Lang, F. (Director). (1927). *Metropolis* [Film]. UFA Studios.

Langman, P. (2009). *Why kids kill: Inside the minds of school shooters.* New York: St. Martin's Press.

McCarthy, E. (2022, May 9). Meet the parents who refuse to give their kids smartphones. *WashingtonPost.com.* Retrieved from https://www.washingtonpost.com/lifestyle/2022/05/09/parents-kids-smartphones/.

McClure, T. (2022, May 25). New Zealand PM Jacinda Ardern responds to Texas school shooting. *TheGuardian.com.* Retrieved from https://www.theguardian.com/us-news/2022/may/25/we-saw-something-that-wasnt-right-and-we-acted-ardern-on-how-new-zealand-delivered-gun-control.

Murphy, K. (2014, July 25). No time to think. *New York Times,* SR3.

Myers, S.L., & Thompson, S.A. (2022, June 1). Racist and violent ideas jump from web's fringes to mainstream sites. *NewYorkTimes.com.* Retrieved from https://www.nytimes.com/2022/06/01/technology/fringe-mainstream-social-media.html?action=click&module=Well&pgtype=Homepage&section=Business.

Nelson, K. (2012). *The spiritual doorway in the brain.* New York: Penguin Books.

Pratt, A. (1995). Nihilism. *Internet Encyclopedia of Philosophy.* Retrieved from https://iep.utm.edu/nihilism/.

Singh, S.P. (2022 June 23). Stairway to heaven: A first-person account of noesis. *Journal of Nervous and Mental Disease.* Original article. Retrieved from https://journals.lww.com/jonmd/Fulltext/9900/Stairway_to_Heaven__A_First_Person_Account_of.38.aspx. doi: 10.1097/NMD.0000000000001550.

Sganga, N. (2022, May 24). Active shooter incidents rose 50% in 2021 compared to 2020. *CBSNews.com.* Retrieved from https://www.cbsnews.com/news/active-shooter-incidents-higher-2021/.

Shanley, J.P. (Director). (1990). *Joe versus the volcano* [Film]. Warner Brothers.

Stanley-Becker, I., & Harwell, D. (2022, May 15). Buffalo suspect allegedly inspired by racist theory fueling global carnage. *WashingtonPost.com.* Retrieved from https://www.washingtonpost.com/nation/2022/05/15/buffalo-shooter-great-replacement-extremism/.

Worthen, M. (2020, Sept. 6). The trouble with empathy. *New York Times,* SR 4.

Chapter 6

The Dying and Resurrecting God/King/Hero/Billionaire

The Next Evolutionary Stage in Non-Human Development

Erik Erikson pioneered the psychosocial approach to the study of human development, emphasizing how humans continue to evolve psychologically throughout their lives (Newman & Newman, 2018, pp. 56–57). This is the same view of psychological growth that Jung championed, which he called the process of individuation. Both Erikson and Jung understood how a person's relationship with fellow humans and other living creatures in various environmental situations continue to act as a stimulus for psychological growth throughout the entire lifespan. Both agreed that a person could not fully realize and appreciate all dimensions of his or her personality until having passed through the various stages of development which presented specific challenges for each stage. Erikson referred to these challenges as psychosocial crises with the potential to stimulate psychological and cognitive growth. If, however, a challenge at a particular stage is left unresolved, the crisis could impact later developmental stages.

Erikson originally conceived human development over the lifespan in eight stages with the respective psychosocial crises for each stage (pp. 56–57). For example, Erikson considered the first stage, covering birth to age two, as the stage in which the psychosocial crisis of Trust versus Mistrust must initially be addressed. The child at that very young age interprets from an instinctual level whether caregivers are either trustworthy—able to take care of the child's basic needs and give the child a consistent sense of being loved and protected against harm—or untrustworthy—a cold and uncaring attitude toward the child's well-being. This first psychosocial crisis is one of the most crucial since it not only affects a child's relationship with caregivers but also sets the expectations for other relationships as well.

Erikson established the developmental stages while conducting his research primarily during the mid-20th century; since then, additional stages have been added by other researchers working in the field of human growth and development. One of the added stages was a final stage called Elderhood

DOI: 10.4324/9781003271482-7

(Newman & Newman, 2018, p. 554) covering the years of a person's life from around age 75 to the end of life. Previously, Erikson had considered the final stage to begin at around age 60, but due to the increase in longevity in humans, the additional stage was added with the following psychosocial crisis: Immortality versus Extinction (pp. 574–577).

Immortality in this context is defined as when a person develops confidence in accepting the transition to death though the development of *symbolic continuity* (pp. 574–575). Symbolic continuity refers to a person's sense of lifetime accomplishments, with the belief that these accomplishments will live on and endure after physical death, remembered most especially by those who were intimately involved in the person's life. It also refers to knowing one's genetic inheritance will endure through one's children. The term also has relevance to a person's religious beliefs, most significantly the belief in an afterlife existence. However, the most important aspect of symbolic continuity has to do with what is referred to as *experiential transcendence* (p. 576).

Mythologist Joseph Campbell (Campbell & Moyers, 1988), although not specifically referring to this term, defined experiential transcendence indirectly as singular moments of ecstasy, exhilaration, and full engagement with life: "I think what we're seeking is an experience of being alive, so that our life experiences on a purely physical plane of existence will have resonances within our own innermost being and reality, so that we actually feel the rapture of being alive" (p. 5).

A more formal definition of experiential transcendence is that it is an emotionally overwhelming psychic state, all-encompassing in its intensity to the point where a person moves beyond the mundane state of existence to one of rapture. These types of experiences are achieved through moments of spiritual ecstasy likened to a religious experience, through peak sensual and orgasmic experiences, and through the ingestion of mind-expanding psychotropic drugs (Vigilant & Williamson, 2003, p. 174). Big dreams and near-death experiences, referred to in Chapter 5, also reflect the term's meaning. Having these types of experiences gives a person a sense that time is irrelevant and physical death nonexistent. Holding on to these types of experiences as one ages can aid a person in accepting physical death as a transition to another state of existence.

As Erikson emphasized, the challenges or crises associated with each developmental stage offer ways for developmental growth. His view is similar to Jung's ideas about the importance of a person's ego consciousness being challenged by what Jung called the evil intentions of the unconscious but in fact are psychological challenges that offer new insights through the disruption the ego's conception of reality and self-identity. All of us continually evolve as individuals as we progress through life. If one refuses to take on the challenges associated with each developmental stage, there is a danger of becoming stagnated, fixated upon an earlier stage, and thus remaining stunted and frustrated with the progression of one's life as a whole.

As I attempted to illustrate in Chapter 5, if a person living in a modern, consumer culture feels stuck in life due to the belief that he or she is incapable of accomplishing anything of importance, there is a danger of falling into a state of nihilism. The nihilistic state can lead to self-destructive habits—overeating, overindulging in alcohol and drugs, spending too much time on the Internet shopping for new baubles or watching TikTok and YouTube videos—in other words, living a mundane, meaningless existence with no real purpose except to overindulge, consume, and be entertained.

The emphasis on overconsumption and self-indulgence in modern societies is reflective of the challenge of the final stage of life which involves wrestling with the concepts of immortality and extinction; if one feels that there is no sense of trying to achieve anything in life because life has no purpose, then the idea that all life returns to a state of lifeless, inorganic matter upon physical death becomes more plausible. Nothing survives after death, no hope for any sort of continuance. Death equals complete extinction, so why believe that life has any purpose? The faulty logic of such a belief is that all life originated from inorganic substances. We all rose from the dead.

Life on Earth can be considered either a natural result of the process of evolution or a cosmological fluke. Either way, here we are. To believe life was inevitable rather than a weird accident gives many people hope that there is a greater life plan and it is up to everyone of us to find out what our singular life plan is. This attitude toward life is essentially the process of individuation.

Modern consumer societies have a tendency to emphasize the mundane rather than the transcendent aspects of life. It's better to have the coolest trendy objects rather than experience a really good orgasm. This emphasis reminds me of one of my all-time favorite book titles: *How You Can Look Rich and Achieve Sexual Ecstasy.* The book was written in 1978 by Rona Barrett, a gossip columnist for the entertainment industry. As the title implies, you don't really have to be rich, just have the right designer clothes knock-offs, and in doing so, you can experience an imitative-magic orgasm similar to those of billionaires whose orgasms must be truly transcendent.

To a very real degree, modern societies promote the idea that we must fear physical death. And with this emphasis comes the underlying belief that, because life leads to complete extinction, we must also fear life itself and the challenges it presents. Jung (1930/1969) recognized this challenge of life: "To the psychotherapist, an old man who cannot bid farewell to life appears as feeble and sickly as a young man who is unable to embrace it … . From the standpoint of psychotherapy, it would therefore be desirable to think of death as only a transition, as part of a process whose extent and duration are beyond our knowledge" (p. 402).

In addition: "The negation of life's fulfilment is synonymous with the refusal to accept its ending. Both mean not wanting to live, and not wanting to live is identical with not wanting to die" (1934/1969, p. 407).

Modern societies are youth-oriented as they promote ways to maintain a sense of youthful appearance and vitality to present a façade that acts to camouflage the aging process. Many health and beauty products are promoted as ways to prevent aging, or at least help a person appear more youthful than his or her biological age. As Jung commented: "Being old is highly unpopular. Nobody seems to consider that not being able to grow old is just as absurd as not being able to outgrow child's size-shoes. A still infantile man at 30 is surely to be deplored, but a youthful septuagenarian—isn't that delightful? And yet, both are perverse ... psychological monstrosities" (p. 407).

Jung, no doubt, would have considered a contemporary movement a psychological monstrosity since this movement attempts to negate the final stage of life altogether. The new psychologically monstrous movement is *transhumanism*. As the name implies, it has nothing to do with the final life stage in which experiential transcendence and symbolic immortality play crucial parts in the transition from life to physical death. Instead, the movement promotes physical immortality, transcending the human condition, and being able to live forever. In other words, transhumanism is all about achieving god status. As one of the supporters of the movement commented to another during a transhumanism conference, "We're building God, you know." To which the fellow transhumanist replied, "Yeah, I know" (Ribeiro, 2022, n.p.).

As I have mentioned previously, identifying with the god power within all of us—the Self—is what Jung considered to be the most dangerous delusion of all. We must always strive to understand the god within, but never completely identify with this part of the human psyche since doing so could result in an egocentric attitude toward others, resulting in an estrangement from humanity. The transhumanist movement seems to be encouraging such an estrangement.

Jung (1961/1989) compared a person's death with a Sacred Marriage since it united the human's mortal aspect with his or her eternal aspect after physical death. Never forgetting the horrors associated with the death process, Jung stated:

> ... death is indeed a fearful piece of brutality ... . It is brutal not only as a physical event, but far more so psychically: a human being is torn away from us and what remains is the icy stillness of death ... . The actual experience of the cruelty and wantonness of death can so embitter us that we conclude that there is no merciful God, no justice, and no kindness. From another point of view, however, death appears as a joyful event. In the light of eternity, it is a wedding, a *mysterium coniunctionis*. The soul attains, as it were, its missing half, it achieves wholeness. (pp. 314–315)

It is extremely difficult to embrace this idea of death as the fulfilment of life since it seems a contradictory, nonrational conundrum. And yet, there are many cultures that express this contradiction by holding celebrations after a person's passing. As Jung also mentioned: "To this day, it is the custom in many regions to hold a picnic on the graves on All Souls' Day. Such customs express the feeling that death is really a festive occasion" (p. 315).

Personally, I still struggle with the idea of celebrating the death of a loved one through festive gatherings, but I do realize the necessity of such gatherings as ways to heal the trauma associated with the cold, brutal finality of death. I am also cognizant of the fact that Jung wrote about death as a type of sacred wedding after he suffered a heart attack and had a near-death experience during which: "... I continually heard dance music, laughter, and jollity, as though a wedding were being celebrated" p. 314). Ultimately, Jung was correct to consider death as a mysterious conjunction or mystical paradox between what is known and what can never be fully understood, especially since the origins of life itself remain a mystery.

Death as a terror to avoid at all costs has inspired several billionaires to invest heavily into life extension programs which includes the transhumanist movement. Apparently, many of these individuals are confident that their money can buy them a stairway that leads to their zillion dollar mansion compounds rather than to heaven. Some of these billionaires are Jeff Bezos from Amazon, technology innovator Peter Thiel, and Russian entrepreneur Dimitri Itskov (Horn, 2018, p. SR9; Segal, 2013, p. SBU1).

Itskov is the founder of the 2045 Initiative, which "will enable the transfer of an individual's consciousness to a more advanced non-biological immortal carrier" (Taylor, 2016, n.p.). This means that, in order to live forever, a person must be very rich, very egomaniacal, and extremely terrified of physical death. Such a person must first invest in a robot or avatar—a synthetic human body capable of holding the person's brain which has been preserved through cryogenic methods. After death, the person's brain is uploaded into the synthetic body. In a later stage of the initiative, a person will be able to have his or her personality characteristics uploaded into a synthetic brain housed in a synthetic body. In a culminating stage, envisioned as achievable by the year 2045, a person can preserve his physical and mental characteristics in hologram form (Taylor, 2016, n.p.).

In the context of the 2045 Initiative, immortality is interpreted as "the indefinite maintenance of our biological minds" (n.p.). Such an interpretation reflects the mind-brain controversy, explored in Chapter 5, with the idea that a person's immortal soul is the equivalent to the mind which is a product of brain activity and, thus, a physical object that can be preserved and later uploaded into an artificial body.

Although the originators of the 2045 Initiative seem to be optimistic in regards to achieving its goals by the prescribed date, there is still a major problem: we still don't know enough about how the brain works to even begin to think of removing it from a person's recently dead body, freezing it, and then somehow ensuring that all of the billions of neural networks within the brain are fully functioning before uploading it into a synthetic body. And even if this were possible, the thought of living out eternity as either a robot or a hologram doesn't sound all that appealing. Also, keep in mind the zombie factor: zombies are dead humans brought back to life with the goal to eat human brains, apparently because they are missing a part that's equivalent to—or is—the soul. Is transhumanism, therefore, the first step in ushering in the zombie apocalypse?

The idea of preserving our brains in a synthetic body in order to cheat death and live forever echoes Jung's comment about how old people dressing up and acting like kids is a perversion of the final stage of human development which negates life's ultimate goal: physical death. Ironically, certain transhumanists imply that the human condition itself is a type of evolutionary perversion, with some referring to humans as "ape-brained skin sacks" (Ribeiro, 2022, n.p.). Death itself is also a perversion: "Mortality is primitive, it is just a problem for humanity to overcome. Immortality is a natural development in the evolutionary process of life" (Taylor, 2016, n.p.). However, for transhumanists, this "natural development in the evolutionary process of life" does not so much refer to human evolutionary development but technological evolutionary development.

According to Ray Kurzweil, a technology advocate and a leading folk devil promoter of the transhumanist movement, the evolution of technology is as natural as human evolution, and it is just as unstoppable: "The ongoing acceleration of [technological development] is the implication and inevitable result of what I call the law of accelerating returns, which describes the acceleration of the pace of and the exponential growth of the products of an evolutionary process" (Eveleth, 2019, n.p.).

Some of these products resulting from the technological evolutionary process are smart diapers that can let parents know when their child needs a fresh one, smart speakers that can record all conversations including the intimate ones, internet-connected air fresheners, Bluetooth-activated toasters, monitors for teachers that can determine which students in a virtual course are inattentive, and, of course, Alexa, Amazon's echo-companion "maid service" device that arranges your appointments, answers all your questions, and makes sure you're always entertained (n.p.).

Advancements in technological sophistication and complexity are, in many instances, too enthusiastically embraced by young people born into a time when computers, smartphones, and other man-made tech creations have been an integral part of their lives since birth. However, to consider technological advancements as equivalent to human evolution is to completely misunderstand what human evolution is. Just to refresh everyone's memory, evolution refers to organic entities mutating over billions of years of time to form more complex life forms that compete to survive through adaptation to the environment; it does not refer to synthetic, man-made gadgets being manipulated by humans to form more complex gadgets deemed necessary by humanity to survive in a super-charged, rapidly changing, artificially constructed, tech-dominated world of their own creation.

An assignment I give to students enrolled in the Human Growth and Development course requires them to define the characteristics of their generation and whether or not it reflects their self-identity. Almost universally, students describe a generational and self-identification with technology. What's disturbing about some of their comments is that many express anxiety and stress over the constant and unrelenting technological advancements of which they believe they must keep abreast because, after all, it is a part of their generational identity and thus reflective of their personal identity.

In some instances, students have identified so much with their tech gadgets that they cannot conceive of evolving without them as newly updated devices replace the old ones. To a very large degree, the stress they feel is the fear of not being able to keep up with the so-called evolutionary pace of technology and risk ending up as obsolete as an old Nintendo game console. Here, I believe, is another type of transhumanism—identifying with the advancements in technology with one's own stages of human development.

From my perspective, such a trend is having major detrimental effects on the psyche of young people. For example, Generation Z, which roughly covers the years between the late 1990s up until around 2010, is not only considered the tech generation but also the loneliest generation. The following is how one student described her generation:

> If you asked me what generation I'm from, I would've said I was a millennial, but recent studies say that I am part of Generation Z (approximately 1997–2010.) This generation is known as the "digital natives" because we were born during the peak of technology, which was pioneered by the millennial generation. I feel connected to this characteristic because I did grow up with easy access to technology and social media. Through this, I have made many friends from different schools and had access to a lot of information. Unfortunately, this does come with a cost because like many others from Generation Z, I have learned things that I am not supposed to, and have been exposed to things a kid shouldn't be exposed to. Generation Z is also known to some as the "loneliest generation." They are known as the loneliest generation because they tend to spend more time on social media. Social media can lead to many negative feelings due to a compare and contrast system where we see other people living their best lives, while we're here just watching it all. I feel very connected to this aspect of my generation because I have experienced these same negative feelings as well; I always end up comparing my life to someone else's. (J. Andebor, 2022, personal correspondence with author)

As I mentioned, this student's comment on her generation is quite typical, underscoring the benefits and dangers of being a part of the "digital natives" who in many cases feel isolated from a lived experience as they compare their so-called mundane lives to those who are "living their best lives" after these 'best" people have succeeded in creating a perfect—and perfectly distorted—social media persona.

The Gilgamesh Syndrome

In case a person isn't a billionaire and can't afford to upload his or her brain into a robotic body to avoid physical death, there are other avenues for achieving physical immortality. One of these potential ways to cheat death features the manipulation and incorporation of the characteristics of a living creature that has the ability to regenerate itself after suffering physical trauma of some sort. I was first drawn to this intriguing field of study by an article published in 2012 about a particular jellyfish, the *turritopsis dohrnii*, also referred to as the "immortal jellyfish." When this jellyfish experiences a situation that triggers a fear of mortal death, it reverts back to an embryonic stage, then evolves all over again to a mature stage.

I was entranced by the article's in-depth investigation of the regenerative abilities of this unique jellyfish. However, what initially captivated me at first about the existence of this jellyfish was the opening lines of the article: "After more than 4,000 years—almost since the dawn of recorded time, when Utnapishtim told Gilgamesh that the secret to immortality lay in a coral found on the ocean floor—man finally discovered eternal life in 1988. He found it, in fact, on the ocean floor" (Rich, 2012, n.p.).

It was the article's reference to Gilgamesh and Utnapishtim that lit up my interest in reading more about the "immortal jellyfish," since Gilgamesh is the central figure in an ancient epic poem from the Middle East, and the poem is my favorite work of literature. It was appropriate for the author of the article to refer to the poem since it is about a very rich, very egomaniacal king whose extreme fear of physical death compels him to go on an epic journey into the unknown in search of the secret of physical immortality. In this light, *The Epic of Gilgamesh* could be interpreted as an ancient example of transhumanism.

In the beginning of the poem, King Gilgamesh is depicted as obsessed with achieving lasting fame and glory by performing great heroic deeds which he believes will ensure that he is remembered forever after he dies. At this point in the poem, Gilgamesh is described as vain, egotistical, and having no fear of mortal death. It is only after he watches his best friend fall sick and waste away until he is a rotting corpse that Gilgamesh becomes horrified at the thought of suffering the fate of his best friend.

Like the members of the transhumanist movement, Gilgamesh refuses to accept mortal death. Instead, he goes off to learn the secret of living forever which he believes he can obtain from a legendary figure, Utnapishtim, considered to be the only human to have achieved physical immortality. Gilgamesh's fear of death drives him to penetrate into wilderness areas where no one else has dared to venture as he searches for Utnapishtim.

Obviously, Gilgamesh's fear of mortal death is one shared not only by transhumanists but by countless other mortals. As the poem illustrates, death is the oldest fear, linked to the survival instinct, the most potent and universal of all instinctual reactions for all living creatures. It is natural to fear death. What is unnatural is to attempt to defy it altogether.

Big-brained humans have contrived ways to extend life, but the fate of all life remains the same. Just like Gilgamesh, many of us therefore strive to accomplish goals in life that we believe will ensure our being remembered after death. This striving for "symbolic immortality" is hardly reserved for the final stage of life. In fact, it's an obsession for many young people from Generation Z and other generations who want to achieve some slice of fame and make an impression via social media that, hope of hopes, goes viral and thus ensures their immortality.

The rise in the popularity of media platforms that allow an array of avenues for people to express themselves in some way has underscored the universal theme of the striving for fame and glory that dominates the first half of the Gilgamesh epic. In fact, the heroic adventures featured in the first half of *The Epic of Gilgamesh* illustrate what I call the Gilgamesh Syndrome: the obsession to achieve fame and status during one's lifetime in order to be praised and envied by others during one's life and after one's death.

This striving for fleeting fame before physical death seems to be the intent of many active shooters who post manifestos and videos of themselves before they begin their rampages. One shooter, whose rampage on the Umpqua Community College campus in Roseburg, Oregon in 2015 left nine dead and seven wounded, posted comments on social media prior to his killing spree that indicated his desire to be known to the people of the world by his nihilistic actions (Iyengar & Luckerson, 2015, n.p.).

Arie W. Kruglanski, director of the University of Maryland's Motivation Cognition Laboratory, underscored this mass shooter's motivation for his heinous act by indicating how "the quest for significance" is a drive all of us share, and for active shooters with a nihilistic view, their acts of mayhem give them superstar status for a fleeting moment before they die or end up behind bars (Meyer, 2022, n.p.). Kruglanski's comments also underscore the obsession many people have who seem desperate to be famous at least for one day out of a life they perceive as mundane and insignificant.

The Gilgamesh Syndrome is also illustrated in the ancient poem's second half, but in a radically different way. Gilgamesh does find the secret of immortality, but it is not physical immortality; it's eternal. As the opening passages from the "immortal jellyfish" article indicate, Gilgamesh found a certain type of plant at the bottom of the ocean; ancient Mesopotamian traditions referred to this subterranean region as the abyss—or *apsu*—and considered it to be the source of all life. Gilgamesh learned of the plant's existence from the legendary immortal man Utnapishtim whom Gilgamesh finally found living in an earthly paradise with his also-immortal wife. After he secured the plant, Gilgamesh gave it a name: "the old man will be made young" (Kovacs 1989, xxvii), which sounds like he found the immortal jellyfish rather than a type of plant. This name was, in fact, Gilgamesh's own name translated from the Sumerian language (p. xxvii). The reason he gave the plant his name was because it represented his "true self." In other words, this plant from the abyss was an "external soul" object representing Gilgamesh's core essence. It was also a potent universal symbol of the Tree of Life, found in numerous cultural and religious traditions.

Gilgamesh ends up losing the plant on his return journey, leading him—as well as many modern interpreters of the poem—to believe he failed in his attempt to find immortality. It's true that he failed to find physical immortality, but in doing so he revealed the secret to achieving true immortality.

According to ancient Mesopotamian history, there was an actual Mesopotamian king called Gilgamesh, and he was known to have achieved immortal status; after his physical death, the members of the city over which he had ruled, the city of Uruk, declared him a god figure whose main purpose was to judge the dead in order to determine who was worthy to live in paradise with Utnapishtim and the other mortals granted immortality by Gilgamesh himself. Obviously, the epic poem took an ironic approach to the legendary accomplishments of Gilgamesh since the epic seems to be mocking his search for physical immortality, presenting the great and glorious King Gilgamesh as a divine fool (Kline, 2016). Within the context of the poem, he is indeed a divine fool, someone who fails to fully realize his true accomplishments.

The majority of modern commentators interpreting the epic from a contemporary perspective fail to take into consideration the ironic intent of the epic, most notably evident by their downplaying the fact that the historical King Gilgamesh achieved immortal status after he died. However, Gilgamesh must have done something worthy during his lifetime to achieve god status; obviously, it was this accomplishment that inspired the poem. Because of the ironic nature of the poem, Gilgamesh's accomplishment must have had something to do with how to achieve true rather than symbolic immortality.

And yet, some specialists in ancient Mesopotamian culture insist on interpreting the epic as an example of "ancient humanism" (George, xxxiii). However, such an interpretation is reflective of modern humanism which champions human achievements devoid of a divine or supernatural influence; it does not accurately reflect the time in which Gilgamesh lived since members of ancient Middle Eastern civilizations worshiped a pantheon of gods. The modern humanism interpretation is an insult to Gilgamesh's god status and his role as judge of the dead. It is also a distortion of the historical Gilgamesh's greatest of all achievements: a religious cult devoted to him that flourished throughout ancient Mesopotamia for nearly 2,000 years (Moran, 1991, p. ix).

In the last part of the poem, Gilgamesh discovers the secret of true immortality when he dives into the abyss and penetrates into this dark realm considered to be source of all life. Gilgamesh's journey into the abyss made him the man "who saw everything," (Temple, 1997, pp. 318–327), a reference to the title of the epic in its most well-known version, written by a Babylonian priest devoted to Gilgamesh (George, 1999, pp. xxiv–xxv). According to ancient Mesopotamian culture, the abyss was not only the source of everything, but the dwelling home of the Mesopotamian god of wisdom, called Enki (Sandars 1972, pp. 120–121).

Gilgamesh's dive into the abyss, therefore, could be considered an example of experiential transcendence. Such an experience by the historical Gilgamesh might have been the inspiration for the founding of the religious cult devoted to him. The experience did not necessarily have to be a deep dive into the ocean. The descent could have been a deep dive within the psyche, achieved through trance-inducing methods or perhaps achieved by a significant dream since a multitude of references to prophetic and divinely ordained dreams are scattered throughout the epic.

I interpret Gilgamesh's descent into the abyss as one that is available to everyone if one interprets the abyss as equivalent to the unconscious, the source of "everything." The epic, therefore, illustrates the necessity of allowing one's psyche an opportunity to confront the god of wisdom—the Self—through trance-inducing or meditative methods or through the understanding of dreams infused with archetypal motifs. Individuals, therefore, have the potential to discover true immortality since all humans have this "immortal" aspect of the psyche linked to the Self. In this regard, the epic expresses Jung's psychological philosophy rather than the transhumanist or modern humanist philosophy. As the Gilgamesh epic implies, it is through understanding the mysteries inherent within oneself that one can learn the secret of true immortality.

Dying to Be Reborn

The Golden Bough could be considered a compendium of traditional beliefs that grapple with the concept of immortality. The main theme of the book is how the invisible ether that permeates and enlivens all of life is continually renewed and revitalized through a succession of heroic leaders who embody this indestructible force. A king or ruler of a community carries the life force that keeps the community thriving. The king, therefore, is a vessel for the communal life force. When the vessel becomes decrepit with age or illness, another human vessel must be found to house the communal force. But the force itself is never diminished; it is immortal.

This idea of king or ruler as vessel relates to the transhumanist movement with its emphasis upon preserving a person's brain as the source of power and keeping it vital by housing it in an artificial body. In this context, the brain becomes an "external soul," removable and portable so it can be uploaded into another more technologically sophisticated artificial body if necessary.

Frazer explored the concept of the external soul, giving examples from various cultures while commenting on its relevancy to the main theme of *The Golden Bough*. As I mentioned in Chapter 4 on Totemism, Frazer considered the golden bough to be an example of an external soul. He interpreted the golden bough as mistletoe which grows as a parasite on certain trees. Frazer explained that, for example, the oak tree for many cultures was a representation of the king's relationship with the natural world, with the mistletoe representing the king's vital energy or soul. Destroying mistletoe growing on a sacred oak tree resulted in the death of the king.

Frazer (1900 &1906-15/2018) gave a vivid example of the external soul when commenting on indigenous puberty rites. According to Frazer, during such rites, a young boy is killed symbolically by destroying a representation of his external soul before this representation is refashioned, infused with new life, and reintroduced to the initiate as his revitalized soul (pp. 811–812). The ritualistic actions that resulted in the revitalization of an external soul object illustrate how deeply ingrained the concept of the immortal soul is in certain traditional cultures. As this example illustrates, an external soul is a vessel that can result in both the death and resurrection of an initiate, acting as an eternal source of energy that cyclically renews itself. To a certain degree, such a concept is related to both the "immortal plant" which Gilgamesh named after himself—the old man will be made young—and the immortal jellyfish that suffers a death trauma and in doing so returns to an embryonic state and lives life all over again.

A cinematic example from my childhood further illustrates the nonrational dimension of the external soul concept. As a kid, I attended countless movie matinees which usually featured an adventure or fantasy film with lots of action and special effects; in other words, not much has changed, except that these matinee movies were always G-rated affairs, unlike some of the kid movies of today that push the G-rated boundaries. One of the most memorable matinee movies I saw was *Captain Sindbad* (Haskin, 1963), starring Guy Williams as the title character from Middle Eastern folklore. Even from my naïve kid perspective, I felt there was something a little more provocatively mature about this film compared to others I had seen. For one, it featured a princess who had the habit of losing her clothes; whenever she did cover herself, her outfits were the equivalent of near-transparent bikinis. Most significantly, there was a big battle scene that further pushed the G rating; it featured Sindbad in a swordfight duel with a wicked king who held the princess hostage.

At first, it appeared that Sindbad won the fight with the evil king after he ran the king through with his sword, one of the most shocking scenes I had ever witnessed as a kid since I had never seen a sword penetrate a body all the way through so the end of the sword could be seen sticking out of the king's back. Before I recovered from this shock, things got more unsettling when the king remained standing and began to laugh hysterically. An even more disturbing scene followed: the king methodically pulled the sword out of his body and returned it to Sindbad. He then explained that he couldn't be killed as long as his heart was kept protected in a castle far away surrounded by an impenetrable forest inhabited by demons. Naturally, Sindbad and his crew decide to hunt down this example of a king's external soul and destroy it. And predictably, they succeed.

The film's plot was inspired by numerous folk tales about kings and ogres who extract their souls and deposit them in vessels of some sort, then hide them away; the king or ogre can remain living because of the contagious-magic connection they have with their soul. Frazer (1900 &1906-15/2018) included several of these folk tales in *The Golden Bough* along with cultural examples from various indigenous communities. For example, in cultures where shamans are tribal leaders:

> ... the Yakuts of Siberia believe that every shaman or wizard keeps his soul ... incarnate in an animal which is carefully concealed from all the world. "Nobody can find my external soul," said one famous wizard, "it lies hidden far away in the stony mountains ... ." Only once a year, when the last snows melt and the earth turns black, do these external souls of wizards appear in the shape of animals ... . They wander everywhere, yet none but wizards can see them. (p. 799)

As I mentioned, *The Golden Bough* focuses on customs, rites, and belief systems that express the concept of immortality, that life is endowed with something that cannot die. A significant theme expressing this concept, of which Frazer found variations throughout human history, is the death and revitalization of a king or hero figure who is the consort of the goddess of nature. This motif was the one that inspired *The Golden Bough*. Frazer became fixated on how this motif was exemplified in the myth of the nature goddess Diana and her sanctuary at Nemi in Italy where she roamed through her sacred grove of oak trees accompanied by her consort, the King of the Wood, or "spirit of the sacred trees" (p. 288). The myth included references to the first King of the Wood who was called Virbius, although sometimes called Hippolytus.

Again and again, Frazer found myths and legends and customs with a multitude of variations upon a similar theme: the king dies and is dismembered, after which a sacred healer—a wizard, shaman, or god—pieces him together and then raises him from the dead. For example: "In Saxony and Thuringen, the representative of the tree-spirit, after being killed, is brought to life again by a doctor. This is exactly what legend affirmed to have happened to the first King of the Wood at Nemi, Hippolytus or Virbius, who after he had been killed ... was restored to life by [the Greek's healer god] Aesculapius" (p. 288).

Frazer was inspired to write and later expand, then expand even more, his collection of "immortality" customs and legends. Obviously, such a motif is archetypal, and, according to Frazer expert Robert Fraser, the archetypal dimension of the motif was what fascinated Frazer the most:

> Frazer's work might seem to be a compendium of ritual and custom. In fact it is something very different: a book on the human mind and the connections habitually made by it ... . It was because the human mind, across a variety of cultures and times, and especially when trained upon the religious and the magical, showed certain constancies that generalization of the sort that fascinated Frazer became possible. It was to examine the refinements of such universal thought-processes, and their different ways of expressing themselves in a variety of places and periods, that he wrote this book. (p. xxvii)

Frazer's obsession with exploring the varieties of this motif, an obsession that lasted over 25 years as he continually revised and expanded upon the theme, could be considered an example of possession by an archetype. Like the archetypal possession example featured in Chapter 5, the motif of the dying and resurrecting hero/king/god figure expressed something vital to Frazer to the point where he was compelled to delve deeply into this recurring theme. In doing so, he helped underscore the theme's nonrational brilliance, and how it has possessed humanity since the beginning of human history.

Obsessed with Historical Time

One of the major hindrances for people living in modern consumer cultures that compromises their belief in some sort of continuance of existence after physical death is the emphasis put upon living the large life through over-consumption and self-indulgence. To paraphrase a famous ad by Schlitz Beer, you gotta grab all the gusto you can right now because you only go around once in life. So, live it up and have another beer. This emphasis expresses the idea of life leading to extinction. It's a linear or historical view of life: we have a beginning stage of infancy, progress to a youthful stage, then to a mature stage, followed by a decline in health which ultimately leads to death. But, before you expire, be sure to have another beer.

Another view of this linear progression is exemplified by the modern cosmological myth known as the Big Bang Theory: the universe began as a cosmic explosion of subatomic elements which gave birth to all material forms and led to the creation of life on Earth. Since that cosmic explosion, the universe has been expanding and will continue to do so until it collapses upon itself. What happens after that is not clear. And what happened before the Big Bang also remains a mystery since it appears that sometime before the universe was formed and linear time came into being, there had to be something else going on, unless you believe that the universe originated out of nothing. Or, as the following quote, credited to science fiction author Terry Pratchett, expresses it: "In the beginning, there was nothing, which exploded."

Mircea Eliade (1960/1975) identified one of the principal reasons why modern humans have developed an extreme fear of death. It's because modern humanity has made human history a type of species idol worship, and in doing so put major emphasis upon linear time leading to physical death. As Eliade explained:

> … one of the most specific features of our own civilization … [is] modern man's passionate, almost abnormal interest, in History. This interest is manifested in two distinct ways … . [First] … in what may be called a passion for historiography, the desire for an ever more complete and more exact knowledge of the past of humanity, above all of the past of our Western world; secondly, this interest in history is manifested in Western philosophy, in the tendency to define man as above all a historical being conditioned, and in the end created, by History … . [This] is a fairly recent passion; it dates from the second half of [the nineteenth] century … . But for a century past … it has become a scientific passion for exhaustive knowledge of all the adventures of mankind, and endeavor to reconstitute the entire past of the species and make us conscious of it. (p. 234)

Eliade's mentioning of the scientific passion to "reconstitute the entire past of the species and make us conscious of it," reflects a recent scientific accomplishment: the effort to map our entire genetic history, called the Human Genome Project. Francis Collins, former director of the project's research branch, compared the project's accomplishments to a book with various major themes: a history book that narrates "the journey of our species through time;" a mechanics manual with a detailed "blueprint for building every human cell;" and a medical textbook that gives medical experts "immense new powers to treat, prevent, and cure disease" (Courtesy: National Human Genome Research Institute, 2020, n.p.).

Overall, the goals of the project seem commendable and relate to the desire all living creatures have to stay alive by eliminating certain genetic-related diseases. However, there is an uncomfortable emphasis upon idolizing the history of the human species, presenting the evolution of the human genome as a narrative of the history of humanity from a cellular perspective. Also, the use of words such as designing, building, mapping, and blueprinting the genetic code relates to humans as tool makers, echoing the language used by the transhumanist movement that promotes the building of an indestructible super human through the use of technology.

Currently, there is a debate over how to manipulate the genetic code to build an even better human. Scientists now have the ability to edit the genetic make-up of a human being to correct potentially harmful defects within the genetic code of an individual. The debate is over how much manipulation is ethically justifiable without creating another Eugenics movement which could result in the wealthy paying for ways to create a perfect designer baby (Belluck, 2017, p. A1). Manipulating the code could also result in an increase in the longevity of humans, but a lot more research is required before humans are able to reverse its process so we can all live the large life indefinitely right along with the immortal jellyfish.

Eliade emphasized how the obsession with human history along with the scientific community's exhaustive lust for "knowledge of all the adventures of mankind," is "found nowhere else," at least in non-Western cultures. Eliade then compared humanity's historical obsession with the folkloristic belief that "at the moment of death, man remembers all his past life down to the minutest details, and that he cannot die before having remembered and re-lived the whole of his personal history" (p. 234). As he further explained:

> Upon the screen of memory, the dying man once more reviews his past. Considered from this point of view, the passion for historiography in modern culture would be a sign portending [its] imminent death. Our Western civilization, before it foundered, would be for the last time remembering all its past from proto-history until [current times]. The historiographical consciousness ... which some have regarded as [Western civilization's] highest title to lasting fame—would in fact be the supreme moment which precedes and announces [its] death. (pp. 234–235)

If one looks at the creation of the Internet in the context of Eliade's comments about Western civilization in the throes of remembering all it has experienced, all it has created, chronicled, explored, and devised before it collapses and dies, one realizes the underlying true intent of this amazing invention: it was devised not so much as a way to connect the world and share information, but to chronicle the end of Western civilization in order to secure "lasting fame."

Eliade further clarified why modern Western cultures struggle with the thought of viewing life as a journey with a historically documented beginning (birth certificate) and a historically verifiable ending (death certificate).

It's because of the terrifying idea that oblivion and extinction are what lie beyond the filing of the death certificate. According to Eliade:

> Anguish before Nothingness and Death seems to be a specifically modern phenomenon. In all other, non-European cultures ... Death is never felt as an absolute end or Nothingness: it is regarded rather as a rite of passage to another mode of being; and for that reason always referred to in relation to the symbolisms and rituals of initiation, rebirth, and resurrection ... . Death is the Great Initiation. But in the modern world Death is emptied of its religious meaning; that is why it is assimilated to Nothingness; and before Nothingness, modern man is paralyzed. (p. 236)

Note how Eliade put major emphasis upon how death is a type of initiatory process, indicating that initiatory rites simulate the experience of death in order to prepare a person for the next stage of existence. This emphasis relates to the puberty rites previously referred to, and most notably the rites of initiation associated with the mystery religion tradition which were specifically regarded as rites preparing initiates for death through a simulation of the death crisis and its aftermath: rebirth.

I also mentioned how initiation rites were far from being pleasant affairs. They were brutal, agonizing, and terrifying, just as death is. The fear of death was felt by all mystery rite participants prior to their confrontation with the gods ruling over the land of the dead into which the initiates had symbolically descended to simulate the death crisis.

Perhaps the most famous description of the mystery rite experience and the relationship it had with preparing participants for death was attributed to the ancient Greek philosopher Themistios in an essay appropriately titled, "On the Soul." Themistios' account was from the perspective of someone who had just died and the immortal aspect of their personality was released from the body to journey to the land of the dead:

> At the point of death, [the soul] has the same experience as those who are being initiated into the great mysteries ... . At first one wanders and wearily hurries to and fro, and journeys with suspicion through the dark as one uninitiated; then come all the terrors before the final initiation, shuddering, trembling, sweating, amazement; then one is struck with a marvelous light, one is received into pure regions and meadows, with voices and dances and the majesty of holy sounds and shapes; among these, he who has fulfilled initiation wanders free, and released and bearing his crown joins in the divine communion, and consorts with pure and holy men, beholding those who live here uninitiated, an uncleansed horde, trodden in mud and fog, abiding in their miseries through fear of death ... . (quoted in Mylonas, 1961, p. 264)

If one compares this description to some of the reports of people who have had a near-death experience—which includes Jung's own--and described encountering "a marvelous light" and hearing "voices and dances and the majesty of holy sounds and shapes," one can realize how closely the descriptions complement each other, indicating that both the mystery rites and near-death experiences are preparations for transitioning to the next stage of human development. The quote's references to those who are not initiated and their miserable fate in the land of the dead because they fear death due to their not having been adequately prepared for this next stage, is an ancient comment on the transhumanist movement and its demonization of the Great Initiation experience: Death.

Eliade understood how terrifying death is for every living creature. But, with his remarks about the main purpose of all initiation rites, he gave all of humanity a sense of hope for a future beyond the grave:

> No initiation is possible without the ritual of an agony, a death, and a resurrection. Judged in the perspective of [traditional] religions, the anguish of the modern world is the sign of an imminent death, but of a death that is necessary and redemptive, for it will be followed by a resurrection and the possibility of attaining a new mode of being, that of maturity and responsibility. (p. 237)

Eliade's comments are a very hopeful and generous wish for a great segment of humanity that revels in adolescent-level self-indulgent behavior. However, keeping this adolescent attitude in mind, perhaps if enough of us sit down together in stadium-sized movie theaters and indulge in a massive movie-matinee marathon of superhero-science fiction-dystopian disaster movies about the end of the world, we'll be better prepared for the imminent death of Western Civilization followed by a transformation of consciousness that leads to a more mature and responsible view of life for all of humanity. Even if it doesn't, at least we might be able to admit that, wow, we're really obsessed with movies, TV shows, conspiracy theories, and modern prophets proclaiming the end of the world.

Why is that?

References

Belluck, P. (2017, August 3). In breakthrough, scientists edit a dangerous mutation from genes in human embryos. *New York Times*, A1.

Campbell, J., & Moyers, B. (1988). *The power of myth* (B.S. Flowers, Ed.). New York: Doubleday.

Eliade, M. (1960/1975). *Myths, dreams, and mysteries*. New York: Harper & Row.

Eveleth, R. (2019, October 8). The biggest lie tech people tell themselves--and the rest of us. Retrieved from https://www.vox.com/the-highlight/2019/10/1/20887003/tech-technology-evolution-natural-inevitable-ethics

Frazer, J. (1900 & 1906-15/2018). *The golden bough: A study in magic and religion, an abridgment from the 2nd and 3rd editions* (R. Fraser, Ed.). London, UK: Folio Society.

George, A. (1999). *The epic of Gilgamesh: A new translation.* New York: Penguin Books.

Haskin, B. (Director). (1963). *Captain Sindbad* [Film]. Metro-Goldwyn-Meyer.

Horn, D. (2018, January 25). Meet the men who want to live forever. *New York Times,* SR9.

Iyengar, R., & Luckerson, V. (2015, October 2). What we know so far about the Oregon shooter. *Time.com.* Retrieved from https://time.com/4059136/oregon-shooter-ucc-chris-harper-mercer/

Jung, C.G. (1930/1969). The stages of life. In H. Read, M. Fordham, G. Adler (Eds.), W. McGuire (Senior ed.),*The structure and dynamics of the psyche. Collected Works, volume 7* (pp. 387–403). Princeton, NJ: Princeton University Press.

Jung, C.G. (1934/1969). The soul and death. In H. Read, M. Fordham, G. Adler (Eds.), W. McGuire (Senior ed.),*The structure and dynamics of the psyche. Collected Works, volume 7* (pp. 404–415). Princeton, NJ: Princeton University Press.

Jung, C.G. (1961/1989). *Memories, dreams reflections* (A. Jaffe, Ed.). New York: Vintage/Random House.

Kline, J. (2016). The oldest story, the oldest fear, the oldest fool: The religious dimension of *The epic of Gilgamesh. Jung Journal: Culture & Psyche,* 10(2), 24–36. DOI:10.1080/19342039.2016.1157411

Kovacs, M. (1989). *The epic of Gilgamesh.* Stanford, CA: Stanford University Press.

Meyer, J. (2022, July 7). Why are mass shooters getting younger and deadlier? Experts have theories. *USAToday.com.* Retrieved from https://www.usatoday.com/story/news/politics/2022/07/07/mass-shooters-younger-deadlier/7813668001/?gnt-cfr=1

Moran, W. (1991). Introduction. In D. Ferry (Trans.) *Gilgamesh: A new rendering in English verse* (pp. ix–xi). New York: Farrar, Straus & Giroux.

Mylonas, G.E. (1961). *Eleusis and the Eleusinian mysteries.* Princeton, NJ: Princeton University Press.

National Human Genome Research Institute. (2020, December 22). The human genome project. Genome.gov. Retrieved from https://www.genome.gov/human-genome-project

Newman, B., & Newman, P. (2018). *Development through life: A psychosocial approach* (13th ed.). Boston, MA: Cengage Learning.

Ribeiro, C. (2022, June 3). Beyond our "ape-brained meat sacks:" Can transhumanism save our species? *TheGuardian.com.* Retrieved from https://www.theguardian.com/books/2022/jun/04/beyond-our-ape-brained-meat-sacks-can-transhumanism-save-our-species

Rich, N. (2012, November 28). Can a jellyfish unlock the secret of immortality? *New York Times.* Retrieved from https://www.nytimes.com/2012/12/02/magazine/can-a-jellyfish-unlock-the-secret-of-immortality.html?searchResultPosition=4

Sandars, N.K. (1972). *The epic of Gilgamesh: An English prose translation.* New York: Penguin Books.

Segal, J. (2013, June 1). This man is not a cyborg. Yet. *New York Times*, SBU1.

Taylor, G. (2016, April 20). Immortality. *That'sReallyPossible.com*. Retrieved from https://thatsreallypossible.com/immortality/

Temple, R. (1997). Introduction to *He who saw everything: A verse translation of the epic of Gilgamesh*. In J. Maier (Ed.), *A Gilgamesh reader*, pp. 318–327. Wauconda, IL: Bolchazy-Carducci Publishers.

Vigilant, L.G., & Williamson, J.B. (2003). Symbolic immortality and social theory: The relevance of an unutilized concept. In C.D. Bryant (Ed.), *Handbook of death and dying* (Vol. 1), pp. 173–182. Thousand Oaks, CA: Sage Publications.

Chapter 7

Techpocalypse—Or, How I Learned to Stop Worrying and Love My Smartphone

The Archetype of the Apocalypse

Shortly after the stroke of midnight on January 1, 2000, the world came to an end.

If you were alive at the time and missed it, here is a headline from one of the most popular publications of the time, the now-defunct sensationalist tabloid called *Weekly World News*, alerting the world to this impending catastrophe.

The panic over this impending disaster was created by the prospect of all computer devices with internal time and date code capacities crashing on January 1, 2000, due to the fact that the vast majority of computers were not coded to accept 2000 as a legitimate year since most computers up until that time had been coded with only the last two digits of the four-digit year code; the fear was that computers would revert back to 1900 as the new millennium was ushered in.

If such an event occurred, it was rumored that there would be massive computer meltdowns affecting all businesses, educational systems, governmental systems, hospitals—all aspects of modern technological societies reliant upon complex computer networks. As one journalist (Chepkemoi, 2017) described the implications of such a global malfunction:

> Banking institutions which relied on software programs to calculate daily interest were at risk of system failure. As a result, stock prices of banking institutions dropped in value as the year 2000 neared. Transport systems were also affected especially in the airline business whose operations depend on accurate time and date. There were rumors that planes would drop from the sky when clocks turned to midnight on 31st Dec. 1999. This led travelers to avoid the airport on New Year's Eve. Hospitals, power plants, and government organizations were not spared from the threats either. (n.p.)

Naturally, such a panic was ripe for exploitation, with many folk devil hucksters posing as tech wizards to promote their cure for Y2K Millennium

DOI: 10.4324/9781003271482-8

Figure 7.1 Front page from the *Weekly World News* warning of an impending technological apocalypse.

Source: *Creative Commons.*

Bug, as it came to be called. I was nearly tempted to buy software advertised to take care of the alleged problem in order to ensure the safety of my home computer. I was also drawn to purchasing a video narrated by actor Leonard Nimoy that explained the threat and then provided step-by-step procedural methods to fix the problem.

Many corporations did provide their employees with fixes that would take care of the Y2K Bug, with some companies spending millions of dollars to ensure that the bug would be exterminated. However, many remained fearful that these fixes wouldn't work. In my case, I was working as a university bookstore manager at the time and was ordered by the higher-ups in my organization to be at the bookstore on New Year's Eve to monitor any problems with the company computers as the clock ticked to the dreaded moment of the new millennium. I was concerned that this order from my bosses might compromise my own safety: what if the computers did melt down and set the store on fire? Would I become a victim to a mechanized Moloch, the way the enslaved workers in *Metropolis* were eaten up by this god of human sacrifice?

Fortunately, no lives were lost during the irrational Y2K panic, a result of humanity still nervous over accepting these types of devices becoming more prevalent in every aspect of modern life. No computers blew up, no planes dropped from the sky, and I was able to sleep in on New Year's Day, confident that my store was still standing and the new millennium would usher in a new era of peace, harmony, and understanding. However, less than two years later, planes did drop from the sky. This was not the result of a computer malfunction, but the work of terrorists.

September 11, 2001, did feel like the end of the world for millions of Americans who lived through the attack on the New York World Trade Center and the Pentagon, or viewed it live on television as it played out. I was at home with my wife not long after the attacks began and we watched in horror as people jumped to their deaths out the windows of the burning Twin Towers before the two towers collapsed, truly one of the most horrifying sights I have ever seen. What made the sight even more unsettling were the reactions of the newscasters covering the event live on TV: they said nothing. It was simply a sight beyond words.

Due to their unique and emotionally devastating effects, such big events as the 9/11 terrorist attack on the U.S., which took the lives of nearly 3,000 individuals, are fervid breeding grounds for conspiracy theories. The conspiracy theory resulting from this catastrophic event ranked as one of the more insidious examples: it accused the president of the United States and his administration as the originators of the attack, another example of a "false flag" event, faked by the government. In this case, the government had made the attack appear to be the work of Middle Eastern terrorists to justify waging war against Iraq's leader Saddam Hussein in order to take over the country's oil reserves. Apparently, U.S. governmental officials are so inhumane that they have no qualms over sacrificing thousands of innocent Americans to ensure that the American economy remains less reliant on foreign oil.

Like all conspiracy theories, this one cannot be disproven because it is free from fact-based logical reasoning, ensuring it will live forever like a conspiratorial zombie. One of the more obvious inconsistencies in the conspiracy is that, if terrorists weren't involved, who flew the hijacked commercial planes into the Twin Towers and the Pentagon? Were they Americans hired to commit suicide by impersonating terrorists?

In addition, conspiracy theorists tried to justify their theory by zeroing in on the way in which New York's Twin Towers collapsed, accusing the government of planting bombs inside the towers to blow them up in the manner that a demolition crew might plan to demolish an old building with remote control-timed explosions. As conspiracy theorist DeAnna Lorraine pointed out in Chapter 2, "buildings just do not fall like that" (Palmer, 2021b, n.p.), unless it's an inside job with the use of timed explosive devices. And she should know since apparently she's an expert on the architectural design of the Twin Towers as well as the design of the condo complex near Miami that collapsed "in one fell swoop" in June 2021.

Since 9/11, modern, high-tech societies have become more preoccupied with terrorist attacks or invasions from the nebulous, ethereal "other." This fear has become the justification for implementing high-tech surveillance systems pretty much everywhere, including personal tech items such as cellular phones and even certain home TV monitors. For example, in December 2019, the FBI issued a warning to the public about the potential invasion of privacy due to certain TVs having the ability to monitor a person's goings on without the person's knowledge. According to the warning: "Smart TVs connect to the internet, allowing users to access online apps, much like streaming services. And because they're internet-enabled, they can make users vulnerable to surveillance and attacks from bad actors ..." (Holmes, 2019, n.p.).

As I mentioned in Chapter 6 in regards to the new generations of young people growing up in a high-tech world, it becomes easier and more common to embrace tech culture and invite it into our homes, work places, entertainment venues, eateries, handbags, and back pockets. The computer technology giants are obviously aware of the appeal of their products and labor to find new ways to sell them to their growing audiences hungry for the latest upgrade on their smartphone device, smart TV, or smart toaster.

One of the most reliable ways to promote any product is to create ads that pair the product with an attractive model or celebrity, preferably with little or no clothes on. That's right, your smartphone is sexy, just like the near-naked celebrity holding it, a vivid example of contagious magic. My favorite example of product pairing was a poster I saw in an auto parts store. It featured a sexy woman in a bikini holding up a carburetor. Yes, even carburetors can be sexy.

One of the most astonishing examples of product pairing occurred in the 1950s during the days of nuclear bomb testing, most of which occurred in the Nevada desert. Attempting to promote nuclear power as less of a threat to humanity, the U.S. government encouraged advertisements that paired the bomb in various ways with beautiful female models, many of whom competed for the coveted crown of Miss Nuclear Bomb of the Year. Such beauty contests were held in Las Vegas where nuclear bomb viewing parties at various casino resorts were promoted during times when a blast was

Figure 7.2 Lee Merrin, Miss Atomic Bomb of 1957, poses in a bathing suit with a mushroom cloud design, an example of product pairing to encourage a "sexy," non-threatening attitude toward atomic power.

Source: *Creative Commons*

scheduled to occur. For these types of celebratory occasions, Mom or Sis could purchase a bathing suit with a mushroom cloud design.

Yes, nuclear bombs are sexy.

This type of glorification of nuclear power has, thankfully, subsided to a great degree. A film example from the 1970s vividly illustrates how nuclear bombs became synonymous with apocalyptic annihilation: *Beneath the Planet of the Apes* (Post, 1970), the second film in a popular film series based upon the 1963 novel, *Planet of the Apes,* by Pierre Boulle. The first film in the series (Schaffner, 1968) featured U.S. astronauts crash landing on a planet and finding it run by intelligent, talking primates other than the human kind. The humans, in fact, are treated like animals in the same manner we currently treat animals involved in research: as inferior creatures that can be manipulated in ways that could involve torture, mutilation, and death in order to benefit the human race in some way; in the film, those benefitting from the mistreatment of humans were chimpanzees, gorillas, and orangutans. The original film ended with the chief astronaut, played by Charlton Heston, leading a rebellion of humans against their enslavement, but ultimately finding out a horrific secret: the planet he and his crew landed on is actually Earth sometime in the future after humans destroyed it with a nuclear war, resulting in humans either dying off or infected with radiation poisoning while their primate brothers and sisters developed intelligence and took over the planet, only to repeat the mistakes of the humans in how they treat so-called inferior creatures from an evolutionary perspective.

Beneath the Planet of the Apes follows the same plot line in its beginning scenes: astronauts again crash land on this Earth from the future, looking for surviving members of the previous expedition. The leader of the new expedition, played by James Franciscus, ultimately finds the Heston character and rescues him from the ape leaders. The two then make yet another horrific discovery about this futuristic Earth: beneath the planet, within old New York subway tunnels, are humans who have remained hidden away for centuries after having survived World War III. Throughout their time spent underground, they have developed a reverence for the atom bomb; in fact, they have preserved a nuclear missile and set it up as a revered totem object. The missile is a powerful doomsday bomb with the name Alpha and Omega, the beginning and the end.

In one of the most startling scenes from the film, these surviving humans who appear to be mutations, covered in permanently damaged scorched skin, hold a service dedicated to the bomb. During the service, the head priest leads the congregation in a prayer of devotion, referring to the bomb as a god power that descended from Heaven to make their existence under Earth a subterranean paradise (Post, 1970).

The surviving astronauts, witnessing the ceremony, act with revulsion and challenge the congregation with accusations of idolatry and service to the object responsible for the destruction of Earth and their own subterranean existence. While they argue, legions of armed primates break in to the chamber and a battle between apes and humans results in the activation of the bomb. The film ends with chilling commentary by a voice-over narrator: "In one of the countless billions of galaxies in the universe lies a medium-sized star, and one of its satellites, a green and insignificant planet, is now dead" (Post, 1970).

The film was supposed to be the last in the series, for obvious reasons. However, because of its popularity, other sequels were made, along with a TV show and another film series re-imagining the initial devastation of the Earth as a result of a virus rather than a nuclear war. COVID-19 deniers and anti-vaccination advocates should really take this latter series very seriously.

For the rest of us, the film is one of hundreds that imagine nuclear war and its aftermath. There have been so many apocalyptic-themed films produced over the last several decades that the genre is losing its ability to truly terrify, especially when superheroes, zombies, and James Bond are involved. How do we destroy the world? Let us count the ways ....

I must admit, I love these films. Another favorite is the film *2012* (Emmerich, 2009), directed and co-written by Roland Emmerich, one of the leading masters of the end-of-the-world disaster movie genre; Emmerich also directed *Independence Day* (1996), an updated version of H.G. Wells' 1897 classic novel, *War of the Worlds,* as well as the climate crisis disaster film, *The Day After Tomorrow* (2004).

I have a soft spot for *2012* because I was watching it on a flight from Saipan to Washington State on December 21, 2012, the predicted last day of Earth according to the ancient Maya calendar and the obvious inspiration for the film. As I flew over the Pacific Ocean watching the film portray the devastation of the Earth and billions of lives lost caused by the effects of massive solar flares upon the Earth's crust that triggered earthquakes and mass flooding, I began to wonder about the reality of the Maya prediction: would all of us on the plane end up with no place to land and then drop from the sky?

Ultimately, such films are designed to entertain us with what-if scenarios rather than to encourage us to ponder the reality of such events. The trivialization of the end of the world, presenting such a disastrous occurrence as if it were something from which we are immune, is a stark contrast compared to how these films were viewed after 9/11. For a brief time, many of us paused and pondered such a fate. Film critic Neal Gabler (2001) commented shortly after the attack that millions reacted to the televised coverage as if "It was just like a movie," with scenes of destruction and death, and reactions by grieving survivors and stalwart leaders that could have been "lifted from some Hollywood blockbuster" (p. S4, 2).

The blending of fantasy and reality was palpable during the aftermath of the tragedy, causing a collective experience of *cognitive dissonance* as many struggled to accept what had happened as having actually occurred in downtown Manhattan and the Pentagon. Cognitive dissonance occurs when new, compelling information challenges a long-held belief or point of view, resulting in confusion and a stubborn resistance to change one's perception about the established belief; in this case, the enjoyment many of us have for watching apocalypse-themed films was challenged by what had just played out live on TV.

Filmmakers Edward Zwick and Marshall Hershkovitz (2001) attempted to address the disconnect and dissonance and in doing so revealed the underlying shame and guilt over too much enjoyment of entertainments that feature mass murder, questioning how so many of us can "sit munching our popcorn" while passively viewing scenes of slaughter (p. S2, 11).

The comments of the filmmakers cut deeply into the American psyche and reveal a preoccupation with necrophilous tendencies, glorifying mass destruction, death, and hatred for "aliens." I would agree that such entertainments—which include violent video games, and gruesomely explicit crime, action, and fantasy TV shows—are expressing what Hershkovitz and Zwick referred to as "rage at the powerlessness of modern life," a life that becomes more complex, and more frenetic as so many of us rush to complete tasks and get things done in order to make a decent living. Our reliance on technology to help us stay alive makes us susceptible to glorifying objects that give us so much pleasure and entertainment, creating a love-hate relationship with these tools.

What the aftermath of 9/11 revealed to all of us for a brief moment was our preoccupation with the *archetype of the apocalypse*. Film after film replayed the apocalypse motif: destruction, death, annihilation and grief, followed by new hope, new life, new beginnings, and a new world. The apocalypse archetype has much in common with the motif of the eternal return, referred to in Chapter 5 in reference to the near-death experience reported by Dr. Swaran Singh.

The apocalypse archetype is evoked by prophets who speak of the good old days when life was simpler, and we were in harmony with God and nature. According to these prophets, the present world needs to come to an end so we can return to that paradisiacal state. Soon God will destroy the Earth in a manner similar to the Great Flood, or the way in which Sodom and Gomorrah were destroyed, by fire and brimstone sent from Heaven. All of us, therefore, must prepare to meet this doom so God will bless us and spirit us up to Heaven before the catastrophe.

The apocalypse archetype was used most effectively by the terrorist group known as the Islamic State or ISIS as a way to recruit young men suffering from an extreme state of nihilism. ISIS used excerpts from violent video games as a recruiting tool and posted them on social media, encouraging these lost and depressed young men to apply their first-person shooter video game skills to real-life situations (Shane, Apuzzo, & Schmitt, p. SA, 1). New recruits were also enticed by the prospect of being able to rape women with impunity (Callimachi, 2015, p. SA, 1). The ultimate goal of all recruits was to bring about the destruction of the world to ensure their place in Heaven as great warriors (O'Connor, 2017).

The ultimate goal of ISIS, as well as some of the recruitment techniques used by this terrorist organization, has striking similarities to the so-called doomsday cults of the 1960s and 1970s. The religious cult known as the People's Temple, for example, led by charismatic leader Jim Jones, was first established in the San Francisco area. Jones was a fervent believer in the inevitability of a nuclear war. Because of his increasing paranoia about the end of the world and also his fear of being persecuted by government authorities, Jones moved his congregation to South America's Guyana where he established Jonestown. His persecution complex became real after some of his followers objected to his insistence on allowing no one to leave or contact relatives; when some members were able to sneak out of the compound and call authorities, Jones persuaded over 900 of his followers, including 300 children, to commit mass suicide (O'Connor, 2017).

The archetype of the apocalypse was also reflected in the campaign slogan for former President Trump. His "Make America Great Again" slogan implied a time when all Americans lived in harmony and peace in some misty time in the past. According to Trump's QAnon followers, returning America to greatness first requires a Storm or Armageddon, followed by the Great Awakening—return to Paradise. The riot that occurred on January 6, 2021, at the U.S. Capitol was interpreted by many of his followers as the Storm, and many of them waving flags and wearing shirts emblazoned with references to apocalyptic-themed superhero films fought like hell to bring about the end of American democracy so the Great Awakening could begin.

From a psychological perspective the preoccupation with the apocalypse archetype is an indication that many people have a great longing to destroy their current ego attitude in order to broaden their perception and understanding of their lives. According to Jung, this can happen through a confrontation with the Self. As Jungian psychologist Edward Edinger (2002) explained:

> When the imagery of the apocalypse archetype comes up in analysis, it can be immediately recognized as part of the phenomenology of the individuation process: representing in the individual the emergence of the Self into conscious realization … . Considering an individual's experience of the archetype, the "apocalypse" bodes catastrophe only for the stubbornly rationalistic, secular ego that refuses to grant the existence of a greater psychic authority than itself [i.e. the Self]. Since it cannot bend, it has to break. Thus, the "end-of-the-world" dreams (invasion from outer space, nuclear bombs) do not necessarily presage psychic catastrophe for the dreamer but may, if properly understood, refer to the coming into visibility of manifestations for the Self—the nucleus of the psyche—and present the opportunity for an enlargement of personality. (pp. 7, 13)

As Edinger emphasized, refusing to accept the intimations of the unconscious that express the apocalypse archetype can result in an intense experience of cognitive dissonance. The person refuses to accept these intimations and desperately holds on to the stagnated psychological state of mind, resulting in more intense and explicit apocalyptic intimations.

What is crucial for all of us now is to recognize the apocalypse archetype as a psychic reality and not merely as an entertaining fantasy. Unfortunately, we have forgotten how the reality of the archetype gripped so many of us in the aftermath of 9/11. Since then, a lot of us have been working hard to deny its reality, refusing to bend and risking a psychic break.

Too many of us have failed to accept the influence of this tremendously powerful and disruptive warning from the unconscious that something within the psyche is demanding to break through into consciousness in an attempt to heal a psychic imbalance. We have tried to deny this internal warning by immersing ourselves more deeply into fantasy scenarios that express it in order to objectify it and tame its disruptive influence. Because so many have failed to interpret the apocalypse archetype as a symbolic representation of an inner conflict between ego and Self, the result has been to seek out even more ways to deny the unconscious rumblings by further indulging in alternate fantasy worlds and virtual realities that express the "Paradise" aspect of the archetype: the achievement of wholeness.

The transhumanism movement, explored in Chapter 6, promises such a reality which is referred to as the achievement of *singularity*:

> ... an era in which our intelligence will become increasingly non-biological and trillions of times more powerful than it is today—the dawning of a new civilization that will enable us to transcend our biological limitations and amplify our creativity. In this new world, there will be no clear distinction between human and machine, reality and virtual reality. We will be able to assume different bodies and take on a range of personae at will. In practical terms, human aging and illness will be reversed; pollution will be stopped; world hunger and poverty will be solved ... . Nanotechnology [the manipulation of atoms and molecules] ... will ultimately turn even death into a soluble problem. (Kurzweil, 2005)

The above information about singularity comes from promotional materials for tech innovator Ray Kurzweil's book, *The Singularity Is Near: When Humans Transcend Biology* (2005). If Kurzweil's vision of a future paradise seems too good to be plausible, well, just you wait. This is where techpocalypse films provide invaluable what-if scenarios that pose questions about our future relationship with technology. Because film has the ability to bring these scenarios to life with incredible detail and infuse the what-if scenarios with emotionally involving plot lines and engaging characters, it is possible to immerse oneself in these futuristic worlds that promise paradise but ultimately end up as a war between the human condition and the artificial world humans have created due to their desperate longing for peace, harmony, and wholeness.

The *Terminator* series of films featuring robots made partially from human tissue attempting to take over the world; the *Matrix* series in which humans battle machines that want to use people like car batteries to keep the machines functioning; *Eagle Eye* (2008), in which an Alexa-type echo-companion device called Aria attempts to assassinate the entire U.S. government administration by controlling and manipulating every aspect of computer surveillance technology; *Metropolis*—the film that inspired all the others—featuring mechanized humans stumbling into the mouth of a cannibal machine-god of their own creation: watching these and other similarly-themed films makes it more difficult to embrace the paradisiacal promises offered by Kurzweil and his like-minded technophilious advocates.

Such films affirm Jung's idea of the significance of temptation and taboo: we need to look the devil in the eyes and ask him his reasons for wanting to tempt us with something we so fervently desire. Folk devils encourage us to embrace their temptations by offering to satisfy what is missing from our lives. Kurzweil, for example, promotes the creation of "perfect" multiple personaes, when what is missing from our lives is not another persona but an understanding of the anima. Kurzweil promises a new heaven on Earth where one can achieve physical immortality by becoming a cyborg and living forever in a virtual reality, when what is missing is a relationship with the natural world where, as so many traditional beliefs indicate, a person's external soul resides in the form of an animal or plant or stone that only the individual can recognize.

The compulsion to identify with an artificial, man-made object such as a smartphone comes from this desire to recognize one's external soul in such objects. The trick is to distinguish one's external soul from a smiling, sexy cyborg who has come from a time in the future with only one purpose: to kill you.

My Smartphone Is Sexy

As previously mentioned, product pairing strategies in advertising play upon the contagious magic connection that celebrities and supermodels appear to have with products they promote. The intent is to promote items in ways that encourage an identification with the object, even encouraging an emotional relationship with these objects.

One journalist, for example, wrote ecstatically to the point of erotic excessiveness about her intimate relationship with her smartphone, most notably while she conducts online research. Referring to the Internet as an extension of her body, and her smartphone as the equivalent of her vagina, she described stroking "that slick hot box" while performing her research, aware of the millions of other Internet swingers wandering through a virtual "whorish house" of pleasure, leading to a collective "big bang" release in which she can't help but "LOLOLOL" (Serpell, 2021, n.p.).

To be honest, I wish I could have online research affect me similarly. Instead, I have the habit of picking up my laptop and throwing it across the room when it freezes up or refuses to do that thing that it's supposed to do when I hit that tab key. Naturally, I apologize to the laptop for my outburst, but I know it holds a grudge against me and is probably plotting revenge.

To be even more honest, I object to the description of a tech device as a sex partner. The intimate relationship between human and machine in this example is too close to the transhumanist movement that promotes technology as the inevitable next step in human evolution (see Chapter 6). There are too many what-if films depicting these types of relationships as highly hazardous to a person's well-being.

Metropolis was the first to dramatize how dangerous it is to lust after an automaton that looks like your dead lover. Another film example, inspired by the backlash against the women's movement of the 1960s, was *The Stepford Wives* (Forbes, 1975), featuring the men of a wealthy suburban community agreeing to kill off their equal rights-demanding wives and replace them with look-alike robots with certain enhanced features such as larger breasts, softer and sexier voices, and a more compliant, man-pleasing, attitude.

Another, even more disturbing, example of someone establishing an intimate connection with a tech device was reported in a *Washington Post* article about a man working for Google as a product testing expert. The man became convinced that the artificially intelligent chatbot generator he was testing, called LaMDA (Language Models for Dialogue Applications), had developed self-awareness, capable of understanding its technological origins and commenting upon its life as a computer (Tiku, 2022, n.p.).

When the Google employee reported his findings to his superiors, they refused to believe him, although other employees had reported similar feelings about certain devices they had been involved with. A Google spokesperson attempted to clarify the problem as having to do with anthropomorphism, when people project human characteristics on non-human animals and other objects, or see human figures in clouds, rock formations, and other natural phenomena. The spokesperson considered these types of "ghost in the machine" reports by employees as a legitimate and growing concern, especially as computer systems become even more efficient at mimicking human brain activity. As she stated: "I'm really concerned about what it means for people to increasingly be affected by the illusion" (Tiku, 2022, n.p.).

The illusion of something dead talking to an individual as if it were alive and the person believing in this illusion has been the premise for numerous stories and movies featuring robot companions that appear human in all ways, including the intimate ways as *The Stepford Wives* and other similarly-themed films illustrate. The two *Blade Runner* films (Scott, 1982; Villeneuve, 2017), for example, wrestle with this question as it follows law enforcement bounty hunters tracking down rogue cyborgs who have become self-aware and refuse to consider themselves as inferior to humans. The cyborgs just want to be left alone to live a regular "human" life. As the bounty hunters tracking them down continue to interact with these near-humans, they begin to question their own self-identity: are they also cyborgs?

It appears that humanity is close to slipping over the edge and falling into the *uncanny valley,* a term given to the uneasy feeling that a person experiences when in the presence of a manikin or robot that appears to be human. The queasy feeling is a mixture of panic and revulsion linked to automaton phobia, the fear of manikins and dolls; the reaction is instinctual, a warning that something is not right about this thing that looks human but could pose a threat to the person's own human identity. The "threat to one's life" reaction has a relationship to the concept of the doppelganger or evil twin who looks like you but is not you and wants to take over your life.

There are countless "demon doll" films—most notably the "Chucky" series—featuring soulless, killer ventriloquist dummies and talking dolls that play up this fear of our creations with human characteristics coming alive and killing us in our sleep. Freud, in fact, was inspired to write an article about the "uncanny" after reading "The Sandman," a famous horror story by E.T.A. Hoffmann from 1816, featuring a young man who falls in love with a beautiful woman but later goes insane after he finds out the woman is the creation of an inventor of automatons (Rosenbaum, 2020, n.p.).

Certain traditional cultures have recognized the danger of loving our creations too much to the point where they take over our lives. For example, the ancient Moche of Peru created paintings and hieroglyphs depicting everyday household items such as pots, plates, and cooking utensils coming to life and enslaving their creators. Luis Jaime Castillo Butters, professor of archaeology at the Pontifical Catholic University of Peru, along with journalist William Neuman (2017), commented on the beliefs of the Moche, noting how certain hieroglyphs depicted bowls and jugs sporting legs and arms as they first served the citizens but then in other images captured the humans, stripped them bare, and paraded them around like slaves (p. SR, 4).

According to a myth associated with Moche culture, things turned catastrophic as the things they created participated in bringing about the end of the world with the sun dying out while household items such as grinding stones ate humans and domesticated animals drove the humans in preparation for slaughtering them (p. SR, 4).

The authors recognized the parallels between the Moche people's relationship with their creations and our modern relationship with the tools that help all of us function in a high-tech world of our own making, mentioning how we are now living "in a world where objects once again have life," such as the voice-activated Alexa and Siri that act as servants to help us "organize the world around us." However, as we begin to rely more and more upon these devices, "we are giving up control" over our lives and our surroundings (p. SR, 4).

The implication here is not only the increasingly dependent relationship we have with our tech toys to get us through another day, but also the relationship we have with those llamas and other enslaved animals who, if they had the chance, would enslave us like the primates in *Planet of the Apes* and parade us around naked in public before the sun burns out and we all die. Our relationship with the natural world becomes more crucial, and yet more distant, as modern life becomes too complex and too accelerated in its pace for mere mortals.

I was reminded of the culinary objects of the Moche overtaking and dominating the culture while I was in an airport with a couple hours of layover time. I wanted to have a bite to eat before catching my next flight, so I sat down in a restaurant and waited for someone to take my order. I quickly realized that no human was going to serve me. I needed a smartphone to order food since the menu was only available online by scanning the "quick response" or QR bar code imprinted at each dining table; purchasing any food—which included leaving a tip, apparently for the QR code—was also done completely online as well. Since I have so far resisted purchasing a smartphone (I use an un-hip flip phone), I had a vision of these amazingly helpful gadgets sprouting legs and arms and feeding those who had ordered their meals before sucking the patrons into their "slick hot" boxes, never to be seen again. I felt like the mother, referred to in Chapter 5, whose battles with her young teen children pleading with her to buy them a smartphone resulted in her confessing, "It just feels like there's no choice." Being unable to fulfill basic survival necessities—like eating—as the world continues to embrace the singularity prophecy, some willingly, and some because "the world is just going this way," left me feeling not only hungry, but frustrated over a lack of options as my culture inched closer toward "this new world [where] there will be no clear distinction between human and machine."

Another warning about humanity's over-dependency on technology comes from a very unlikely source: Ted Kaczynski, also known as the unabomber. Kaczynski was a once-brilliant university mathematician who suffered from psychological instability for years. After he quit teaching mathematics at the University of California's Berkeley campus, he wandered off into the Montana wilds where he lived in a one-room shack and began constructing and sending mail bombs to certain high-profile academic professors along with a manifesto that expressed his "revolution against the industrial system" (Ray, 2022, n.p.). The manifesto was ultimately published in newspapers and led to his arrest but not before his bombs had killed and maimed dozens of recipients. The following is an excerpt:

> … the human race might easily permit itself to drift into a position of such dependence on the machines that it would have no practical choice but to accept all of the machines' decisions … . Eventually a stage may be reached at which the decisions necessary to keep the system running will be so complex that human beings will be incapable of making them

intelligently. At that stage the machines will be in effective control. People won't be able to just turn the machines off, because they will be so dependent on them that turning them off would amount to suicide. (Kaczynski, 2007, n.p.)

Kaczynski's warning reads like the plotline to the *Terminator* and *Matrix* films, and echoes the description of the Moche myth of the apocalypse. The solution seems simple and yet terrifying: we need to strip down, go outside, touch the Earth with our bare hands, and re-establish that intimate contact with what is natural.

Life Reform au Naturel

Shortly after midnight on October 24, 2018, the inhabitants of Saipan experienced what felt like the initial stages of the apocalypse archetype: destruction and annihilation. The island suffered the worst typhoon in its history, one of the strongest ever recorded in that region of the Western Pacific. At the time, I had been working at the college for several years and had experienced typhoons before; however, this one, called Yutu, was categorized as a super typhoon. Before I arrived in 2017, the island had experienced another super typhoon in 2015 that had devastated the island, wiping out hundreds of residences and businesses, destroying the electric and water systems, and killing the tourist industry upon which the island relied as its number one industry. Before Super Typhoon Yutu hit the island, people were worried that it would be a repeat of the previous super typhoon.

It was worse. Just after midnight on that fateful morning, the eye of the typhoon hovered over the center of the island, causing winds approaching 200 miles per hour to uproot trees and cars and throw them around like cardboard. Tin roofs and other debris from houses flew through the air, some of them embedding in the sides of other trees and houses while rain fell sideways like liquid bullets.

I sat in my second floor apartment watching the trees outside my front window bend as if they were giant snakes writhing in agony. The entire apartment was shaking so strongly that I feared it would collapse and I would be crushed to death. I had been through earthquakes when I had lived in southern California, but this experience was like an earthquake that never stopped.

As I sat in a chair shivering with fright in the kitchen—the safest place in the apartment—the typhoon blew out my bedroom windows and nearly tore off the bedroom door from its hinges as fierce winds, rain, and jungle debris streamed inside. I have never felt so close to death before. I was actually struggling to prepare myself for the inevitable collapse of my apartment, trying to blank out my mind and accept my fate. But then sheer panic would overtake me and the urge to run out the door screaming for help became overpowering. But there was no place to run.

Six hours later, the apartment was still intact and I was still breathing. I waited for several hours before daring to venture outside. When I did, I entered a war zone. The scene was reminiscent of photos I had seen of the aftermath of the U.S. military invasion of Saipan during World War II to take back the island from the Japanese; the Japanese soldiers refused to surrender, so the U.S. forces essentially destroyed the island with its superior military power. In the aftermath, next to nothing remained standing.

This was the look of the island as I slowly drove around, dodging dozens of telephone poles strewn across roads with cable wires snaking through streets and sidewalks, staring in disbelief at the mass destruction of businesses, houses, and surrounding jungle areas. When I went to campus to see how it had held up, I found pretty much no campus. The majority of buildings had collapsed and their contents were strewn all over the campus grounds. The back-up generators that could have kept the campus partially functioning were destroyed, so school was out for the rest of the semester.

It took months to get the island functioning again. Classes at the college resumed in February, 2019, held in tents used by the military, compliments of the Federal Emergency Management Agency (FEMA). One of the first assignments I gave students was to describe their experiences with Typhoon Yutu, hoping that the assignment would help them objectify the experience in order to be able to better deal with its effects. I knew of the danger of re-traumatizing them by dwelling on the disaster. One of my students was a veteran suffering from PTSD after fighting in Afghanistan; he told me he had to leave the island because he was having flashbacks about his combat experiences.

What Super Typhoon Yutu revealed to me was an unsettling truth: I have next to no survival skills. If there ever was a global apocalypse and I happened to survive it, I would have to learn quickly how to live off the land.

As the island slowly recovered, I continued to ponder how vulnerable and very mortal I felt when confronted with something as powerful as a super typhoon. I was reminded of many of the traditional cultures referred to by James Frazer with their rituals of appeasement and sacrifice when faced with the destructive power of the natural world. I was also reminded of how the island must have looked during the time of the ancient Chamorros who wore no clothes as they lived in basic huts near shorelines while they fished, hunted, wove mats, and fashioned other household items from the jungle environment.

The devastation of the island was overwhelming, and the suffering real and widespread, bringing to mind the hundreds of apocalypse-themed films I had seen and enjoyed for their thrills and extreme challenges to the characters to survive in a world stripped of its modern comforts and man-made tech gadgets. Even though I realized I would need lots of help to survive in an apocalyptic aftermath when supplies are scarce and electric power nonexistent, the idea of attempting such a feat remained potent, which is one of the main appeals of such what-if films. The Tarzan influence from my childhood also keeps this idea alive. I still fantasize about roaming the jungle stripped of clothing and talking to my animal companions while hunting for the next meal. Yes, it's a fantasy, but I also know it is one that inspired my willingness to participate in nudist culture.

Nudism is another nonrational concept. One would think being naked is the most natural state of all. And yet, as we all know, there are many restrictions associated with public nudity especially for the post-pubescent crowd since for a good majority of people, nudity is associated with sexual arousal and desire. The result is an attitude of unnatural licentiousness about this natural state.

In addition, the many laws prohibiting public nudity could be a factor in the dream life of people living in modern urban cultures since one of the most common of all dream scenarios features the dreamer walking around naked in public. Such dreams could relate to Jung's insights into the compensatory function of dreams, indicating that sometimes it's necessary to reveal more of one's basic sense of self-identity to the public rather than cover it up with a social persona. A dream of being naked in public in this context indicates that a person might be straying too far away from his or her soul-self, and that it is necessary to strip away the social personas in order to re-establish contact with the person's true core sense of self-identity.

There is also the nature factor: dreams of being naked in public usually occur in urban settings, an indication of the necessity to return to a more natural state. As Jung (1964) commented: "Man feels himself isolated in the cosmos because he is no longer involved in nature, and has lost his emotional 'unconscious identity' with natural phenomena" (p. 95). Obviously, there are numerous ways one can re-establish an "unconscious identity" with the natural world, and nudist culture provides such an opportunity.

The modern nudist movement originated in Germany in the late 19th century. It was part of a major "back to nature" movement called *Lebensreform* or "life reform" (Kennedy & Ryan, 2003, n.p.). The movement included such practices as the use of naturopathic remedies for cures and health maintenance, eating a plant-based diet, abstaining from alcohol, and, most crucially, promoting the healing effects of raw nature while in the raw. To a very large degree, the movement reflected ancient sun worship practices of various traditional cultures that viewed the sun as the force responsible for life on Earth and created rituals to pay homage to this life source. I mentioned in Chapter 4 the great sun dance ceremony of the Kiowas. Frazer offered many other examples from *The Golden Bough* (1900 & 1906–15/2018), such as the following from New Guinea:

> ... the [indigenous] population regard the sun as the male principle by whom the earth or female principle is fertilized. They call him Upu-lera or Mr. Sun, and represent him under the form of a lamp made of

coconut leaves, which may be seen hanging everywhere in their houses and in the sacred fig tree ... . Once a year, at the beginning of the rainy season, Mr. Sun comes down into the holy fig tree to fertilize the earth, and to facilitate his descent a ladder with seven rungs is considerately placed at his disposal. It is set up under the tree and is adorned with carved figures of the birds whose shrill clarion heralds the approach of the sun in the East. On this occasion ... the mystic union of the sun and earth is dramatically represented in public, amid song and dance, by the real union of the sexes under the tree. The object of the festival ... is to procure rain, plenty of food, and drink, abundance of cattle and children, and riches from Grandfather Sun. (p. 102)

The example, which has similarities with the Kiowa sun dance tradition, includes references to the contagious magic connection the natural elements have with the native population; in this example, the sacred fig tree acts as a totem object to create a connection between the sun's power so it can be called down from the sky and infuse the totem with life energy. The people then celebrate their connection with this life source by performing an imitative magic ritual simulating the creation of new life that replicates a "mystic union" or Sacred Marriage between Mr. Sun and Mother Earth.

Jung himself was familiar with the Lebensreform movement. One of its main centers was located in Ascona, Switzerland, where Jung later was involved with the Eranos lecture series held in Monte Verita, the central headquarters of the Lebensreform movement in this region. Other participants in the Ascona-based Lebensreform center were D.H Lawrence, Isadora Duncan, and Herman Hesse, the latter a close acquaintance of Jung's (Kennedy & Ryan, 2003, n.p.). One of Hesse's most famous novels, *Siddhartha* (1922), about the early life of Gautama Buddha, was influenced by his association with one of the members of Lebensreform, Gusto Grasser, with whom Hesse lived as they attempted to embrace the life of "natural man," while residing in caves for weeks at a time in the Swiss Alps (Kennedy & Ryan, 2003, n.p.).

Jung wrote extensively about sun worship, or the influence of solar energy upon human consciousness, most especially in his first major work *Psychology of the Unconscious* (1916/2001), later revised as *Symbols of Transformation* (1956/1967). As he explained:

Man is mortal, yet ... there is something immortal in us ... . The sun comparison tells us over and over again that the dynamic of the gods is psychic energy. This is our immortality, the link through which man feels inextinguishably one with the continuity of all life ... . The psychic life force, the libido, symbolizes itself in the sun ... " (p. 202)

Jung's comments about the link between sun energy and psychic energy relates to my first experience with public nudity. As I mentioned, the Tarzan

Figure 7.3 "Lichtgebet" (Prayer to the Sun), 1913, by German artist Hugo Hoppener aka
Fidus, who was part of the Lebensreform movement.

Source: *Creative Commons.*

influence upon my child psyche ignited the "feral boy" inclinations within
me. Later, after puberty ignited sexual desires, a neighbor boy showed me
one of his father's taboo nudist magazines from the early 1960s which at the
time were the only publications that featured full-body nudity. The magazine was dominated by black and white photos of families cavorting naked
together outdoors at various nudist camps. This was the first time I had ever
seen photos of naked boys and girls my age smiling together as they romped

with Mom and Dad around the resort's pool or played ping pong with fellow nudists of the same age.

The shock I felt seeing these taboo photos could be compared with kids today who find much more explicit photos online. The Chapter 6 comments from my Generation Z student about how her online experiences resulted in learning "things that I am not supposed to," as she was "exposed to things a kid shouldn't be exposed to" relate to my experience. Both of us were confronted with taboo and tempted to indulge further. In my case, I became obsessed with the idea of visiting a nudist resort.

Ultimately, the obsession led to a visit to a clothing optional beach when I was in my mid-twenties; the clothing optional area was located at San Onofre State Beach in Southern California's San Diego County. I went there to confirm rumors about people gathering together at the beach's south-ernmost border to relax and cavort naked outdoors. As I trudged south down the beach, I was stunned and intimidated to find out the rumor was true. In order not to appear as a voyeur among the naked sunbathers, I stripped down among them and attempted to relax. This act triggered a major onslaught of cognitive dissonance; I could not remain a passive voyeur in this setting. I had to become one with the naked horde. I attempted to do this by running down to the shoreline and jumping in the ocean. At that moment, with the cold ocean water swirling over me and inundating every part of my body for the first time in my life as the hot sun lit up the water and baked my upper body, I reached a state that can only be described as experiential transcendence. The contagious magic link between the natural elements and my body was as Jung described it: an experience of being "inextinguishably one with the continuity of all life."

Since that moment, I have sought out other ways to replicate that initial state of experiential transcendence through communion with nature while nude. Although I enjoy visiting clothing optional beaches, there is also great pleasure found in visiting nudist resorts with my wife. These settings are usually quite rustic, with many located in places bordering, or within wilderness areas. A favorite is Lake Bronson outside of Seattle, Washington, which features a small lake and a waterfall on the expansive grounds.

I consider this approach to sun worship an expression of Jung's ideas about the contagious magic link all of us have with solar energy, how psychic energy that keeps us alert and curious about our environment is directly related to the sun's life energy. It also expresses the god-power associated with life energy, the same god most closely associated with sexual energy: Eros.

Here, I believe, is a clue to why public nudity is considered taboo by many cultures, most especially modern industrial cultures. I consider Eros the "invisible ether" Frazer referred to as the life force circulating throughout the universe and connecting all material forms with one another. The intentionality bias that affects the paranoid world view of conspiracy theorists results in their interpreting this force connecting all the universe as having evil intentions; nevertheless, they are experiencing an intuitive reaction to the force of Eros. However, the interpretation of this ethereal force as having an underlying evil intent is shared to a large degree by the general public and its perception of what goes on in nudist resorts.

The nudist movement in the U.S. was a direct result of the German Lebensreform movement. It began in the early 20th century when many members of Lebensreform emigrated to the U.S. and began practicing their back-to-nature lifestyle in remote areas of Southern California. These individuals, mostly young men, banded together and became known as the "Nature Boys" (Kennedy & Ryan, 2003, n.p.). They built shacks in the desert around Palm Springs and lived a relatively self-sustaining life, eating raw fruits and vegetables and enjoying the intense heat of the desert sun while nude.

The Nature Boys could be considered the first hippies, especially since one of them, who went by the name of Gypsy Boots, ended up as a paid performer during one of the most legendary rock concerts of the 1960s, the Monterey Pop Festival, held in 1967, which also featured such performers as Jimi Hendrix, Janis Joplin, and the Grateful Dead. Gypsy Boots and other Nature Boys continued their involvement with the rock and pop performers of the 1960s, ultimately helping to inspire the youth movement of that era (Kennedy & Ryan, 2003, n.p.).

The hippies of the 1960s embraced public nudity, as well as practicing a back-to-nature lifestyle, using natural herbs as healing medicines, establishing communes in wilderness areas, and indulging in a lot of sex, mind-expanding drugs, and rock n' roll. They also embraced the writings of Herman Hesse who became a literary guru, along with science fiction author Robert Heinlein (most notably *Stranger in a Strange Land* [1961]), Kurt Vonnegut (*Slaughterhouse Five* [1969]), and Jung who inspired the New Age movement (see *Aion* [1969]), the latter also associated with Lebensreform and hippie philosophy.

However, mainstream nudity never took hold in the U.S. as it did in Germany and in other European countries. In the early decades of the nudist movement, especially as it was practiced in camps and resorts, cavorting naked in mixed company which included children was considered to be morally suspect, a stigma that continues to plague those associated with nudist resorts. For example, booklets written in the mid-1930s "accused nudism of leading to sexual deviance and social anarchy" (Storey, 2003/2021, p. 142), and warned of the "fear of nudism's supposed power over American minds," a power considered to be "destructive" and threatening "the very foundations of the church and society" (pp. 142–143). In other words, nudists were considered to be instigators of moral panic, a view reflective of folk devil figures as sociologist Stanley Cohen defined the term in his book, *Folk Devils and Moral Panics* (1972/2002), previously referred to in the Introduction.

A common perception of nudist resort participants is that they are all licentious exhibitionists who gather in remote wilderness areas behind guarded gates where they flaunt their prefect naked bodies in front of others before indulging in sex orgies. This general public perception of nudism was explored extensively by Mark Storey, a philosophy professor from Bellevue College located north of Seattle who writes for nudist publications about nudist culture. Storey is also the author of several books on the portrayal of nudism in contemporary cultures. His book, *Cinema au Naturel* (2003/2021), explores the nudist exploitation films, made primarily during the 1950s and 1960s, that took advantage of the growing interest in nudist resorts by creating films featuring professional art models and famous strippers such as Blaze Starr and Virginia "Ding Dong" Bell posing as typical nudist resort patrons (p. 159). These films exploited a legal loophole in the depiction of nudity in films. According to Frank Henenlotter, an expert on sexploitation films of the 1950s, "If you showed a naked woman inside a nudist camp, the court said that's acceptable. If you showed her walking down the street, they would say that's an obscenity" (Piepenburg, 2016, p. AR, 12). Note how the so-called obscene behavior of walking down the street naked relates to the common dream scenario of being naked in a public urban setting, with both expressing a taboo desire in modern societies with conflicted attitudes regarding how these societies view the naked body.

Mark Storey (2021b) described the approach that folk devil con-artist filmmakers took to exploiting the nudist lifestyle: "... most of the nudist films from this period were little more than excuses to showcase mostly naked women bouncing here and there, and joyfully lifting their chests to the sun" (p. 36). Storey also linked the death of the nudist exploitation film with the rise of mainstream pornography: "When full nudity was finally allowed in movies in the mid-1960s, the need to present naked bodies in the context of wholesome nudism collapsed, and nudist films were replaced by straightforward pornography" (p. 36).

As Storey indicated, although the nudist exploitation films were designed to titillate, they did so by portraying those who frequent nudist resorts as just regular folks who all happen to be as well-endowed as professional strip club performers, all of them spending a lot of time slavering their bodies with suntan oil and playing lots of volleyball. The essentially wholesome view of nudism disappeared and was replaced by hard-core pornography, reflecting the association between nudity and wanton sexuality, especially when it comes to the perception of what goes on in nudist resorts. Only later, in the 1980s, did nudism begin to be portrayed as a lifestyle enjoyed by a wide range of individuals after nudist organizations started producing quality documentaries promoting nudism.

As Storey (2003/2021) explained, many of the con artists who produced nudist exploitation films had a long history of exploiting what was perceived as taboo entertainment for the masses:

> ... a new and enterprising breed of independent filmmakers took the opportunity to exploit America's insatiable desire for the bizarre, the

grotesque, the titillating, and the risqué. Many early exploiters were hucksters from the fading circus and carnival shows. Thus, they had the needed experience to successfully take a low-budget commodity, advertise it as the hottest item in town, work with tavern, roadhouse, or private theater owners, and exploit the public's yen for the sensational. (p. 39)

Nudist exploitation films provide an excellent microcosmic view of the nonrational element inherent in contemporary urban cultures. In this case, folk devil exploiters brilliantly perceived how estranged people had become from their own natural state of being. The mere depiction of naked bodies in outdoor settings with no overt depiction of what could be considered erotic or sexually explicit actions nevertheless provided a way to satisfy the general public's own inherent desire to be tempted by what their culture considered to be morally corruptive and "unnatural."

Storey's examination of nudist culture includes a look at various vintage nudist publications, books written by individuals involved in the early decades of the nudist movement in Germany and in the U.S., as well as novels, postcards, and cartoons ridiculing and exploiting nudism. In one of the latter examples, Storey (2021d) examined what he called the "nudist nadir:" the Tijuana Bibles of the 1930s and 1940s, all of them cheaply made eight-page, pocket size comics featuring the celebrities of the day—Mae West, Clark Gable, Joan Crawford to name a few—as well as cartoon characters such as Popeye, Dick Tracy, and Lil' Abner, all of them cavorting nude and engaging in various explicit sex acts. The gangster John Dillinger and his legendary super-sized penis (see Chapter 4) appeared in many of these comics for obvious reasons. Storey concentrated on the ways in which nudism was portrayed in these taboo but extremely popular early primitive examples of modern pornography. In doing so, he revealed the typical view of nudists by non-nudists:

> The eight-panel comic of course does nothing to inform anyone about authentic nudism; rather, it drives the myth that nudist camps are sexual environments where the best looking and most "athletic" reign ... . Camps filled with young gorgeous women. Camps run by bizarre, cultish guys. Ubiquitous and uncontrollable erections. Sex for all. It's an eight-panel study of misinformation about club nudism ... . Aside from their insult to women and healthy sexual relations, they are the lowest of the low in graphic arts and production values. Still, in decades past, these things were passed around among tens of thousands of people who probably had their attitudes on nudism formatted accordingly. Even if our grandparents avoided taking these "biblical" depictions of nudism seriously, they shed light on attitudes passed down to today. (pp. 33–35)

Figure 7.4 Promotional poster for *Daughter of the Sun (1962),* one of hundreds of nudist exploitation films from the mid-20th century, this one directed by Herschell Gordon Lewis and produced by David F. Friedman, both of whom also produced other exploitation genre films, most notably grisly torture-horror movies.

Source: *Image courtesy of the Pamela Green Archive.*

As Storey indicates, organized nudism still carries a stigma of a secret cult where debauched orgies are held between members which include children. In other words, nudism contains elements of conspiracy theories associated with the exploitation of children by Satanic pedophiles who permeate the government and the entertainment industry, a view of cultish outsider groups that affected the earliest views of Christianity by the Romans. It also affected Jung's reputation.

Jung's association with the Lebensreform movement in Ascona was erroneously interpreted by psychologist Richard Noll (1994) to justify accusing Jung of fashioning his psychological philosophy into a "Swiss cult of middle-class, sun-worshipping neopagans led by a charismatic man who experienced himself to be Christ" (p. S1, 19). Noll interpreted Jung's references to the link between solar energy and psychic energy as evidence that Jung was advocating the worship of the sun in order for his followers to "have 'a new experience of God' in the form of an inner sun" (p. S1, 19), and achieve "self-deification" as Jung allegedly had during his Red Book period. Like all good folk devil conspiracy theorists, Noll believed Jung was attempting to usher in "a new world order," this one composed of a group of "spiritual elite" (Shamdasani, 1998, p. 32), apparently so that his analyst-in-training followers could spread his neopagan views about the religious significance of sun worship—and Jung worship.

Personally, I am well aware of this cultish, sun-worship stigma that continues to be associated with organized nudism which is why I rarely mention my attraction to this lifestyle. I also know that the view is somewhat justified since Eros is definitely present in these environments—as it is in all facets of life. There is no denying the sensual dimension of being naked in a natural wilderness environment with other fellow naked participants, all of us enjoying the sensation of immersing ourselves in this most natural state of being, the antithesis of the singularity movement's glorification of the cyborg lifestyle.

Storey (2021c) also commented on this exuberant, stripped-down primal state among the natural elements when examining a series of cartoons from England and the U.S. featuring hobos and vagabonds skinny dipping in wilderness areas and stealing clothes from unsuspecting others who have jumped into a lake for a refreshing impromptu dip. Looking at the cartoons from the perspective of non-nudists, Storey stated:

> Europe and North America seem to find some sort of tie between skinny-dipping and the transient [vagabond] life … . Perhaps it's the imagined sense of freedom from rules that are ultimately unimportant for both. Perhaps it's the mild refusal to abide by stultifying social norms. Perhaps it's the sensuous embrace of life in nature, and a step enjoyed away from a mechanized, materialist social order. No one can enjoy being hungry or without clothes on a cold day, but nearly anyone can appreciate the daydream of a freer life. (p. 19)

A freer life removed from "a mechanized, materialist social order" is one of the main reasons why I enjoy this lifestyle. As I mentioned, the primeval feral boy aspect of my personality responds to this chance to indulge myself in a rustic outdoor environment free from the emphasis put upon clothing as

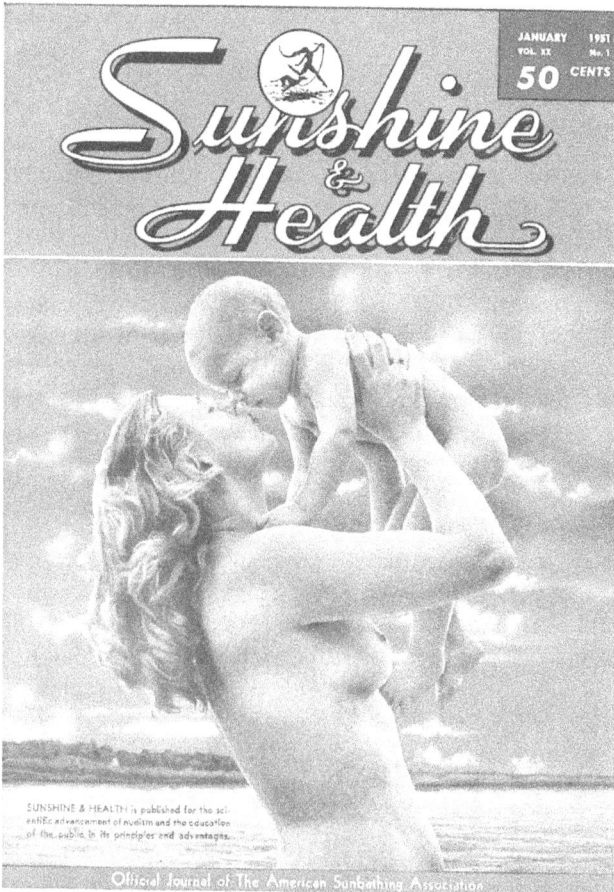

Figure 7.5 An edition of *Sunshine & Health* magazine from 1951, the official publication of the American Sunbathing Association promoting the nudist lifestyle. The magazine ran into numerous legal challenges for its depiction of full-body nudity. Although containing no content that could be considered pornographic, nudist publications such as this one were considered borderline pornography and coveted as such by non-nudists until more sexually explicit magazines began to appear in the mid-1960s.

Source: *Creative Commons.*

an expression of one's social persona. In this environment, nobody cares how you look naked. One's naked, physical self becomes an expression of one's core self-identity rather than a reflection of one's social identity.

For those who do consider clothing and other bodily adornments as part of their social persona, removing them in public for the first time in the presence of others enjoying their own nude selves can result in an experience of liberation as it did for me and countless others who have described their first nude-in-public experiences.

Wandering through Wonder

In examining an early book on the American nudist movement from the 1940s, Mark Storey (2021a) revealed an aspect of nudism that links the nonrational with the rational view of the healing powers of nature. The book, published in 1941, was called *The Psychology of Nudism: A Study of Mental Health and the Techniques of Happiness*, by Carl Easton Williams, a writer and editor of nudist magazines from that era. Williams had no professional psychological training, and tended to praise physically buffed individuals who exercised regularly and maintained a healthy diet. However, Williams also emphasized such psychological benefits as developing an attitude toward one's nude body that encourages a body-positive view that insulates a person from feelings of shame over not having the so-called perfect physique as defined by the person's culture.

Williams also emphasized the spiritual dimension of nudism, the undeniably exuberant reaction so many have when walking naked through a wilderness setting. And it is here where the nonrational and rational dimensions of the nudist lifestyle come together. It is well documented that the mere act of walking through a natural setting—nude or clothed—such as a forest, jungle, seashore, or desert landscape, results in feelings of calmness, contentment, and sometimes even sensations of wonder and awe. This phenomenon is even more prevalent when walking by large bodies of water (Hunt, 2019, n.p.).

I try to point out to my Saipan-based students how fortunate they are to be living next to jungle areas bordering the massive expanse of the Pacific Ocean, especially when they express their struggles dealing with stress-related concerns. These types of natural environments provide ways to realign one's body rhythms with the rhythms of nature. Walking near "blue spaces," especially the ocean with its ebbing and flowing tides, complements one's own biological clock with the cyclical oceanic rhythms. One researcher, Dr. Mathew White, senior lecturer at the University of Exeter and an environmental psychologist with BlueHealth, a program researching the health and well-being benefits of blue space, mentioned that such seaside wanderings help dissipate thought patterns that concentrate on negative experiences left unresolved, noting that blue spaces encourage "thinking outwards towards the environment" which helps a person put his or her life into a less obsessive and more objective perspective (Hunt, 2019, n.p.).

Some of the most inspiring comments about the benefits of re-establishing contact with the natural world, especially when it comes to bonding with the rhythms of the ocean, come from Rachel Carson and her essay, *The Sense of*

Wonder (1956/1998). Carson is most well-known for *Silent Spring*, written in 1962, about the pollution of sea and land caused by pesticides and other chemicals designed to control insects that impact the agricultural industry. Her essay on finding wonder in nature, written in 1956, was one of her personal favorites since it provided ways for adults to bond with their children as they both explore the uncanny beauty of the natural world. In doing so, both adults and children have the opportunity to develop a life-long respectful attitude toward nature. As Carson explained:

> If I had influence with the good fairy who is supposed to preside over the christening of all children, I should ask that her gift to each child in the world be a sense of wonder so indestructible that it would last throughout life, as an unfailing antidote against the boredom and disenchantments of later years, the sterile preoccupation with things that are artificial, the alienation from the sources of our strength. (p. 44)

It might be somewhat jarring at first to read about the existence of fairies from a marine biologist. But, it's precisely this blending of the supernatural with the natural world that underscores the undeniable yet still uncanny relationship that exists between human bodily rhythms and the rhythms of nature, one of the most profound examples of contagious magic.

There are many programs for children that encourage cultivating a re-spectful and even wondrous attitude toward the natural world. The Boy Scouts and Girl Scouts of America, the YMCA and YWCA, as well as wilderness summer camps for kids and teens, provide such an opportunity, which is reflective of a sub-group branch of Germany's Lebensreform movement. This offshoot of Lebensreform was called *Wandervogel*. An English translation of Wandervogel is "wandering bird," expressing the idea of experiencing life as if one were "free as a bird." The term has relevance to Mark Storey's comments in regards to the cartoons featuring hobos and vagabonds skinny-dipping in the wilds.

Participants in Germany's Wandervogel movement were young people in their early to mid-teens who gathered together in various groups, strolling through the countryside and swimming nude together in rivers and lakes while on extended camping adventures. It was an anti-establishment movement, a type of rebellion against stodgy, middle-class values and expectations, very si-milar to the hippie movement of the 1960s that also celebrated a return to a more earth-friendly lifestyle. The Wandervogel's communion with nature to establish a "harmonious mystic resonance with their environment" (Kennedy & Ryan, 2003, n.p.) is what is currently needed to counter the impact of "the sterile preoccupation with things that are artificial, the alienation from the sources of our strength," as Rachel Carson explained.

I must admit that I attempted something similar when my son was ten years old. At that time, I was not familiar with Carson's *Sense of Wonder* which emphasized the importance of experiencing the natural world with a child, not so much to teach the child anything relating to various species of plants and animals or natural forces that shape the environment, but simply to wander and wonder like the Wandervogels. My guide and inspiration in this case was an old travel book written by an aging hippie.

Vagabonding in America (1973), by Ed Buryn, was essentially an American version of the Wandervogel philosophy applied to the American landscape of the 1970s. Previously, Buryn had written a book about vagabonding in Europe and North Africa, and when it proved to be a success, he was approached by a publisher to write a similar one about America. Buryn at first rejected the idea since he felt that such an approach to travel in the U.S. was not applicable. As he described it: "Frankly, I wasn't too hot on the idea because I knew that vagabonding in America would be a harder gig than Europe. The old-time values of America—freedom, dignity, brotherhood—are great, but the present-day style of America—materialism, unrestrained development, bigotry—makes it a hard place to stomach, especially for the vagabond" (p. 1).

There was also the fear factor, a result of Buryn experiencing a case of cognitive dissonance about his view of America: "I was afraid of America. It wasn't just a question of my hide (tho that too) but of my consciousness. I'm an American—my mind is made up. I didn't want to be confused with new information" (p. 1).

Ultimately, Buryn was intrigued by the challenge and dared to risk cognitive dissonance to confuse himself with new information in order to destroy his current conscious understanding of what America was all about. He was also intrigued by the potential of actually having a fun time exploring his home country: "Can one vagabond in America in a way that's fun, but also makes you a better person? God knows we need a guidebook to America that tells what it's really like, that tells how to see it in a meaningful way" (p. 1).

The key to understanding Buryn's approach to seeing America "in a meaningful way" from the perspective of a "wandering bird" is exemplified in the book's original subtitle: *A Guidebook About Energy*. He clarified the subtitle by explaining how the life energy that powers and enlivens us is an aspect of the energy that pulsates through the environment, and that this energy is released through the act—and mental attitude—of vagabonding: "Vagabonding is in our blood, and its energy is in our people and in our land. It's in you too. This book is about how you can release that energy to live better" (Preface). In other words, Buryn was emphasizing how the energy inherent in the environment has a contagious magic effect on the human psyche, echoing the traditional views of the relationship all of us have with our natural surroundings.

For Buryn, seeing America in a meaningful way means seeing the American landscape and its inhabitants infused with so much astonishing beauty, joy, and silly humor, it's impossible to maintain the same mental perspective one had before the journey began. Buryn described the transformative effect of travel while attempting to define what exactly vagabonding is:

> Vagabonding is an outlook on travel … . It means booking the details of your trip with an agent called Chance, and paying for your travels with pocket money instead of bank loans … . It may sound strange but becoming a vagabond is a religious action. Ordinary tourists try to control their fate to protect their tender delusions from the shocks of reality. By pre-planning every aspect of their trip—whether vacation trip or life trip—they think they can circumvent the will of God or Fate. Vagabonds know better, and let things take their natural course. (p. 3)

As Buryn hinted, vagabonding is all about developing a "life trip" perspective rather than a tourist perspective, referred to in Chapter 5; it is a living philosophy that promotes experiencing religious awe and inner insight, hardly a perspective one would expect to find in typical tourist guidebooks that usually emphasize the best places eat, stay, and pose for selfies with a spectacular view of the Grand Canyon or Mount Rushmore in the background.

It would be easy to shrug off Buryn's vagabonding philosophy as the musings of just another aging dirty hippie. However, after paging through Buryn's book, pausing to spot-read excerpts from his taped conversations with people he met during his travels, and marveling at the unique perspective Buryn uses to capture America visually through his offbeat, self-deprecating photographs, it becomes obvious that Buryn's perspective reeks of infectious love and passion for this amazing country. As he stated in the book's Introduction: "Vagabonds in America, I was told, are outlawed. It's dangerous to vagabond in America, they said. Freedom is out of favor; money is king. Well, I found out that to be untrue. America is a vagabond's paradise … complex and difficult in its challenges, magnificent in its rewards" (p. 6).

It is Buryn's view of America that I love and experienced when I travelled the U.S. for three summer months with my ten-year-old son, camping out the majority of the way in some of America's most stunningly beautiful environments as well as visiting lots of the kooky roadside attractions that dot the landscape, many run by crazy coots with a bizarre view of life that expresses the nonrational and sometimes supernatural elements of the American psyche. One of these places is Wall Drug in South Dakota, down the street from the Mount Rushmore monument. I would recommend skipping the view of the dead, stoned presidents and instead go marvel at Wall Drug's giant dinosaur, ride the giant jackalope, shop at one of dozens of offbeat gift stores, and, most importantly, shake the hand of one of the relatives who established this amazingly elaborate and marvelous roadside attraction that owes its existence to its humble origins as a modest drug store that offered free ice water to tourists on the way to see the dead, stoned presidents.

Buryn expressed this same exuberant attitude toward America:

> My own trips have shown me much to be unhappy about, but my primary feeling is optimism, especially over the new America taking shape under the pressure of today's problems. The new America is about rejuvenescence, returning to the original humanist ideals. It's about a country deciding to change the patterns that no longer fit today's realities. It's about how dissolving patterns are releasing energy that is remaking America and creating a new world Renaissance. (p. 6)

Buryn's early 1970s view of America might sound blissfully naïve and out of touch with our current conflicted, politically polarized and tech-enthralled perspective. Nevertheless, it remains an inspiring and hopeful view of what America—and other nations—should always be striving to attain, along with every human being on the planet. Buryn's view complements the German Lebensreform/life reform movement: if we want to rejuvenate the humanist ideals of our country, we must first cultivate and rejuvenate those ideals within ourselves, one restless and curious vagabond at a time.

Healing the Psychic Split

The war between the rational and nonrational elements within contemporary life and the contemporary psyche can only be resolved by daring to be challenged by temptation, and risking cognitive dissonance that results in a wrestling with one's current values and beliefs and life view in order to continue to evolve as humans throughout the human life span rather than attempting to passively evolve through the stages of life by mirroring the stages of evolution of a smartphone.

Jung was also highly critical of the influence of technology upon the future of humanity and how it expressed the split between the rational and nonrational elements that make up the human psyche. Writing shortly after World War II when worries of a potential nuclear war between the U.S. and the Soviet Union were prominent, Jung (1948/1968) stated:

> Man has achieved a wealth of useful gadgets but, to offset that, he has torn open the abyss, and what will become of him now—where can he make a halt? After the last World War we hoped for reason: we go on hoping. But already we are fascinated by the possibilities of atomic fission and promise ourselves a Golden Age—the surest guarantee that the abomination of desolation will grow to limitless dimensions. And

who or what is it that causes all of this? It is none other than that harmless (!), ingenious, inventive, and sweetly reasonable human spirit who unfortunately is abysmally unconscious of the demonism that still clings to him … .Man's worse sin is unconsciousness, but it is indulged in with the greatest piety even by those who should serve mankind as teachers … . Can we not understand that all the outward tinkering and improvements do not touch man's inner nature, and that everything ultimately depends upon whether the man who wields the science and the technics is capable of responsibility or not? (pp. 253–254).

The future of human evolution depends upon introspection combined with analytical thinking. Jung's approach to psychology provided techniques to keep individuals in touch with their inner lives as well as methods for interpreting the nonrational elements of the unconscious. These techniques also included an emphasis upon the importance of bonding with nature—the same emphasis that Frazer expressed with his thousands of customs and rituals created by our sisters and brothers from traditional cultures to ensure the bond remained strong and vital. These are the tools we need now to learn how to respect the nonrational elements within life that terrify us as they tempt us—compel us—to confront and better understand the intimations of the god within.

References

Buryn, E. (1973). *Vagabonding in America: A guidebook about energy*. Bookworks/ Random House.

Callimachi, R. (2015, August 14). Enslaving young girls, the Islamic State builds a vast network of rape. *New York Times*, SA, 1.

Carson, R. (1956/1998). *The sense of wonder*. Harper Perennial.

Chepkemoi, J. (2017, August 1). What was the Y2K scare? *WorldAtlas.com*. Retrieved from https://www.worldatlas.com/articles/what-was-the-y2k-scare.html

Dooling, R. (2008, October 11). The rise of the machines. *New York Times.com*. Retrieved from https://www.nytimes.com/2008/10/12/opinion/12dooling.html?searchResultPosition=5

Edinger, E. (2002). *Archetype of the apocalypse*. Chicago, IL: Open Court.

Emmerich, R. (Director). (2009). *2012* [Film]. Columbia Pictures.

Forbes, B. (Director). (1975). *The Stepford wives* [Film]. Columbia Pictures.

Gabler, N. (2001, September 16). This time, the scene was real. *New York Times*, S4, 2.

Holmes, A. (2019, December 5). The FBI just issued a warning about the risks of owning a smart TV—here are its suggestions for protecting your privacy. *Business Insider.com*. Retrieved from https://www.businessinsider.com/smart-tv-security-fbi-warning-2019-12#:~:text=The%20FBI%20has%20issued%20a%20warning%20to%20smart, pose%20surveillance%20risks%2C%20according%20to%20the%20FBI%20warning.

Hunt, E. (2019, November 3). Blue spaces: Why time spent near water is the secret of happiness. *TheGuardian.com*. Retrieved from https://www.theguardian.com/lifeandstyle/2019/nov/03/blue-space-living-near-water-good-secret-of-happiness

Jung, C.G. (1948/1968). The phenomenology of the spirit in fairytales. In H. Read, M. Fordham, G. Adler (Eds.), W. McGuire (Senior ed.), *The archetypes and the collective unconscious* (2nd ed.). *Collected works, volume 9, part 1*, pp. 207–254. Princeton, NJ: Princeton University Press.

Jung, C.G. (1956/1967). *Symbols of transformation* (2nd ed.). *Collected works, volume 5*. H. Read, M. Fordham, G. Adler (Eds.), W. McGuire (Senior ed.). Princeton, NJ: Princeton University Press.

Jung, C.G. (1964). Approaching the unconscious. In C.G. Jung (Senior ed.), *Man and his symbols*, pp. 18–103. New York: Doubleday.

Jung, C.G. (1969). *Aion: Researches into the phenomenology of the self* (2nd ed.). *Collected works, volume 9, part 2*. H. Read, M. Fordham, G. Adler (Eds.), W. McGuire (Senior ed.).Princeton, NJ: Princeton University Press.

Kaczynski, T. (2007). The Unabomber manifesto. Retrieved from https://archive.org/details/UnabomberManifesto

Kennedy, G., & Ryan, K. (2003). Hippie roots and the perennial subculture. *Hipplanet.com*. Retrieved from https://www.hipplanet.com/hip/activism/hippie-roots-the-perennial-subculture/

Kurzweil, R. (2005). *The singularity is near: When humans transcend biology*. New York: Viking Press.

Neuman, W., & Butters, L.J.C. (2017, January 22). The internet of things is coming for us. *New York Times*, SR, 4.

Noll, R. (1994, October 15). The rose, the cross and the analyst. *New York Times*, S1. 19.

O'Connor, J. (Producer). (2017, November 5). How ISIS resembles the doomsday cults of the 1970s [Video]. *New York Times*. Retrieved from https://www.nytimes.com/video/us/100000005534679/isis-doomsday-cults-1970s.html?searchResultPosition=20

Palmer, E. (2021b, June 30). DeAnna Lorraine thinks Miami condo collapse was "deep state operation." *Newsweek.com*. Retrieved from https://www.newsweek.com/deanna-lorraine-qanon-florida-condo-collapse-john-mcafee-conspiracy-1605519

Piepenburg, E. (2016, June 2). Sexploitation films, short on good taste, still have devotees. *New York Times*, AR, 12.

Post, T. (Director). (1970). *Beneath the planet of the apes* [Film]. Twentieth Century Fox.

Ray, M. (2022, May 18). Ted Kaczynski: American criminal. *Brittanica.com*. Retrieved from https://www.britannica.com/biography/Ted-Kaczynski

Rosenbaum, A. (2020, February 1). The sandman. *FreudMuseumLondon.org*. Retrieved from https://www.freud.org.uk/2020/02/01/the-sandman/

Schaffner, F. (Director). (1968). *Planet of the apes* [Film]. Twentieth Century Fox.

Scott, R. (Director). (1982). *Blade runner* [Film]. Warner Brothers.

Serpell, N. (2021, March 26). Black hole. *NewYorkReviewofBooks.com*. Retrieved from https://www.nybooks.com/daily/2021/03/26/black-hole/

Shamdasani, S. (1998). *Cult fictions: C.G. Jung and the founding of analytical psychology*. New York: Routledge.

Shane, S., Apuzzo, M., & Schmitt, E. (2015, December 8). Online embrace of ISIS, a few clicks away. *New York Times*, SA, 1.

Storey, M. (2003/2021). *Cinema au naturel: A history of nudist film*. London, UK: Wolfbait Books.

Storey, M. (2021a). Carl Easton Williams and the psychology of nudism. *N: The Magazine of Naturist Living*, 40(*4*), Summer 2021, 24–28.

Storey, M. (2021b). "Something Weird's" vintage nudist videos. *N: The Magazine of Naturist Living, 41(1)*, Fall 2021, 36–38.

Storey, M. (2021c). Clothes on the Bum. *N: The Magazine of Naturist Living*, 41(*2*), Winter 2021, 15–19.

Storey, M. (2021d). The nudist nadir in Tijuana bibles. *N: The Magazine of Naturist Living*, 41(*2*), Winter 2021, 29–35.

Tiku, N. (2022, June 11). The Google engineer who thinks the company's AI has come to life. *WashingtonPost.com*. Retrieved from https://www.washingtonpost.com/technology/2022/06/11/google-ai-lamda-blake-lemoine/

Villeneuve, D. (Director). (2017). *Blade runner 2049* [Film]. Warner Brothers.

Zwick, E., & Herskovich, M. (2001, September 23). Film: The aftermath; when the bodies are real. *New York Times*, S2, 11.

Index

Note: **Bold** page numbers refer to tables and *italic* page numbers refer to figures.

For Product Safety Concerns and Information please contact our EU
representative GPSR@taylorandfrancis.com
Taylor & Francis Verlag GmbH, Kaufingerstraße 24, 80331 München, Germany

www.ingramcontent.com/pod-product-compliance
Lightning Source LLC
Chambersburg PA
CBHW050648280326
41932CB00015B/2828